Legacy of Stone

This book is dedicated
to the memory of
Ian T. Kenyon, 1946–1997,
a brilliant scholar, mentor, and friend.

Legacy of Stone

ANCIENT LIFE ON THE NIAGARA FRONTIER

Ronald F. Williamson
and
Robert I. MacDonald

Foreword by Wayne Hill
Executive Director, Fort Erie Native Friendship Centre
Fort Erie, Ontario

Published in association with
"The Peace Bridge"
The Buffalo and Fort Erie Public Bridge Authority

eastendbooks
Toronto 1998

Designed by Melissa McClellan, Tanya Saari
Printed in Canada by Metrolitho

Canadian Cataloguing in Publication Data

Williamson, R.F. (Ronald F.)
         Legacy of stone : ancient life on the Niagara Frontier

Includes index.
ISBN 1-896973-08-6 (bound)   ISBN 1-896973-10-8 (pbk.)

1. Indians of North America – Ontario – Niagara Peninsula – Antiquities.
2. Stone implements – Ontario – Niagara Peninsula. 3. Niagara Peninsula (Ont.) –
Antiquities. I. MacDonald, Robert I. II Title.

E78.05W88 1998   971.3'3801   C97-932002-X

Front cover: *Longhouse Interior*, Ska-Nah-Doht Indian Village, Longwoods Road Conservation Area.
Back cover: Black slate fragment with etched thunderbirds.

Unless otherwise indicated, the source for all illustrations is Archaeological Services Inc.

eastendbooks is an imprint of Venture Press
45 Fernwood Park Avenue
Toronto, Canada
M4E 3E9
(416) 691-6816 telephone
(416) 691-2414 fax

Contents

Acknowledgements

Since the spring of 1992, Archaeological Services Inc. (ASI) has conducted almost constant archaeological investigations along the shore of the Niagara River within the Town of Fort Erie. During the course of our work, the Buffalo and Fort Erie Public Bridge Authority provided every form of logistical support within their power. In large part this support was due to the sincere interest taken on the part of their staff — particularly Stephen Mayer, Ron Lampman, Cliff Elwood, Brian Benner, and Bob Smith. Their genuine efforts at effective communication and collaboration with the project engineers and contractors, the Fort Erie Native Friendship Centre and ASI staff, during an ambitious campaign of redevelopment, also resulted in a model of cooperation between the development, aboriginal, and archaeological communities. We also conducted investigations during this period for the Town of Fort Erie. That work was also undertaken in the same spirit of cooperation and we extend our thanks to Mr. Bill Packer, of the Department of Public Works, for his support and interest.

A large number of other individuals and organizations have also contributed to the successful completion of this project. Mr. Wayne Hill, Executive Director of the Fort Erie Native Friendship Centre, and Mr. Neal Ferris, of the Ontario Ministry of Citizenship, Culture and Recreation, provided assistance and advice in developing the overall strategy adopted for the investigation of the site. Further support and assistance was provided by Harry Rosettani, Jim Flake, and Peter Flake.

The members of the overall contracting team are to be acknowledged for their flexibility, patience, and unfailingly good-natured response to situations with which they were not familiar. Our thanks go to Sto Tritchew, as well as Doug Campbell and Rob Bivollotto of Stephens and Rankin Construction Inc. and their crew; Diarmuid Nash, John Snell, and Ted Teshima of Moriyama and Teshima Architects; John Brucato of Merit Construction; and Alf Beam and his crew. We would also like to acknowledge the technical assistance provided by Kevin Smith and Jack Holland of the Buffalo Museum of Science, Douglas Perrelli of the Archaeological Survey, University at Buffalo, State University of New York, and Jim Pengelly of Port Colbourne.

Our particular thanks, however, must go to Bob Smith, of the Public Bridge Authority, for his interest and his unflagging willingness to provide logistical and technical support to the study team in the field and to accommodate their work within the overall operations of the customs facilities and the construction project.

We would also like to thank Richard Douglas, formerly of the *Niagara Falls Review*, Mike Vogel of the *Buffalo News*, Mike Robinson of the *Times-Review*,

Leonard LePage of *The Standard,* and Harry Rosettani (freelance) for their thoughtful media coverage of our investigations over the years. A number of images taken by these journalists have been included in the volume. Mike Robinson also kindly provided access to the archives of the *Times-Review.*

Finally, this project would not have been possible without the remarkable efforts of the ASI staff members who completed the fieldwork, laboratory processing, data analyses, and report preparations. A detailed technical volume reporting on the site, entitled *In the Shadow of the Bridge: The Archaeology of the Peace Bridge Site (AfGr-9) 1994–1996 Investigations,* is available at most regional agencies and libraries.

The graphics for this volume were prepared by Andrew Clish, Jane Cottrill, and David Robertson. The illustrations in the graphic on the prehistory of the Niagara Frontier were drawn by Andrew Clish, and adapted from the Ontario Archaeological Society's poster on Ontario's prehistory. The artifact illustrations are by Monicke Thibeault. The artifacts were photographed by Martin Cooper, Bruce McGaw, and Robert Pihl. We are also grateful to Debbie Steiss, Christopher Watts, Martin Cooper, Andrew Stewart, and Julie MacDonald for their editorial assistance, and to Jeanne MacDonald, Nadine Stoikoff, and Randall White for their helpful comments on an earlier draft of this book and for their patience with a couple of archaeologists.

Finally, we would like to acknowledge the tremendous interest that Ron Lampman has shown in the conservation and public interpretation of the archaeological heritage of the Niagara Frontier. Without his help and the support of the Peace Bridge Authority, the public would not have had access to the complete story.

Ronald F. Williamson
Robert I. MacDonald

Foreword

As the field archaeologist's sharp spade pierces the stratigraph of Mother Earth's epidermis, the ages of time come forth. To the trained eye of the archaeologist the different strata reveal an age, an environmental condition unto itself. The duty of the archaeologist is to transfer the unheard and unremembered ages (fires) through a mirror of a reflected time capsule until the physical, the mental, the spiritual, and the emotional are seen and heard in the present, loud and clear.

To the Aboriginal observer of the dig, the sound of the beat (drum) ever so faintly emerges from that distant past to the present. The beat is soundless to all except that distant relation who carries the beat deep within. As the dig moves on, the memory and sound of the beat of the drum (heart of the Aboriginal soul) increases in frequency and vibration. All this and much more is found in this book, *Legacy of Stone: Ancient Life on the Niagara Frontier.*

When I picked up this book to read and review, I was pleasantly surprised that the detailed graphic description and in-depth interpretation of recent experiences and findings held my interest, page after page; I didn't put the book down until it was finished. The excavation has been a balance of hard, laborious work, often under extreme weather conditions and the occasional reward of that work. An example of these rewards is the discovery of the ancient cooking pot, pottery with the contents recognizable enough to be translated into a recipe. The book introduces us to what it takes to be a field archaeologist, and I would suggest that it could be required reading for a student interested in becoming an archaeologist. It should also be of great interest to avocational archaeologists as well as mainstream readers interested in this field or in the geographic changes of the land base over periods of time.

The book is greatly enhanced by photos, illustrations, and particularly the sidebars, which contain valuable additional condensed, descriptive information and detail, but which stay within the parameters of the mainstream of the story. Throughout the book there are intriguing tidbits which continuously arouse the interest of the reader, such as the description of the mass emigrations of squirrels. On page 16 there is a very good description of an ossuary burial, and on page 33 an interesting account of the geographical changes over vast time periods. There is a diversity of information such as the comparison between a modern-day mall to the knowledge of plant uses. There is an acknowledgement of the information and knowledge which has been lost; knowledge which was the product of thousands of years of experience and refinement and which has re-emerged in the past 10 to 15 years in the medicinal uses of natural plants and herbs. The Aboriginal had, and still has that knowledge which has been, for the most part, outlawed from mainstream society.

I would like to take this opportunity to express my sincere gratitude to the authors for their sensitivity to the integrity, spirituality, and respect to Aboriginal Peoples of the past and present. It is clearly documented that if proper procedures are employed by the archaeologist and land developers with respect to these very vital issues and concerns of Aboriginal Peoples, then the development will be smoother, more efficient, and ultimately more successful. As stated in the book, "archaeological conservation and construction need not be mutually exclusive enterprises."

As alien and abhorrent as it is to Aboriginal People to cut into Mother Earth and dig up the past, I find myself somewhat between a rock and a hard place. Being an oppressed race in an ever-oppressing society, the proof that we were here thousands of years ago, are here, and shall be here justifies, to a small degree, this study of our past behaviours, habits, and customs.

In dealing with the vast expanse of time in man's eye and with humans of the past, in closing let me pass on this quote: "Every atom in your body, except for those of hydrogen, was manufactured by nuclear reaction inside a star and spread across space in a supernova explosion." We are literally made of stardust. The man or person who wishes to make a success of life will continue to learn. He knows that he needs more education and that his education did not cease when he left school or university. "The time will most assuredly come, and the best and wisest know not how soon, when all distinction, save those of goodness and virtue, shall cease, and death, the leveller of human greatness, shall reduce us all to the same level."

Wayne Hill
Executive Director
Fort Erie Native Friendship Centre

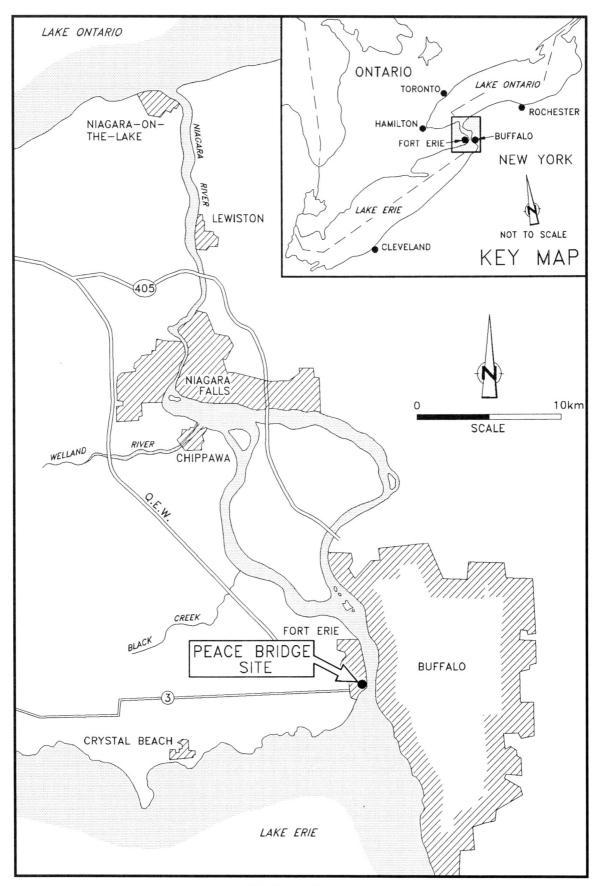

The Niagara Frontier.

Prologue

Echoes of the Past

SEPTEMBER 1814

When Private Neely opened the flap of the field hospital tent, the sun was beginning to rise above the horizon. He looked out across the lake and could just make out the wisps of smoke from the houses of Black Rock. It was an unusually calm day, but the temperature was nippy and his uniform was so ragged that the early morning air seemed to chill him to the bone. He had been on duty all night and had just checked on his friend, Morrow, who had been hit by shrapnel the day before. It had been Morrow's seventeenth birthday and the British had celebrated the occasion by scoring a direct hit on his tent with a 24-pound cannonball. One soldier had died miserably while several others, including Morrow, had been seriously injured.

Neely was eager to go to his own quarters and get some rest, since he was exhausted, but before he managed to step out of the tent the surgeon's mate, John Lawrence, yelled at him to find Semple. That could mean only one thing — that someone had just died and that Semple and he were going to have to bury him in the graveyard behind the field hospital. Tired and hungry, he cursed beneath his breath, knowing he would be up until at least noon.

As Neely emerged from the tent, his senses sharpened and he began to walk towards Semple's quarters. Climbing behind Captain Towson's battery on the big sand knoll known as Snake Hill, he could hear the constant rumble of explosions of both the British and American guns across the camp. The air was thick with smoke and the smell of gunpowder. The Americans had been under siege in this wretched fort since the beginning of August, and hundreds of rounds of British artillery fire rained down every day on the camp, killing or wounding at least half a dozen men. On one of the worst days, near the end of August, there had been over 20 American casualties from the bombardment and there was no escaping it. The British fired on any target, visible or imagined, including the American work parties that were burying the dead. He wasn't looking forward to the next few hours

The camp was huge, almost 30 acres in size, and as he descended the east side of Snake Hill, the fort buildings were still half a mile ahead. As he glanced to his left he saw a work party repairing a section of the perimeter breastworks that linked the fort with Towson's battery. Men were hauling in timbers to close a section of the wall that was likely breached by British artillery fire, while others were shovelling dirt to deepen the ditches in front and behind. Beyond the outer rim of the ditch, other work parties were dragging in tree limbs, saplings, and brush, and sharpening their ends to points, orienting them outwards to re-form the abattis. He was glad he wasn't a

"Brit," ordered to fight his way through that threatening barrier.

The tents for Semple's unit were just ahead and as he reached the mess area he spotted Semple sitting alone, eating a piece of hard bread and some salt pork — a meagre breakfast to fuel an eight-hour day of hard toil. It, nevertheless, reminded Neely of the fact that he hadn't eaten in 12 hours. There was no time for that now, however, as there was a grave to dig and he knew Lawrence would expect them back at the hospital at any moment.

Semple responded to the orders with little enthusiasm but within 10 minutes they were back at the field hospital looking for Lawrence. They found him helping to restrain a writhing patient who was having his left hand amputated. Neely shuddered when he realized the patient reminded him of his little 12-year-old brother who he hoped was safely back on the family farm in Vermont. It didn't look to Neely like the shot of whiskey, which was usually given prior to surgery of this nature, was doing its job. With a snap, the surgeon completed what he had started with a saw, and then cut through the remaining flesh with a scalpel. Much to the horror of the groaning teen, the surgeon threw the hand on the ground and while tying off some arteries, told Lawrence to bury it with Warren, the soldier who had died earlier that morning.

Neither Neely nor Semple had known Warren; he had arrived with the New York Militia less than a week ago and had been with a party sent to probe the British lines the day before. Almost all of the force had returned, with the exception of an officer from the Twenty-first who had been killed, and Warren, who had been reported missing in action. While the officer had been shot dead by a British picket, Warren had been wounded by a shot to his shoulder, and had managed to crawl and stumble his way back to the fort buildings. He had only just returned when a British round hit the side of a bastion, sending brick fragments into his back. When he was found, he was bleeding profusely and barely alive. They rushed him to the field hospital adjacent to Snake Hill and near his own camp. He made it through the night but died just as Neely was leaving the tent earlier that morning.

Neely and Semple quickly grabbed a couple of shovels and headed to the graveyard beside the hospital. The wind had picked up and the waves were crashing into the rocky shoreline, adding to the constant noise of the bombardment. They started to dig a hole, about six feet long and a few feet wide, next to the grave they had dug about a week ago. That grave had been a large one, taking almost half a day to dig, since it had to accommodate three soldiers, all shot in a skirmish with the British. They, too, had been rushed to the field hospital, and although the surgeon had tried his best — including removing a leg from one soldier in a complex amputation — they all died and were buried together.

A few hours later they were almost finished, although the hole was still a little narrow. As the British rounds were getting close, they agreed they would rather make the body fit the hole than the other way around. While Semple rested on his shovel, Neely decided to widen the hole just slightly on one end but stopped abruptly as a strangely formed rock fell into the hole. Neely leaned over and picked up the piece of stone, examining it closely. It was ovoid in shape, about the size of his palm, and was made of a variety of flint that he had noticed outcropped along the shoreline. It had been purposefully shaped somehow on both faces until it was regular in outline. Neely had just tossed the piece to Semple, asking him what he made of it when another two identical pieces fell out of the wall of the hole.

Just as Neely was about to pick up the other two, a British artillery round landed about 50 yards away and the two men ran for cover, forgetting for the moment their odd discovery. Since the hole was completely excavated — at least in their opinion — they made their way back to the hospital and reported to Lawrence that the job was done. When they told him about the specially shaped flint pieces that they had found, showing him the one that Semple still had, they asked him what he thought they were. All Lawrence had to offer was, "How the hell would I know, they must have been important to someone if there's more than one of them; now get Warren into that hole and don't forget the lad's hand!"

NOVEMBER 1987

It was a typical November morning in Fort Erie — bitterly cold and blustery with winds gusting off the lake. Although the tents covering the dig were flapping wildly and the propane heaters were running at full blast creating quite a din, you could still hear the scientists talking as they huddled over the exposed skeletons. The excavation complex was a hive of activity with a half dozen archaeologists uncovering a number of bodies, two biological anthropologists examining the bones of three individuals that had been interred in a common grave pit, a conservator working on a small metal object near the shoulder of one set of remains, and a number of United States Army officers looking on. In the corner of one of the tents, Sgt. Jay Llewellyn, a forensic photographer with the Armed Forces Institute of Pathology in Washington, was videotaping the activities.

It had been a strange fall for the crew from Archaeological Services Inc. (ASI), culminating in their work here amid colleagues from across northeastern North America. They had been retained by the Town of Fort Erie to get to the bottom of the mystery of the human remains that had turned up at a construction site along Lakeshore Road, south of the old fort and adjacent to what was known locally as Snake Hill. While neighbours had reported the discovery of bones to both the police and media the previous spring, it had taken six months for the various levels of government to sort out a course of action. Archaeologists hadn't arrived on the scene until early October. In the dirt left over from the construction that spring, the ASI crew had found part of a human jaw, some teeth, and a piece of an arm bone, an ominous sign of what lay ahead. While it wasn't possible to determine the origin of the fragments, which had obviously been disturbed from their original context, the crew hoped that other remains might offer clues to their origin.

Within a few days of those initial finds, a number of intact skeletons were found, revealing an interesting pattern. The bodies had been placed in graves on their backs with their heads to the west, fully extended and often with their hands folded neatly across their pelvis areas. This pattern was recognizably European and once the small, pewter disks, inscribed with a script "I" or "US," were found on the bodies, and identified as the remains of buttons that had fallen through the body cavity as flesh and clothing had rotted away, it quickly became apparent that they were American soldiers from the War of 1812.

It turned out that the graveyard was in the area of some of the bloodiest fighting of the fall of 1814, during the American occupation of Old Fort Erie. Luckily, the officer responsible for constructing the defensive works at the fort during the American occupation had left records that included a detailed map of American fortifications. Their defensive lines had been anchored at the southwest end of the camp with an artillery battery on Snake Hill, just a few yards east of where the graves were discovered. The British had laid siege to the fort, determined to drive the Americans back across the river, constantly bombarding the fort and associated camp for most of the late summer and fall of 1814.

Once it had been determined that the burials were those of US military personnel from the War of 1812, the crew was caught up in a whirlwind of international diplomacy, science, and media attention, resulting in an offer of unlimited support for the project by the US army — a most astounding but valuable result. Now, several weeks later, with an international team of experts in place, the project was humming along at a steady pace.

That was, until this morning. Archaeologists Debbie Steiss and Andrew Clish had found a relatively small grave stain the day before. Grave stains are easy to spot once topsoil is removed because the mixture of topsoil and subsoil, used to fill in a grave, remains a slightly different colour from the surrounding earth. They had documented the stain and had proceeded to expose the skeletal remains within the grave when they noted some darker stains near the foot of the grave.

Steiss went to find Ron Williamson, who was in charge of the dig, to report that it looked like the grave had perhaps intruded upon deposits from an earlier time period and that the site might be multicomponent. When they returned, they found that Clish had already recovered several aboriginal artifacts in the area of the darker stains. He had discovered a smooth ground stone tool that resembled a modern whetstone, as well as some charcoal and animal bone that had been calcined in some ancient fire. Within minutes, the entire research team had descended upon the burial location and a discussion ensued to determine how to document both occupations of the site. It was decided to complete the exposure of the remains and to investigate the prehistoric deposits once the body had been removed.

Steiss and Clish had the body fully exposed by the late afternoon, having carefully avoided any further disturbance of the prehistoric deposits. Despite having been in the ground for 173 years, the skeleton showed clear signs of a traumatic death. An iron ball was found next to his right shoulder blade and a fragment of brick rested along his upper spine, as if he had been exposed somehow to an explosion that had sent a brick fragment deep into his back. His position within the grave, however, was somewhat odd. The west half of the grave was simply too narrow for the body and he had been placed so that his left shoulder was slightly higher than his right side. Steiss had just left to inform Llewellyn that he could photograph the burial when she heard an audible gasp from Clish. Again, various team members gathered around the grave. Clish had discovered that an additional lower forearm and hand of a very young teenager had been placed below the body in such a way that it now appeared beside the right elbow of the individual. It looked, for all intents and purposes, like his third hand, except that it had been sawn off at the wrist. The surgeon must have been in a hurry though, given the little tab of bone at the end of the cut where the hand had been snapped off.

The amputated limb confirmed the suspicions of Williamson and some of the other team members — that the graveyard had been a burial ground for a nearby field hospital. The historian for the project, Dr. Joseph Whitehorne, had found references in American military records to a small graveyard that was described as being "just back of Towson's Battery" near a field hospital and the camp of the New York Militia. Further evidence of medical intervention was present in some of the other graves. A few of the bodies, for example, had included straight pins that were probably used to fasten bandages, and the positioning of the ankles on a number of the skeletons indicated that they had been bound together before burial to make it easier to carry the corpse, a practice typical of preparations for burial after death in a field hospital, rather than one associated with the burying of dead in a battlefield.

Clish trowelled the wall above the burial site, making final preparations for photographing the skeleton. Within seconds, three large, identical flint tools, much larger and cruder than arrowheads but clearly shaped by human hands, fell into the grave, barely missing the skull of the individual. The archaeologists knew instinctively that this was a very significant discovery, but they decided to completely define the prehistoric find before announcing it to the rest of the team. There was a small, almost indistinguishable stain in the wall, about two feet below the surface and three feet above the grave, where the crew could make out several more of the stone tools. There was one part of the stain that they figured had been disturbed when the grave had been dug in 1814 and they wondered if any of the artifacts had been removed. At the very least, two pieces had been previously dislodged since they found them while trowelling behind the skull.

As Clish and Williamson excavated around the tools, they were careful to control their mounting excitement, not wanting to miss any of the details of their orientation and distribution, details that might be clues to their origin. By the time they were finished, they had unearthed 20 of these large tools, as well as a roundish fist-sized stone that Williamson figured had been used like a hammer to shape the stones. What was most exciting, however, was that the objects had clearly been cached or hoarded in this secret location sometime in the very distant past, perhaps as part of some ceremonial offering. In fact, Williamson guessed that they may not have been held by human hands for nearly 4000 years. As thrilling as that prospect was, the archaeologists were even more interested in speculating about the ancient human drama that had ultimately led to this curious discovery and about the possibility that other treasures from the past lay hidden from view along this stretch of shoreline, on what is known as the Niagara Frontier.

Peace Bridge site stratification in truck pad area, looking east towards Niagara Boulevard. Note the two layers of granular overlying the paleosol. Rob MacDonald is trowelling the interface between the paleosol and the subsoil in the area of a cultural pit feature.

1 Layers in the Sand

Little did we know then that within five years, many of us would be back investigating one of the richest prehistoric aboriginal sites in northeastern North America, and only a kilometre or two northeast of where we had been in 1987. On the other hand, we had been very aware of the significant potential for encountering vestiges of ancient life on the Niagara, if only on the basis of what we had been recovering at Snake Hill.

Indeed, a myriad of aboriginal artifacts, including ceramic pot fragments and flint tools, had been found scattered around the various soldiers' remains. If the relevant government agencies, the media, and the general public had not been so focused on the admittedly dramatic discoveries dating to the War of 1812, they may have been interested to learn of the other finds we had made at the site.

Perhaps the most spectacular prehistoric aboriginal discovery made at the Snake Hill site was the mysterious cache of half-made flint tools called bifaces, which dated to about 1800 BC. Bifaces represent an early to middle stage in the reduction of large blocks of flint into usable, fashioned tools such as spear points. The absence at the find of the small flake debris, created when the flint block is reduced, suggested that the tools had been made elsewhere and deposited there, perhaps as an offering.

However they came to be there, these items indicate that aboriginals had used the area as a source of stone for their tools and weapons. There was also evidence of a fishing camp at the site, used by Iroquoians, but in more recent times — it appeared to be only about 600 years old!

The point illustrated so strikingly at the Snake Hill site was that the past is both hidden from view and layered, and that it is possible to travel through time by simply excavating a hole in our backyards with a shovel. It is also quite apparent that in some places that hole might land you in completely different eras, depending on the depths at which you stop digging. The historian and geographer David Lowenthal once wrote that the past is a foreign country. While he was actually commenting on our inability to know with any certainty what went on in the distant past, since it is shaped by us in our interpretations, the metaphor can be applied to archaeologists in a different way.

Archaeologists regularly travel to many foreign countries while working at essentially the same place, assuming that people at radically different times in the past viewed their surroundings in radically different ways. How dissimilarly, for example, did the aboriginals of 4000 years ago, the occupants of that fishing camp 600 years ago, the soldiers of 1814, or the archaeologists in 1987 for that matter, view the world, despite sharing that same piece of landscape along the Lake Erie shoreline? The essential task of the archaeologist is to answer that question while travelling through time.

A cache of 20 early stage bifaces was recovered from the Snake Hill site among the remains of American soldiers from the War of 1812. The bifaces, seven of which are illustrated here, were made of Onondaga flint. The absence of any accompanying flake debris indicates that they were made elsewhere and deposited at the site, perhaps as an offering.

It was five years later, in 1992, that we were called back to that shoreline to conduct what we thought would be a routine predevelopment assessment. Within hours of arriving, however, we found ourselves embarking on a scientific journey that would challenge our abilities over the course of several years. Not only would we travel through time at a dizzying pace, but on occasion we would have no idea where or when we had stopped and with whose past we were dealing.

The Buffalo and Fort Erie Public Bridge Authority, the international agency that operates the Peace Bridge between Fort Erie, Ontario, and Buffalo, New York, initiated the assessment. They were involved with an ambitious redevelopment of their commercial customs facilities, situated adjacent to the Niagara River and north of the Peace Bridge, in Fort Erie. It was the intention of the Peace Bridge Authority to close Walnut Street, at Niagara Boulevard, to allow greater room for trucks to turn as they exited newly constructed customs inspection booths in the truck yard and made their way either to the highway or to detailed inspection bays in a large, also newly constructed customs facility. The need for the redevelopment was clear since the commercial truck traffic had been increasing dramatically since the Canada-US Trade Agreement took effect in 1989. Whether one agreed with the legislation or not, the need for more spacious and efficient customs facilities was undeniable.

A few days before we arrived, substantial quantities of aboriginal artifacts had been accidentally discovered under a rear concrete garage slab during demolition of the house at 9 Walnut Street, on the northwest corner of Walnut Street and Niagara Boulevard. Further earth-moving activity on the property had been suspended by the Peace Bridge Authority in order to allow us time to conduct an assessment of the property. It was not only the discovery of the new artifacts, however, that prompted the study. Many of the older residents of Fort Erie could recall two well-publicized excavations in the mid-1960s, when archaeologists from both Canadian and American universities unearthed hundreds of aboriginal skeletons nearby and shipped them to the National Museum in Ottawa where they had been for decades, a fact with which the local aboriginal population was uncomfortable.

Those events had occurred just a few blocks north of where the Peace Bridge Authority was planning to construct their new facilities. The legislation governing the discovery and analysis of such remains had changed substantially in the intervening decades. The Peace Bridge Authority wanted to do the right thing, from the perspectives of both government legislation and their aboriginal neighbours.

Our objectives were, therefore, simple — to determine the nature and extent of

FLINTKNAPPING
The Craft of Chipping Stone Tools

As any stonemason will tell you, there are basically two ways to shape stone for any given purpose: you can break it with a sharp blow, or you can grind it with something abrasive. Over 2 million years ago, our far-distant ancestors discovered that by breaking certain types of stone, they could fashion cutting tools with extremely sharp edges. Unfortunately, the popular image of stone tools tends to dwell on the crude, early forms and the prehuman beings that used them.

Most would be surprised to learn that the trade of flintknapping was practised in some industrialized societies well into the current century. For example, the town of Brandon, in England, was once the gun-flint production centre for the British military, and many historic buildings in that part of East Anglia are made of knapped blocks of flint. In Cyprus, the traditional method of threshing involved spreading the grain on the ground and running over it with a toboggan-like sled with flint blades embedded in the bottom. Even today, a few specialized craftspeople make a living by chipping flint, although most are producing replicas of prehistoric tools for collectors, museums, and universities.

Flint is chemically similar to glass, composed mostly of the mineral, silica. Indeed, wherever a volcanic glass called obsidian was available, it was a favourite material for stone tool manufacture. Although flint and obsidian are relatively brittle, they are harder than steel. This is why sparks, which are actually white-hot metal filings, are produced when they strike steel. At the same time, being like glass they produce extremely sharp edges when broken. In fact, the electron microscope has revealed that an obsidian blade is sharper than a surgical scalpel made of stainless steel. Since flint has microscopic crystals and no grain or preferred direction of cleavage, it can be worked into complex shapes by flaking or chipping it along the edges. The process of flake removal is highly predictable, so the experienced and adept flintknapper can produce any number of shapes.

Most formal chipped stone tools are bifacial, meaning they are more or less flat with two sides or faces. In fact, archaeologists refer to bifacially worked tool preforms as bifaces. Some examples of traditional stone tools include knives, projectile points (spear, javelin, and arrowheads), drill bits, axes, hide scrapers, spokeshaves, and engraving tools. In some cultures, however, flintknappers also produced artistic items, including jewellery, animal effigies, and other representational art.

Since flintknapping is a process involving the reduction of a large block of flint into a much smaller tool by flaking, it results in vast quantities of waste flakes called debitage. Characteristics of these flakes and the flake scars left on the tools allow the archaeologist to determine whether any given flake was detached by a hard blow from a hammerstone, by a soft blow from an antler hammer, or by pressure applied with a pointed antler flaker. Many inferences can be drawn from this information, including: how certain tools were made; what flintknapping tool-kits were used; what flintknapping techniques were employed; whether or not flintknapping was a generalized or specialized skill; whether the particular site inhabitants were sedentary, based on the ratio of carefully prepared versus expedient tools; what the preferred raw materials were and how available they were; and whether or not conservation of raw material is indicated through resharpening and reuse of tools.

In addition, by analyzing the wear patterns and organic residues on tools themselves, inferences can be drawn concerning how specific tools were used. It is even possible that once the more prosaic issues of technology and function have been considered, the size and shape of the artifacts can be examined in the context of "style," a concept that, while difficult to define, is used frequently to identify ethnic affiliations.

Guild Hall, Norwich, constructed from knapped blocks of flint — another example of East Anglian flintknapping in England.

the archaeological deposits and to recommend the necessary actions to reduce, if not eliminate, any potential adverse impacts posed by the redevelopment plan, to the deposits containing the artifacts.

When we arrived we began by screening the backdirt stockpiled during the initial demolition, in case artifacts that could be linked with a particular time or culture in the past had been uncovered by the construction activities. Using a mechanical sorter that separated the soil from rocks and artifacts, which were spewed down a chute and onto a tarpaulin, we began to recover a number of ceramic pot fragments and flint tools, some of which were thousands of years old. While the recovery of these items gave us a head start on the time periods that were represented in the deposits in this location, we had no idea of the extent or richness of the site. We, therefore, also excavated a number of controlled test units to examine the stratigraphy or the history of soil deposition in the area, and to measure the artifact yield for a test area of known size.

We were not prepared for the results from the first test unit. In fact, we were simply astounded. A one-metre-square test unit had been hand-excavated in the lawn, just metres from the intersection and adjacent to the sidewalk, and it had yielded almost 5000 artifacts. At other sites throughout North America, archaeologists would literally jump at the prospect of excavating a site that promised to yield even 100 artifacts from a unit of similar size. This was our first glimpse of the incredibly rich deposit we now called the Peace Bridge site. The unit had also revealed a complex stratigraphy involving a number of buried soil layers. A black organic soil layer was detected at a depth of 40 centimetres, extending 50–55 centimetres below the modern lawn surface.

In a second test unit, excavated in the area of the former concrete pad about 30 metres west of the first test unit, artifacts were recovered from the same organic soil layer, which appeared there at a depth of approximately 60 centimetres, below a series of disturbed modern strata.

This black organic artifact-laden soil is called a

The study area. The closely spaced contour lines on the left side of the map represent the large ridge of glacial sediment deposited by the Laurentide Ice Sheet during the last glaciation, about 13 000 years ago.

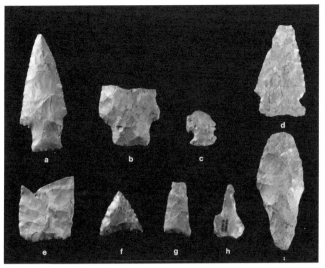

paleosol, and it was this paleosol that would become the focus of archaeologists, planners, and construction crews in this part of Fort Erie — at least until all of the Peace Bridge's plans had been realized.

We were also interested to note that pit features had been excavated through this paleosol into the sterile sands below. These pits had been excavated by the prehistoric inhabitants of the site and used to store foods or bury their refuse. Since the pits were originally dug through the dark organic soil into the subsoil, their shapes and depths were forever recorded in the lighter-coloured sandy subsoil, as the holes were filled with the darker soil leaving discernable stains. In addition to organic soils and ash, some of these pits were found to contain ceramic vessel fragments, while others seemed to contain only flint chips and tools.

The ceramic fragments found on the site included small sherds from the rims of nine separate vessels. Ceramic vessels first appear in the Niagara Frontier about 500 BC. They were used daily as water storage containers or cooking pots. The craftswomen who made these vessels did not use a potter's wheel, but skilfully coiled and pinched the clay to the form of the pots, and then smoothed them and applied decoration to the interior and exterior surfaces of the upper rims. These decorative attributes have traditionally been used by archaeologists in an effort to identify the ethnic affiliations of their makers and to date the site on which they are found.

The designs on six of these vessels consisted of oblique impressions made along the upper rim with a stick that had been wrapped with a cord. A row of circular holes had also been punched into the interior surface of the vessels, resulting in raised nodes on the opposite surfaces. Vessels with that type of decoration are known to be 1200 to 1300 years old. The remaining three pots had poorly shaped collars and were decorated with linear impressions on the collar and interior, some of which had been made with a fingernail and some with a piece of flint or bone. They are more recent, perhaps dating from AD 1200 to 1400.

The flint items included seven spear points and two arrow points, encompassing thousands of years of occupation of the site. The earliest spear point was of a Late Archaic culture called Genesee, dating to between 2000 and 1500 BC. Most of the other projectile points were also from the Late Archaic and Early Woodland periods, suggesting the site was occupied mainly by hunter-gatherers before the introduction of corn into the region. On the other hand, the recovery of the ceramic fragments as well as two arrow points, one dating to the latter half of the first millennium AD, just after the introduction of corn, and the other to the Late Woodland period, indicated more or less continuous prehistoric use of the site over at least 4000 years.

THE OLD WORLD
Before It Became the New World

The Western scientific tradition has a habit of viewing phenomena from its own perspective. This is why Europe and Asia became known as the Old World, while the Americas were known as the New World. In reality, the New World is as old as the Old World and some would argue that people have lived in the Americas for as long as anywhere else.

Since most of what has happened in the Great Lakes region occurred well before there was any kind of written history, both aboriginals and non-aboriginals have had to rely on archaeology to tell the story of that distant past. The earliest evidence suggests that small bands of nomadic hunters moved into the region as the continental glacier was retreating 11 000 years ago. Known as Palaeo-Indians, these people pursued caribou, mastodon, and other game, in what was then an open boreal forest or tundra-like environment. Although very few of their camps have ever been found, archaeologists can readily identify their stone tools. The most diagnostic feature of the large spear-heads of this period are the prominent flutes or grooves on each face of the points.

The replacement of fluted spear points with side-notched forms at about 10 000 years ago marks the beginning of the Archaic period. By this time, hunter-gatherer bands had likely settled into familiar hunting territories. The landscape, however, continued to change, with much lower water levels in the Great Lakes and the expansion of more temperate forests.

Over the following millennia, technological and cultural change is evident in the wide variety of tools produced, which in turn are reflections of the shifts in hunting strategies necessitated by a constantly evolving environment. From about 3000 years ago, however, an increasing number of these tools assume additional social and symbolic functions, as indicated by their use as grave offerings. Some are made of banded slate and rival any of the art produced anywhere in the world.

The arrival of ceramics around 2800 years ago represents the beginning of the Woodland period,

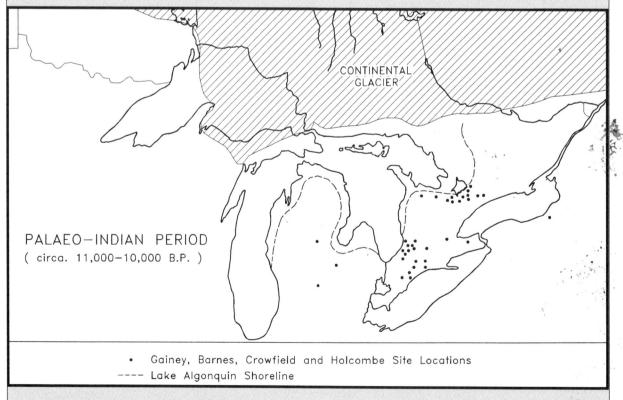

PALAEO—INDIAN PERIOD
(circa. 11,000—10,000 B.P.)

CONTINENTAL GLACIER

- Gainey, Barnes, Crowfield and Holcombe Site Locations
---- Lake Algonquin Shoreline

Distribution of Palaeo-Indian sites in the southern Great Lakes region, 11 000 years before present.

The Prehistory of the Niagara Frontier

PALAEO—INDIAN PERIOD
(c. 9,000 B.C. — 7,000 B.C.)

- first human occupation of the area
- hunters of caribou and now—extinct Pleistocene mammals
- small camps
- band level society

ARCHAIC PERIOD
(c. 7,000 B.C. — 1,000 B.C.)

Early (c. 7,000 B.C. — 6,000 B.C.)
Middle (c. 6,000 B.C. — 3,000 B.C.)
Late (c. 3,000 B.C. — 1,000 B.C.)
- hunter—gatherers
- small camps
- band level society

WOODLAND PERIOD (c. 1,000 B.C. — A.D. 1650)

Early (c. 1,000 B.C. — 400 B.C.)
Middle (c. 400 B.C. — A.D. 600)
- hunter—gatherers
- large and small camps
- band level society with kin based political system
- mortuary ceremonialism & trade networks

Transitional (c. A.D. 600 — A.D. 900)
- introduction of agriculture
- base settlements on floodplains
- introduction of bow and arrow

Late/Iroquoian (c. A.D. 900 — A.D. 1650)
- major shift to agricultural dependency
- villages, hamlets, camps
- development of socio–political complexity

which in turn is usually divided into the Early, Middle, Transitional, and Late Woodland sub-periods.

Although a useful temporal marker for archaeologists, the appearance of these ceramics, known as Vinette 1 ware, does not seem to have profoundly changed the hunter-gatherer lifestyle. There is compelling evidence in the Early Woodland period, however, for an expanding network of societies across northeastern North America that shared burial rituals.

A common practice, for example, was the application of large quantities of symbolically important red ochre (ground iron hematite) to human remains and the inclusion in graves of offerings of objects that represented a considerable investment of time and artistic skill. Moreover, the nature and variety of these exotic grave goods suggest that members of the community outside of the immediate family of the deceased were contributing mortuary offerings.

The most significant change during this and the ensuing centuries, especially during the Middle Woodland period, was the increase in trade of exotic items, no doubt stimulated by contact with more complex, mound-building cultures in the Ohio and Mississippi valleys. These items were included in increasingly sophisticated burial ceremonies that occasionally involved the construction of burial mounds by local groups.

While these developments may have emanated from the need for greater social solidarity among growing aboriginal populations that were competing for resources, the period has come to be regarded as one of the first continental free trade zones documented in the old New World. What is perhaps even more astonishing is that the Niagara Frontier may have served much the same role then as it does today.

The pace of cultural change seems to have accelerated remarkably after about 1200 years ago, having been energized by the introduction of tropical cultigens, such as maize and squash. The appearance of these plants initiated a long and gradual transition to food production away from reliance on naturally occurring resources, a trend that is seen in many places in the world where archaeologists examine the adoption of an agricultural way of life.

The incipient agriculture of these Transitional Woodland communities obviously led to decreased mobility as people tended to their crops. Sites became more intensively occupied and subject to a greater degree of internal spatial organization. These changes ultimately contributed to substantial population growth, increasing reliance on agriculture, and the development of socially and politically complex Late Woodland societies, including the historically recorded Iroquoian-speaking tribal confederacies, such as the Huron, Neutral, and Iroquois.

A detailed analysis of a sample of the flint chips and other flint tools from the site indicated that a considerable amount of time was spent by the inhabitants reducing large blocks of flint into smaller more manageable pieces, and then further refining those pieces. The latter activity was also indicated by the recovery of 36 bifaces, all manufactured from the flint that outcrops along the shoreline, and ranging in quality and degree of flaking from crude, early stage bifaces, like the ones found in the Snake Hill cache, to refined, late-stage bifaces, that resemble arrowheads.

These findings were not surprising and confirmed that the primary reason that people were at the site was to make the stone tools they needed throughout the year. As most were hunter-gatherers, this was only a stop in an annual round of hunting, fishing, and collecting, but perhaps one of the more important stops, since all of the other activities depended to some degree on their having the necessary tools to carry out the other life-sustaining tasks.

The press reports on the Walnut site.

Since the test excavations had provided us with enough information concerning the very rich nature of the deposits at this spot, we recommended to the Peace Bridge Authority that any further soil disturbance of any nature should be preceded by an archaeological assessment. Our main fear was that any construction activity might impact human remains, a likelihood that had been amply demonstrated years ago. Thus, prior to the excavation for a new storm-water catchbasin aside the curb at the same intersection the following spring, we removed the soils down to the paleosol that had contained all of the artifacts. When we had screened through the paleosol, we noticed that there were two large, dark stains in the sandy subsoil, the hallmarks of pit features.

Once we had carefully defined and recorded the stains, we began to excavate down into the features. It was with both surprise and relief that we encountered human remains in each pit almost immediately; surprise — that one of our first areas of investigation had come up with human burials, and relief — that we had advised our clients to check for such remains. Otherwise, the skeletal remains would have been seriously disturbed by the placement of the new catchbasin. An even greater surprise awaited us, however, as we carried on to define the burials in the pits.

The first burial represented the remains of a fully intact woman in her early thirties. The fact that her bones were positioned correctly to one another suggested that she had been put in the pit at death and not sometime after, as is frequently the case with prehistoric aboriginal burials. She had been placed on her left side in a tightly flexed position, like a fetus in the womb. The real surprise came with the second burial. It had been truncated by a Consumers Gas pipeline trench, so that only the lower limbs and hip bones remained. In the absence of detailed laboratory analysis, not enough of the second burial was present to determine gender and age, although it was possible to determine that this individual was also placed in a tightly flexed position, lying on his or her left side.

While no grave goods accompanied either interment, the recovery of ceramic body sherds from the grave fill, that date to the Transitional Woodland period *(circa AD 600–900)*, suggested that the burials related to an occupation no earlier than that period. There was no sign of any of the other skeletal remains of the second burial and it was assumed that they had been lost or dispersed further along the pipeline trench when it had been excavated, probably in the 1980s.

The excavation for the catchbasin had been in a very open area. Sensing the prospect of a good story, various Canadian and US media began monitoring the scene within hours. The discovery of the human remains had become public information by the next day, and crowds awaited us as we continued with our investigations. Ron Williamson, who was leading the investigation for our ASI team, seized the opportunity to inform the general public and the relevant land management and development agencies (including Consumers Gas, the Niagara Parks Commission, and the Town of Fort Erie) about the dangers of any kind of construction in this area. A truncated human body was about as dramatic a warning as it was possible to make.

Officials from all of the agencies, including John Teal, the mayor of Fort Erie, were invited to examine the remains first-hand. Most committed their agencies and corporations almost immediately to ensuring that this sort of debacle would never occur again. Indeed, since that discovery the Town of Fort Erie, like the Peace Bridge Authority, has ensured, wherever possible, that their operations would not impact such sensitive archaeological deposits in this part of Fort Erie. Consumers Gas has had their operations monitored in the area as well.

What began as a rational well-conceived plan on the part of the Public Bridge Authority to pre-check their construction sites quickly evolved almost overnight into a voluntary, local prerequisite for development in this part of Fort Erie. The Fort Erie Native Friendship Centre also shared a vital interest in the two burials at Walnut Street. Upon the discovery of the human remains, officials from the centre were contacted immediately to seek their advice and counsel on a course of action. Under the newly revised Ontario Cemeteries Act, the closest band was to be considered the "friends of the deceased" when the exact cultural affiliation of the remains could not be established. The Friendship Centre was deemed the appropriate contact by Six Nations Council in Oshweken, the closest band.

After consulting with elders and faithkeepers, the local community, under the leadership of Wayne Hill, instructed the Peace Bridge Authority and us to avoid any further disturbance of the burials, if that was at all possible. The Authority responded quickly by changing their plans for the catchbasins and instructing their engineers to make alternative ones. The catchbasin was moved and the remains were reburied without further incident.

First, a tobacco ceremony was held over the burials, asking the souls of the dead for forgiveness for having disturbed them and assuring them that they would not be disturbed again. These decisions and procedures that we followed defined the protocol for the work that was to be undertaken over the subsequent years. With the understanding of the provincial agencies, following the protocol became the *modus operandi* for the project and opened a new era in working relations between the development, aboriginal, and archaeological communities. This new spirit of cooperation would come to be tested over the ensuing years as hundreds of thousands of artifacts were excavated and dozens of burials encountered during the redevelopment of the Peace Bridge facilities.

The relatively small size of the test excavation in the Walnut-Niagara area had still not indicated the true extent of the site. How far did this remarkably rich deposit extend north or south along the Niagara Boulevard or inland from the shoreline? Was it connected with the nearby digs that had been conducted decades previously? Were there other burials nearby? All that we knew for certain was that before anything could be built, further excavation was required.

David Boyle, father of Canadian archaeology, seen here at the Ontario Provincial Museum.

(Ontario Archives)

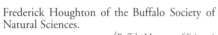

Frederick Houghton of the Buffalo Society of Natural Sciences.

(Buffalo Museum of Science)

2   First Discoveries

The truly memorable moments in archaeology are those associated with the discovery of spectacular sites and the instants at which patterns finally begin to emerge from the muddle of data, hinting at stories of past human lives.

Unfortunately, the latter often occur well after the former. It was only with the insight gained from several years of detailed excavation that we were able to fashion the overwhelming mound of archaeological data from both our initial and subsequent excavations into a picture of what actually occurred in ancient times along that stretch of Niagara River shoreline. On the other hand, the general enormity of what is now referred to as the Peace Bridge site was glimpsed from its very first discovery at the turn of the century.

That story begins in the late 1800s and early 1900s and is known only from fragments of letters, museum accession records, and exploration accounts from institutions in Buffalo and Toronto. It is known, for example, that David Boyle, often referred to as the father of Canadian archaeology, visited the area in 1887, during his initial season as provincial archaeologist for Ontario. In the process of documenting what is now known as an important site dating to the middle of the first millennium AD on Point Abino, in Fort Erie, Boyle made the following remarks in his 1891 report of the Canadian Institute:

> To many people in this country it is a source of wonder where the Indians procured their flint, but to the dwellers along the eastern end of Lake Erie this matter is plain. Immense quantities of chert are found in the limestone forming the outcrops near the shore. Many of the nodules are sufficiently large to yield material for a score or two of arrow-tips or spear-heads, and although the quality in general is not of a character to permit of producing the finest specimens of flaking, there are occasional pieces that present excellent fractures. For miles, along the sandy beach heaps of flakes may be seen. The number and extent of these warrant the belief that here the Indian fletcher carried on his trade both for "home and foreign consumption," as relics of this kind are found in all parts of the country corresponding in appearance with the Lake Erie material.

Boyle, a self-taught archaeologist and former school principal, was Canada's first full-time professional archaeologist. He began his archaeological career with the Canadian Institute, a learned society that was established in 1851 to share and disseminate information about eastern Canada and to provide a forum for discussion of scientific problems and discoveries.

Although its creation was not unique, in that other urban centres in North America were also establishing such organizations at this time, it was the largest in Canada. By the late nineteenth century, the Institute and its museum had been transformed into a multi-disciplinary research agency, housing a growing regional archaeological collection. Boyle went on to fill the position of curator, from 1896 to 1911, at the Ontario Provincial Museum, the collections of which later became part of the Royal Ontario Museum.

Boyle worked diligently at maintaining contacts with numerous museum and university-based American archaeologists, such as W. Beauchamp and William Henry Holmes at the Smithsonian Institution, and F.W. Putnam of the Peabody Museum at Harvard University. Indeed, his archaeological reports for Ontario, which laid the foundation upon which Canadian scientific archaeology was based, were cited widely by American archaeologists. A more obvious reason for Boyle's correspondence with his American counterparts was that he had few Canadian colleagues!

One of Boyle's more junior contemporaries in Buffalo, New York, was Frederick Houghton, a principal in the Buffalo public school system, renowned for his method of teaching English to non-English-speaking adults and children. Houghton was also a self-taught archaeologist, although he had received training in geology at Harvard University. He worked in his spare time for the Buffalo Society of Natural Sciences, describing the geology of western New York and surveying archaeological sites in New York and southwestern Ontario, focusing on the Niagara Frontier. Like Boyle, he was awarded the prestigious Cornplanter Medal from the National Society of Natural Sciences for his efforts in archaeology. He was later instrumental in creating a wildlife sanctuary near his home in Springville, New York.

Boyle and Houghton are unlikely to have corresponded, given the differences in their ages, and the fact that Boyle suffered a debilitating stroke in 1908, during Houghton's work in the Niagara Frontier. Houghton is central to this story, however, for being the first person to actually record the Peace Bridge site. He conducted the first focused research in the region resulting in a comprehensive list of sites in the Niagara Frontier for the Buffalo Society of Natural Sciences. Between 1907 and 1909, Houghton documented and visited hundreds of sites, including many on the western side of the Niagara River.

In his report on this work, he identified a village and quarry site on the shoreline between the village of Fort Erie and the ruins of Old Fort Erie, describing the beach as "one continuous refuse heap in which occurs points, potsherds, and a few bone articles." Houghton was impressed with the quality and abundance of flint on the beach at Fort Erie. He observed that the shoreline was strewn with chips, flakes, blocks, and half-formed implements, all of which constitute the waste of aboriginal quarrying and manufacture. He also noted that caches of oval blanks are sometimes found in such places, and that the site was not so much a village as a great well-established camping place for parties who came there for a supply of flint. He reported that pipes, stone axes, a complete clay jar, a beautiful stone effigy pipe, and a number of graves were found on the terrace above the beach.

This was the first detailed description of the extent and richness of the Peace Bridge site, which was to seize the attention of both the archaeological community and the general public in the 1960s and again in the 1990s. Interestingly, Houghton had also documented what he called a village site and possibly a mound at the point known as Snake Hill, just beyond the ruins at Old Fort Erie.

It was almost 60 years before archaeologists returned to the southeastern Niagara peninsula. In the late 1950s and early 1960s, Marian White, Associate Professor of

Anthropology, State University of New York at Buffalo, and Assistant Curator of Anthropology at the Buffalo Museum of Science, quietly conducted research in the Niagara Frontier, not only re-examining known Neutral sites, but also looking for new sites on both the American and Canadian sides of the Niagara River. White was to become quite a local celebrity, however, when she responded to a panicked call for help from town officials in Fort Erie, in July of 1964.

On July 17, Jim Flake, a local contractor had uncovered a massive quantity of human bone while grading a portion of the first terrace adjacent to the Niagara River, near the intersection of Forsythe Street and Niagara Boulevard. He was working in a grocery store parking lot on private property owned by Antonio Marinaccio. This discovery was made well before there was any clear federal or provincial legislation regarding responsibility for such finds. Decisions regarding the site were made by the Fort Erie council. The mayor in 1964 was John (Jack) Teal, father of the mayor, John Teal, who visited the Walnut Street site 28 years later in the 1990s.

The younger Teal was clearly interested in the history of his city as well. In fact, after witnessing the Walnut Street burials, Mayor Teal forwarded to Williamson an excerpt from a Christmas souvenir booklet which had been prepared for Fort Erie in 1911. While it provides a fascinating historical perspective, it was an important promotional booklet in its day, featuring a story on an old log house, once situated east of Niagara Street, between Forsythe and Princess streets. It was apparently the first building erected in Fort Erie in the eighteenth century, having been surrounded by a dense forest of black ash.

The mayor forwarded the piece, however, since the text mentions:

> an Indian camp located on the flats — or the present site of the Village of Fort Erie, and the arrow making industry was located on the river front near the junction of Goderich and Garrison Roads, as a certain grade of flint suitable for the purpose is found there. A bed of the chippings is still to be seen. Several Indian graves have been discovered on Walnut and Goderich Streets, also on the hill property of the Douglas Estate.

Clearly, the Peace Bridge burials were not the first to be found on Walnut Street, nor would they be the last.

The Teal family was not the only example of a "full circle" coincidence, however, as it was Peter Flake, son of Jim Flake, that we worked with whenever we needed the help of mechanical equipment. Not only did Peter become an honorary member of our crew, but Jim Flake was a welcome visitor to the site and occasional operator when his son was unavailable.

The 1964 discovery led to a difficult situation for the senior Teal, not made easy by the lack of cooperation of the landowner, who almost immediately demanded $50 a day from the town to cover his losses for not being able to use his parking lot. The more crucial issue faced by the town, however, was finding the appropriate experts to deal with Jim Flake's discovery of human bones. After attempting to find advice and assistance from the University of Western Ontario, the University of Toronto, the Royal Ontario Museum, and the National Museum of Canada, the town turned, in desperation, to the Buffalo Museum. Dr. Marian White responded promptly, accompanied by a group of her students as well as members of the Frederick M. Houghton Chapter of the New York State Archaeological Association, many of whom would later become well-known archaeologists.

Dr. Marian White considers a *Times-Review* question on her findings at the Orchid site, while Jim Flake watches the team sifting the fine soil where his bulldozer uncovered the remains.

(*Times-Review*, July 23, 1964)

As time was of the essence, the Buffalo team commenced investigations immediately. They had to work in haste, as the landowner was constantly threatening to shut things down and the town had decided to fund the archaeological work and provide police protection for a 10-day period only.

Almost immediately, the dig was a major local attraction, drawing dozens of people to watch the proceedings daily. The local weekly, the *Times-Review*, ran stories on the dig and the attendant administrative hassles for several weeks. One editorial, entitled "The Human Family," especially captured the spirit and purpose of the dig:

The Bones — brown and brittle — robbed of their thin blanket of fine earth lay in a heap under the blazing Friday sun. Small girls scuffed bare feet in the dry soil giggling as one conjectured loudly on the possibility of their being dinosaur bones. Such a tiny girl for such a long word.

Boys in swim trunks teetered on the edge of the slight decline until a police officer called out "Away you go boys." They edged away but not before one bronzed lad said loftily "Whatsa buncha ole bones matter!"

They matter. In Mexico and Central America, in Egypt and Greece, in any area on this earth old bones revealed by noisy bulldozers or quiet excavators' knowing touch, old bones matter — even in Fort Erie.

Who were these people, and how and when did they live? Did they experience love and hate, fear and frustration, as we do? Relax in the sun; shiver in the cruel frosts? Did plague take their lives? Or starvation or war?

Whoever they were, however they lived and died, their bones matter. They are a part of the chain linking the human family, of which every smallest additional piece of information is important. Not that a small, sun-browned boy would be expected to know that!
Times-Review, July 23, 1964

It was not long after the dig started, however, that local officials and citizens became concerned that it was an American team working on Canadian soil. By the following week Mr. William Noble, then a student at the University of Toronto and

Peter Flake (son of Jim Flake) and his dog, 1997.

later a professor of anthropology at McMaster University, had arrived to assist in the direction of the excavations as an official representative of the National Museum of Canada. Unfortunately, and despite appeals by the town council and the chamber of commerce, to the likes of federal health minister and local MP Judy LaMarsh, and the Ontario premier's office, no funding was ever made available for more detailed investigations of the property and the costs of the fieldwork were assumed by White. Mayor Teal observed that "Legislation is needed to cover protection of such sites and to relieve councils of financial strain."

Twenty-three years later, when the Snake Hill skeletons were found, the situation was no different and it was again the Americans who saved the day. In both cases, however, significant destruction of human remains and archaeological materials could have occurred without the responsible actions of the Fort Erie councils.

Even though 10 days did not provide enough time to complete the excavation of the site and the disinterment of all of the skeletal material, an astonishing amount of work was accomplished under difficult circumstances.

White's investigations were restricted to two discrete areas that remained accessible between the existing structures and deposits of heavy fill on the property. One area consisted of an ossuary, which is a large pit filled with bone, while the other area consisted of a series of individual features and burials within the paleosol. Ossuaries are the final burial place of community members who had died during the occupation of their village as well as deceased from some neighbouring villages, all of whom were reinterred just prior to the main village's relocation.

Archaeologists preparing to pack up their finds for despatch to the National Museum, Ottawa.
(*Times-Review*, July 30, 1964)

"Old Indian burial site. This is the 'heap of bones' uncovered on Forsythe Street as they appeared when the *Times-Review* arrived, following a call from Ken Hunt, *Review* employee, to say that a bulldozer had uncovered what appeared to be human bones. Burt Miller, Constable Jack Barton, Fort Erie Police Department, and a Niagara Parks Commission Police Officer (whose name was unfortunately not learned) talk over the discovery."

(Gordon Marshall, *Times-Review*, July 23, 1964)

Interestingly, the "Black Robes" — French Jesuit missionaries who came to Ontario during the early seventeenth century — had witnessed an ossuary burial in the spring of 1636 among the Huron, and an associated ceremony known as the Feast of the Dead. Jean de Brebeuf, the famous Jesuit martyr, described it in the following manner:

> The people proceeded to the cemetery where those called Aiheonde, those who take care of the graves, removed the bodies from the tombs in the presence of the relatives, who renew their tears and feel afresh the grief they had on the day of the funeral ...They display before you all these corpses ... The flesh of some is quite gone and there is only parchment on their bones; in other cases, the bodies look as if they had been dried and smoked ... and in still other cases they are still swarming with worms ... When the friends have gazed upon the bodies to their satisfaction, they cover them with handsome beaver robes ... after some time they strip them of their flesh, taking off skin and flesh which they throw in the fire along with the robes and mats in which the bodies were wrapped ... as regards the bodies of those recently dead, they leave these in the state in which they are, and content themselves by simply covering them with new robes ... the bones having been well cleaned, they put them partly into bags, partly into fur robes, loaded them on their shoulders and covered these packages with another beautiful hanging robe.

Relatives and friends of the deceased contributed glass beads, wampum necklaces, and other trade goods, as well as food for the journey of the souls to the afterlife. According to Samuel de Champlain, the famous explorer and one of the first Europeans to meet directly with the Huron, the pits were most often placed outside of the villages, were very large and deep, 10 fathoms square (approximately 18.3 metres/60 feet), and were capable of containing all the bones, furniture, and skins offered to the dead. A high scaffolding was erected along the edge to which all the bags of bones were carried. Then the grave was lined on the bottom and sides with new skins and robes, after which all of the presents were placed in the pit with the bundles of bones. At that time the crowd of onlookers raised a great cry of lamentation.

Unfortunately, White and her crew were not given the opportunity to determine whether the Fort Erie ossuary had been surrounded by scaffolding, since the grading

An imaginative illustration of an ossuary burial and the Feast of the Dead, 1724.

activities that led to the discovery of the ossuary also resulted in its severe truncation. Indeed, two feet of soil had been removed before the skeletal material was noted. The burial pit was estimated to have originally measured 4.3 metres (14 feet) in length, 2.6 metres (8.5 feet) in width, and approximately 1.5 metres (5 feet) in depth. It had a flat-bottomed, deep basin-shaped profile and contained three layers, including a basal layer with large quantities of human skeletal material; a middle layer that was largely devoid of bone or artifacts; and an upper layer that also contained dense concentrations of human bone.

As the bodies had been placed in the pit, in most cases years after the death of the individuals, they were in an advanced state of decomposition and their bones were separated from one another. Since the pit contained the bones of hundreds of people, it therefore had the appearance of a large, deep, jumbled mass of bone. White's team had a biological anthropologist or bone specialist on the site named Audrey Sublett, whose almost impossible task was the regrouping of the bones into individuals. She was kept busier, however, just collecting important forensic data, such as age, sex, and disease information, which might not have survived the journey from field to laboratory.

A bundle and flexed burial were thought to have been added later into the upper layer. A bundle burial is a form of interment where the bones of the individual have all become separated from one another, either intentionally through dismemberment or as a result of decomposition over time. The pattern of the burial often involves the placement of the leg and arm bones first, followed by the torso, and then the skull. A flexed burial, on the other hand, involves the placement of the body on its side, shortly after death, and often drawn up into the fetal position. The burials at the intersection of Walnut Street and Niagara Boulevard were flexed burials.

Two additional, discrete, pit features were also identified within the upper layer and found to contain the remains of a minimum of 10 and 19 individuals, respectively. It was suggested that these bodies were deposited at the same time as the main ossuary pit was filled. Five apparently separate bundle burials, representing a minimum of 11 individuals, were documented at the interface of the bottom two layers. The most dense concentrations of bone in the upper and lower layers were thought by White to represent both discrete bundles as well as intentionally mixed remains.

In total, the bones of just over 300 individuals were recovered during the course of the ossuary excavations, although White suggested that up to one-third of the skeletal material in the ossuary may have been removed during the bulldozing of the site. She also estimated that up to 50 individuals remained unexcavated upon the completion of the fieldwork, although other workers suggest even more remains were left behind. As plastic orchids were reportedly placed on the graves when the site was backfilled, the site has come to be known as the Orchid site.

The ossuary included no grave goods, as the vast majority of the artifacts recovered during the excavations were regarded as secondary inclusions in the ossuary fill, having come from the surrounding paleosol, representing centuries of occupation of the site. Indeed, ceramics and flint tools dating to the Transitional Woodland period (AD 600–900) as well as to the Late Archaic period (1800 BC) were found in the fill of the pit. Despite thinking that the majority of the artifacts were not associated with the bones, White, nevertheless, suggested that some of the artifacts may have been included with individual bundle burials and could be regarded as contemporaneous with these interments. Consequently, White assigned the ossuary to the Transitional Woodland period, suggesting that it dated to *circa* AD 900.

White's dating of the ossuary, however, received little support from her colleagues. Even William Noble, her assistant director at the site, argued that the ossuary was probably prehistoric Late Iroquoian, based on its size, the lack of grave goods, and the presence of a "false floor" (the largely empty second layer) that resulted in upper and lower bone chambers. The disagreement was settled several years ago when one of the long bones from the ossuary was radiocarbon dated to AD 1380±90, placing it within the Middle to Late Iroquoian period.

Noble had been correct. The Orchid ossuary is most likely associated with a nearby Iroquoian village. ASI archaeologist Martin Cooper, whose PhD dissertation at the University of Toronto concerned the Iroquoian occupation of the region, has even pinpointed the location of the likely candidate site, situated not far from the Fort Erie racetrack.

Another area at the Orchid site was excavated under the direction of Joseph Granger, one of White's students. Six burial features, and a single non-burial feature were documented within a trench situated about 25 metres northeast of the main ossuary pit. Granger thought that all of the features had been excavated within or through the paleosol and that the deposit was quite extensive. In addition to the intact features, the bones of an infant, two adult males, and a young adult female were also recovered from the bulldozed surface of the site, indicating that additional burial features had been impacted.

Although only a few of Granger's burials could be assigned to a specific temporal or cultural period, they all had fascinating stories to tell. One of the burial features contained the remains of a female, aged 50 years or more. This individual, who was buried in a loosely flexed position, was accompanied by a weasel skull, a small fossil horn coral covered in red pigment, and an ovate flint knife — all located near the facial region. Granger suggested that the weasel skull, painted coral and ovate knife represented the remains of a medicine bag.

Another of the bodies was that of a male of approximately 26–30 years of age. Although not accompanied by formal grave goods, six Transitional Woodland projectile points were distributed around the body, between the vertebrae and in the thoracic and abdominal regions, suggesting that this individual had been deliberately killed and the arrowheads left within the body.

Some of the burials could be dated, however, to the first half of the seventeenth century (1630–1650). These were perhaps burials of Neutrals, Iroquoian-speakers who occupied the Niagara frontier at that time. One of the interments included the remains of a female of approximately 50 years of age who was buried with two red glass tubular beads, a red twisted glass tubular bead, a dog or wolf canine, and the base of a smooth-surfaced globular ceramic vessel.

Another pit contained two adult males, aged 31–40 and 26–30, who were in flexed positions with their legs overlapping. Thirteen netsinkers and seven river pebbles were around their legs. Granger suggested these artifacts represented a fishing net that may have entangled the two after their canoe had upset in the Niagara River, causing them to drown. A notable quantity of grave goods was specifically associated with the elder of the two individuals, including a conch shell gorget inset with nine blue glass beads, 16 copper seed beads, six blue glass seed beads, fragments of fine copper wire, and a turtle shell rattle. Two other kinds of shells accompanied the younger man to the afterworld. The glass beads were items introduced to Iroquoians by French, English, and Dutch traders in the early seventeenth century.

The non-burial feature proved to be a large, deep, refuse-filled storage pit that contained Early to Late Middle Woodland material in the form of Vinette 1 (Early Woodland) pottery — the earliest form of ceramics in northeastern North America — five Meadowood (Early Woodland) bifaces and three Meadowood projectile points, an antler projectile point, a bird bone bead, three Transitional Woodland projectile points, as well as numerous later ceramic pot fragments, all representing a long occupational sequence similar to that documented by our team at the intersection of Walnut Street and Niagara Boulevard, during excavations in 1992 and 1993.

Granger, in his description of the features from this part of the Orchid site, described the paleosol as the Niagara River sheet midden, extending from one end of Fort Erie to the other and representing the accumulated refuse of many cultural groups over thousands of years. This was only the second statement, and the first since Houghton's, recognizing the immensity of the Peace Bridge site.

It was an attempt to redevelop the same piece of land that resulted in our team visiting the site in November of 1988. We had been asked by the Ontario Ministry of Culture and Communications (now Citizenship, Culture and Recreation) to examine the human remains and artifacts uncovered during the demolition of a house to the north of where Joseph Granger had been working. This material was discovered by Mr. Jim Pengelly, an archaeological conservation officer, who had been monitoring construction work around the southeastern Niagara peninsula.

While many local citizens had either forgotten about the site or were too young to have paid it any attention, it was the job of conservation officers, under an innovative provincial program, to keep an eye on sites that still had intact deposits and that might come under private development pressure. While the area in the front portion of the house had been excavated for a basement, Pengelly spotted human skeletal material and artifacts near the demolition line at the back half of the house and called the appropriate people at the ministry in Toronto. The ministry, in turn, phoned us at ASI, and within hours Williamson and Cooper were on site, aware that they were treading on sensitive ground, as had been amply demonstrated almost 25 years previously.

Williamson and Cooper confirmed that the surviving paleosol in the area of the house contained large amounts of human bone and grave goods, including a small brass kettle and glass trade beads. On the basis of his research with historic Neutral sites in the Niagara Frontier, Cooper surmised that the brass kettle and beads had probably been traded to this Iroquoian group through other aboriginal groups who were in direct contact with the Black Robes, the French Jesuit priests who were in Ontario at the time. The goods may also have originated with Dutch and English traders along the New York seaboard.

Numerous pieces of flint and animal bone were also encountered. The area of exposed bone was cleaned and photographed, although none of the material was collected, with the exception of the brass kettle and beads that had been exposed. This material represented too much of a temptation to the local collectors, so the decision was made to ensure their safety. Based on the presence of the trade goods, at least some of these burials date to the first half of the seventeenth century and no doubt represent the northward continuation of the cemetery area documented by Granger.

Following our work on the site, it was capped with a layer of sand fill, to protect the remains from further disturbance, and surrounded by a fence. The Fort Erie Native Friendship Centre and Ganawageh Urban Aboriginal Homes have been maintaining the site since 1988. Unfortunately, the site has remained in exactly the same condition, with a half-demolished house overlying dozens, if not hundreds, of additional bodies. The same problems that plagued the 1964 and Snake Hill excavations remain — assigning responsibility for paying for either protecting the skeletons or for carefully removing the bodies and reinterring them elsewhere. What is certain is that the new cemeteries legislation in the province would preclude the remains being sent to a laboratory for any more than a very brief period of time, unlike what had happened at the conclusion of the 1964 excavation.

In that case, all of the artifacts and the skeletal material were taken to the National Museum in Ottawa. Although White and Granger, the latter now a professor at the University of Louisville, in Kentucky, managed to publish a few articles concerning the site, most of the analyses of the bones were undertaken by Canadian students.

For example, a sample of 133 skulls from the ossuary was included in J. Eldon Molto's PhD dissertation analysis. Molto was attempting to trace biological relationships between various Middle and Late Woodland aboriginal populations in Ontario. He concluded that the Orchid population was somewhat isolated in biological terms from other Ontario Iroquoian populations, and that this pattern suggested a lack of strong historical relationships between Niagara Frontier groups and those from the remainder of southern Ontario. This marginal position of the Orchid population led to the suggestion that the Orchid community's closest ties may have lain with the occupants of western New York State.

The final chapter in the saga of the Orchid site, however, was played out only a few years ago at Old Fort Erie, and involved the skeletal remains taken from the site in the 1960s. The local aboriginal friendship centre had been trying for many years to track down exactly what had happened to the remains and grave goods and had been in contact with the National Museum. It was their intention to rebury the bodies with appropriate ceremony in a place that would never be disturbed again. After many meetings and dealings with various government bureaucracies, Wayne Hill, the executive director of the Fort Erie Native Friendship Centre, and Mayor Teal, also a Niagara Parks Commission board member, finally arranged for a permanent burial site. On September 29, 1995, the human remains and associated grave goods from the Orchid site were reburied at Old Fort Erie in a deerskin-lined pit, quite similar to the size and shape of the original burial feature.

Williamson, who was fortunate enough to have been invited to attend the reburial and "Feast of the Dead" found the tears and sobs of the aboriginal onlookers eerie, not only in their emotional power, but in their resemblance to the descriptions of lamentation in the early seventeenth-century accounts of ossuary burial. This modern event, so like its ancient counterpart, brought to conclusion an interruption to the rest of the ancient ones that had started some 31 years previously.

The Orchid site was not the only archaeological excavation to reach the pages of the local newspaper in the 1960s. Less than one year after the excavation of Orchid, a second extensive cemetery on the Niagara River terrace, known as the Surma site, was uncovered 250 metres to the south of the Orchid site, near the intersection of Niagara Boulevard and Queen Street. This site was also found during grading on the south side of the Queens Hotel. Again, salvage excavations were carried out over a 10-day period, but this time under the direction of J. Norman Emerson, an archaeologist with the University of Toronto, and the field supervision of William Noble.

The other major difference between Orchid and Surma, outside of the fact that an ossuary was not involved, was the level of media coverage. An editorial in the *Times-Review*, dated November 5, 1964, for instance, suggests that the site was actually found that fall and that the discovery was "being kept very quiet." While the editorial goes on to agree that it might be desirable to avoid the hectic scenes associated with last July's Forsythe dig, the concern is raised that the citizens remain informed and that a permanent display of these finds be established in Fort Erie, perhaps at the Historical Society Museum at Mather Arch, a dream that was never realized.

The following April, a brief article reported that three skeletons, a stone pipe and a number of large spear points had been found the previous October by workmen in the area of a new addition to the Queens Hotel. It goes on to state that the proprietors of the hotel, Mr. and Mrs. Surma, had received a letter from William Noble informing them that a grant had been obtained from the University of Toronto for a brief excavation. The article is clear in indicating that secrecy regarding the site had been maintained in order to protect the site from looters, and that the town would be cooperating fully with the excavation team. The owners of the property had rescheduled the proposed renovations and construction in order to allow for the investigation at no cost to the town or the University of Toronto.

Three areas were explored at the site, including the zone immediately adjacent to the south facade of the hotel, a trench between the Queen Street sidewalk and the roadway, and the basement of a residence on the southwest corner of the intersection. While all three locales yielded large quantities of Late Archaic and Transitional Woodland artifacts from the ever-present paleosol, together with pit features and wooden post remains, only the area adjacent to the hotel yielded burials.

BONES OF CONTENTION
How Times Have Changed

A visit to the Ontario Provincial Museum in the Toronto Normal School in 1908 would have provided you with an opportunity to examine the fruits of David Boyle's labours, namely, every type of aboriginal artifact imaginable. You would also have been confronted, however, with the skulls of innumerable aboriginals, displayed like artifacts behind glass on wooden shelving. While such a practice is now considered unethical and immoral by most archaeologists and museum curators, archaeologists and biological anthropologists remain interested in examining the bones of those who came before, but only if they can do so without offending their descendants — contemporary aboriginal people.

As always, the issues attached to such a sensitive topic, especially one involving death rituals, broader religious beliefs, and clashing worldviews, are very complex and, not surprisingly, neither anthropologists nor aboriginals share a common perspective among themselves. There is, nevertheless, a wide gap between the view that scientists who examine human remains are guilty of perpetrating a crime upon the most sacred and the view that science should have unrestricted access to all of the past. This gap has narrowed only in the last two decades as a result of some important initiatives in both the United States and Canada.

In the United States, aboriginal concerns regarding the excavation, analysis, and ultimate disposition of human remains led to the enacting of the federal Native American Graves Protection and Repatriation Act, in 1990. This law directed all public and private museums and laboratories in the United States, with the exception of the Smithsonian Institution in Washington, DC, which is covered under separate but similar legislation, to inventory their human skeletal collections and determine those that may be ancestrally linked to existing tribes.

The museums are then responsible for communicating the relevant information to those tribes and following their wishes in regard to disposition of the collections. In this context, both aboriginals and anthropologists have had the opportunity to partially reconcile their differences and to reach mutual understandings through the discovery of common ground.

Indeed, scientists have become more adept at explaining that there is a great deal to learn about ancient life from human bones including insights into general health, diet, population dynamics, and age-at-death and sex ratios. At the same time, similar analyses can contribute to discussions concerning contemporary issues.

Since genetic relationships and ethnic affiliations are reflected in the skeleton, for example, biological anthropologists are playing increasing roles in the resolution of conflicting land claims on the part of aboriginal groups and in the medical determinations of predispositions for certain diseases, such as diabetes. Aboriginals, on the other hand, are arguing that while these bones may yield valuable information, their permanent disposition in museums is at odds with any native American belief system, regardless of whether they can be linked with a specific tribal entity.

In Canada, a successful consultation process between First Nations and the Canadian Museums Association, and the adoption of a Statement of Principles for Ethical Conduct Pertaining to Aboriginal Peoples, by the Canadian Archaeological Association, has led, in many jurisdictions, to better communication between aboriginal and archaeological communities, aboriginal involvement in directing, undertaking, and interpreting archaeological research, and shared management of aboriginal heritage features. This is perhaps best reflected in the enormous amount of work currently being undertaken by archaeologists for First Nations clients.

Not only has this new era of cooperation resulted, in some cases, in repatriation of human skeletal collections from Canadian museums, as with the case of the Orchid bones, but it has also led to the development of local protocols between archaeologists, municipal leaders, and aboriginal leaders to investigate complex burial sites in the context of ensuring their long-term protection from development impacts.

Recently, for example, Archaeological Services Inc. exhumed over 100 bodies from a partially disturbed, early fourteenth-century Iroquoian ossuary, located in a soccer field in North York, at the instruction of Six Nations council. In the process, important historical data were collected about the way in which the burial feature was formed, all of the skeletal elements were mapped, and detailed forensic and genetic analyses of the bones were conducted. The removal and analyses of the bones were undertaken with the understanding that they would be almost immediately reburied in a ceremony conducted by elders and faithkeepers from Six Nations. Their new resting place and the funding for the project was provided by the city of North York, representing yet another remarkable example of co-management of a heritage feature on the part of archae-ologists, aboriginals, and landowners.

In 1997, the Buffalo and Fort Erie Public Bridge Authority was given a provincial conservation award for exactly the same sort of achievement concerning the Peace Bridge site. Perhaps, most importantly, one of the letters of nomination was provided by the local aborig-inal community, a testimony to the degree to which times have changed.

Display room at the Ontario Provincial Museum in the Toronto Normal School, 1908.

(City of Toronto Archives)

Unfortunately, no plan of the distribution of burials or other features was ever produced, nor are descriptions of the non-burial features available.

The investigations adjacent to the hotel resulted in the discovery of 11 single burials placed in shallow, flat-bottomed pits that were about one metre (three feet) across and excavated through the paleosol. Seven of the interments were flexed while others contained the remains of people who had been dismembered and placed in bundle form. A child burial was also found in a pit feature under the sidewalk in front of the lounge entrance to the hotel on Queen Street. While the child burial was documented, it was not excavated by Noble's crew. Interestingly, we may have rediscovered it in the spring of 1994 and again protected the burial from further disturbance.

Ten other burials appear to have been disturbed by the initial construction activities as they were identified from isolated remains found during the excavations. These included the remains of an infant, a child who was between two and six years of age, an adolescent of indeterminate sex, a sub-adult male, and at least eight adults. Thus, the remains of 22 individuals were encountered from across the site.

There were several spectacular grave goods found with the bodies. One adult male was buried with a ceramic platform smoking pipe; another male, between 27 and 30 years old, with a shell bead necklace, a slate gorget, and 11 broad triangular projectile points known as Levanna points; another male with a whetstone; yet another male with a whetstone, a slate gorget, and a beaver incisor that may have had a handle; a female, between 18 and 21 years old, buried with some pottery and a shell necklace; and three other burials of indeterminate sex who were buried with Levanna projectile points. In addition to these items, the excavators reported that turtle shell ornaments, a bone spatula gorget, and nodules of red ochre were also recovered.

In addition to the funerary items, large quantities of other artifacts were recovered during the excavations from the paleosol layer, although much of it has never been processed and remains in storage at the Department of Anthropology, University of Toronto. The artifacts that were reported upon and illustrated in a 1966 article, however, include a large number of projectile points, the majority of which were of the Late Archaic Genesee period as well as Levanna points, like the 20 specimens recovered from the burials. A few Early Woodland Meadowood and Transitional Woodland points were also found as were other kinds of flint tools such as drills and scrapers and a small number of ceramic fragments from the Early and Transitional Woodland periods.

In an insightful analysis undertaken in the early 1980s of a sample of the projectile points from the site, in particular those from the Late Archaic Genesee period, Ian Kenyon suggested that some of the pentagonal-shaped specimens in the assemblage were actually bifacial preforms. Kenyon went on to identify a three-stage manufacturing process for Genesee projectile points at the site. Not only was this one of the first studies to reconstruct a tool production sequence for this period, but it was the first time that the site was recognized for its important quarry function since the time of Boyle and Houghton.

In summary, artifacts from all of the periods between the Late Archaic and Transitional Woodland periods were recovered from the site. The two major occupations, however, took place during the Late Archaic and the Transitional Woodland periods. The Late Archaic use of the site is evidenced by one of the largest concentrations of Genesee projectile points found up to that date, in the Great Lakes region.

The second major component was that of the Transitional Woodland period, indicated mainly by the inclusion of the Levanna projectile points with a number of the burials. The results of two analyses of the skeletal material from the site are also

Ceramic platform pipe recovered from the Surma site in 1964.

consistent with the assignment of the burials to the Transitional Woodland period. Jerry Cybulski, a biological anthropologist from the National Museum in Ottawa, examined certain traits on the Surma crania that led him to conclude that these individuals were intermediate between Middle and Late Woodland populations.

He also found that the patterns of dental wear and caries among the Surma people suggested a subsistence base that included a developing agricultural diet, typical of the pre–Iroquoian period. A more recent high-tech analysis of collagen stable carbon isotopes, sampled from the bones of some of the adults, likewise indicated that maize was only a limited component of the overall diet. This, in turn, indicated that the burials dated to between AD 500 and 1000, since the earliest corn in Ontario dates from the sixth century and sites in the eleventh century appear to have been fully agricultural.

The Queens Hotel was destroyed by fire in 1986, after which the remaining walls were bulldozed into the basement. In 1992, the London Museum of Archaeology was retained by a private developer to carry out an assessment of the property. Their work included the excavation of test pits in the interior of the former structure, monitoring of the removal of the rubble fill, investigation of the underlying undisturbed soils, and collection of material from the area of several pit features that had been dug previously by looters on the lawn along the east side of the former structure.

The analysis of the material recovered during the assessment is not yet complete. However, the preliminary report notes that the assemblage includes a wide variety of projectile points; Transitional Woodland ceramics; two intact whelk shell columella beads; a tubular bone bead; ground stone items; fragments of mica; other formal bifacial tools; and large quantities of flint flakes, all typical of the paleosol layer and all in quantities that were a pale reflection of what was yet to come.

Surma site excavation in 1965.

3 The Changing Landscape

Many visitors to archaeological site excavations in the Great Lakes region are surprised to find us digging so close to the surface. They are no doubt accustomed to seeing deep, stratified excavations in places like the Middle East or Mesoamerica, as depicted in television documentaries and popular magazines. What they soon learn is that, in most cases, the ground surface we are walking around on today is essentially the same surface that aboriginal caribou hunters were walking on nearly 11 000 years ago. Only in places like river floodplains, where additional sediment has accumulated over time, do North American archaeological sites usually exhibit the sort of layering commonly seen elsewhere in the world.

One of the sites where this layering can be seen is the Peace Bridge site, which sits on the floodplain of the Niagara River. At this location, the Niagara is wide and swift-flowing with a maximum depth of 12 metres and a floodplain about 400 metres wide, at least on the west side of the river. The floodplain terminates at the base of a 10-metre-high moraine scarp to the west, which is a large ridge of glacial sediment that was deposited by the Laurentide Ice Sheet during the last glaciation as it paused during its retreat around 12 700 years ago.

Soils develop as a result of the constant deposition of organic material (plants and animals) on the surface of the ground, over thousands of years. As this material is incorporated into the soil, distinctive layers are produced, which are familiar to most people as the dark brown organic topsoil and the underlying buff-coloured subsoil. On the Niagara floodplain, this process occurs on alluvial sands — sediments laid during periods when the lake levels were high.

The complex layering seen at the Peace Bridge site is a result of sudden interruptions to this gradual soil-building activity. When the decay of organic materials at the surface suddenly ceases, as it does, for example, if floods deposit a layer of inorganic sediment, or when city engineers spread tons of construction fill across the ground, a new soil gradually begins to form at the surface of this new sediment. The now-buried soil is called a paleosol, an "old soil." Interpreting the layering of the soil and other deposits — in archaeological parlance, the stratification — would become a crucial key to understanding the formation of the Peace Bridge site.

The stratification of the Peace Bridge site consists of two principal layers. The lower layer is a paleosol representing the original ground surface as it had existed for several thousand years up until the early twentieth century. In some parts of the site, there appear to be more than one paleosol, probably resulting from partial inundations of the area at various times. The upper layer, on the other hand, consists of various deposits of twentieth-century fill, ranging from clay to sand to crushed stone and asphalt. By building up the land with fill, the people of Fort Erie had inadvertently capped and protected much of the Peace Bridge site from disturbance. While the site has only been damaged where excavations were undertaken for foundations

TIME
The Fourth Dimension

The human mind requires familiar concepts as benchmarks against which to measure and compare new ideas and experiences. For example, if one knew that the distance to the corner store was about a kilometre, a trip of 10 kilometres might be considered in terms of 10 trips to the corner store. Because this process works at the scale of human experience, concepts such as the distance between the earth and the moon tend to fall beyond our immediate grasp.

For this reason, analogies are often used to express these concepts in somewhat more familiar terms. The distance to the moon might be expressed in terms of trips around the world, for example. As those of us who have not travelled around the world will attest, however, the larger the measure the more difficult it is to grasp in human terms.

If relating large values in three dimensional space to human experience is a problem, it is even more difficult when we move into the fourth dimension: time. Individually, our only frame of reference is the length of our own lives. We can extend this somewhat by considering our connections to parents and grandparents, but once we are beyond the scale of the lives of people we have known, time passage becomes less meaningful.

Even archaeologists, who deal with bygone ages on a daily basis, have trouble getting their minds around the fact that people first colonized the Niagara Frontier some 11 000 years ago. Here again, however, analogy can help us out. If we were to convert time into something more familiar, such as distance, and say that one millimetre represents one year, we would see that a human lifespan would average about 70 millimetres or seven centimetres, the length of a human finger.

Continuing this analogy, we can see that European explorers would have first come to the Niagara area around 40 centimetres (400 years) ago, the length of the lower arm and hand, while the first aboriginal colonists would have arrived at the end of the last Ice Age, around 11 metres (11 000 years) ago, the length of a city bus.

Finally, the bedrock underlying the Peace Bridge site would have originated as sediment in an inland sea some 400 kilometres (400 million years) ago, which, to bring it back to human terms, is roughly the distance from Fort Erie to Detroit.

and underground utilities, the landscape has been completely altered in the last few centuries.

In order to really understand and interpret the prehistoric lifeways of the site, we would have to know more about the local environment and how it had changed. It was not enough to imagine the site with trees and meadows in place of buildings and roads, because not only had modern development reshaped the landscape, but natural forces had been remodelling it throughout prehistory. It had never been static. Since the aboriginal residents had, by necessity, adapted to the prevailing environmental conditions, it was important to reconstruct changes in the environment that might have been relevant to the way people had lived.

Like the earlier researchers who had been tantalized by the richness of the Peace Bridge site, we were well aware of what had attracted prehistoric bands of people to this particular location. While any single natural resource might have been enough to draw people there, the Peace Bridge site had many, including flint, fish and waterfowl, potable and navigable water, which avoided dangerous river currents, well-drained sandy soils that might have been valuable to people cultivating plants, and easy access to inland plant and animal resources.

It was the flint, however, that had clearly acted as the principle draw for both aboriginal hunter-gatherers and agriculturalists to the site for thousands of years. To understand how the flint came to be there and why it was the preferred toolstone would take us far from the normal boundaries of our discipline and farther back in time than we would normally travel. Much farther.

In fact, we would have to go back to about 400 million years ago, when plants and animals were first colonizing the land and more than 150 million years before the dinosaurs. At that time, the Peace Bridge site was situated at the margin of a vast inland sea. Sediments accumulated on the seabed, and over time, physical and chemical changes in the sediments turned them into rock. Among the sedimentary rocks formed this way were limestone and chert, commonly called flint.

The primary minerals of these rocks, calcite (calcium carbonate) and silica (silicon dioxide) were concentrated in shallow reef environments by marine organisms which used the minerals to form shells and other body structures. Fossils of these creatures, many of which were microscopic, abound in the limestones and flints of the Niagara region.

By tracing the geological history of the region, we were able to develop an understanding of how these flint beds had come to emerge after hundreds of millions of years to dominate the shoreline in the vicinity of the Peace Bridge site. Since the sedimentary beds were formed, changes in the earth's crust had tilted them, causing them to dip towards the south. Because the various layers contain rocks of differing hardness, exposure of the tilted rocks over millions of years to wind and water produced lowlands where the rock is softer and uplands where it is harder. While the most famous example of such differential erosion is the Niagara Escarpment, there is a smaller version in the southern Niagara Frontier called the Onondaga Escarpment.

Extending across upstate New York through Buffalo and Fort Erie, and continuing westward roughly parallel to the Lake Erie shoreline, the Onondaga Escarpment eventually disappears from view under the clays of the Haldimand Clay Plain near Hagersville, Ontario. We were even able to identify a possible edge of the escarpment as it crossed the vicinity of the site. While examining geotechnical bore hole logs, we noticed that, to the north of Queen Street, the bedrock drops suddenly by several metres, perhaps indicating the edge of the buried escarpment.

Aside from its effect on local drainage patterns – forcing many of the major regional watersheds to flow into the Niagara River rather than Lake Erie – the Onondaga Escarpment was important to prehistoric hunters because it was a source of flint. Occurring as thin beds and nodules, a type of flint called Bois Blanc was available to aboriginal peoples at a number of exposures along the escarpment.

More important than Bois Blanc, however, was another type of flint called Onondaga, the most widely used flint throughout regional prehistory. Named from its association with the Onondaga formation, Onondaga flint is an easily recognized and mapped rock that has eroded away from the edge of the Onondaga Escarpment to the shoreline of Lake Erie. It outcrops at the Peace Bridge site and southward along the edge of the lake. These were especially attractive outcrop locations to people seeking the flint since wave action had fractured and reduced the tabular rock, littering the beaches with large flint cobbles, precluding the need to physically quarry the stone.

We were also interested, however, in identifying the occupational periods represented at the site by temporally diagnostic tools made from the Onondaga flint. It seemed that at other sites in southern Ontario, either Onondaga flint was not always the preferred toolstone for prehistoric hunter-gatherers or that it was unavailable from time to time for some reason or another. Given that this site was one of the major quarries of Onondaga flint and that it was located on a shoreline, we wondered if the flint might have been periodically inaccessible due to shifts in lake levels through time. We had also noted that no artifacts older than 4000 years had been found on the site.

The evolution of Lake Erie since the retreat of the last ice front about 12 400 years ago can be characterized by a complex sequence of fluctuating levels, which seem to have three principal causes. First, the water volume in the Erie basin is closely linked to variations of inflow from the upper Great Lakes. Second, the water level is controlled by bedrock sills in the Niagara River which have changed over the years, as they have been both uplifted by removal of the glacier's weight and downcut by the river. Third, climatic change has varied the water inputs into the Erie drainage basin, thereby affecting lake levels.

In fact, between about 11 200 and 10 300 years ago, water levels in the Erie Basin were as much as 10 metres higher than at present. Not only was the current Niagara River floodplain under water at this time, but an enlargement of Lake Erie — called Lake Wainfleet in Ontario and Lake Tonawanda in New York — covered large portions of the Niagara Frontier. Then, from about 10 300 to 5500 years ago, Lake Erie dropped to elevations estimated to range from modern levels to several tens of metres below modern. With input from the upper Great Lakes cut off for most of this period, the Niagara River outlet may have actually ceased flowing at times. Between about 5500 and 4000 years ago lake levels once again rose to as much as seven metres above modern ones, refilling much of Lakes Wainfleet and Tonawanda.

After that, lake levels fell to roughly modern levels, where they have remained relatively stable ever since. Currently, Lake Erie exhibits annual lake level fluctuations of about one metre, although extreme rises of up to 2.4 metres have been recorded. The fact that it is the shallowest lake and has the smallest volume of the Great Lakes has contributed to the development of a rich biotic environment, as evidenced by its very productive modern fishery. The bounty of the environment would have been even greater in prehistoric times thanks to lush coastal marshes which are now rare.

It is clear that fluctuations in the levels of Lake Erie had periodically flooded the Peace Bridge site, particularly between about 5500 and 4000 years ago. Occasional flooding might have produced swampy conditions that would have allowed only seasonal occupation or prevented use of the site area altogether. Prolonged rising of the river would have not only prevented occupation, but might also have scoured away any archaeological evidence of occupations that may have occurred before about 4000 years ago. Subsequent rises in lake levels can be identified for periods around 2170, 1350, 820, and 430 years ago. Given the evidence of occupation of the Peace Bridge site after 4000 years ago, it is assumed that these latter flooding events were relatively minor, since they were of insufficient severity to remove evidence of prior occupations.

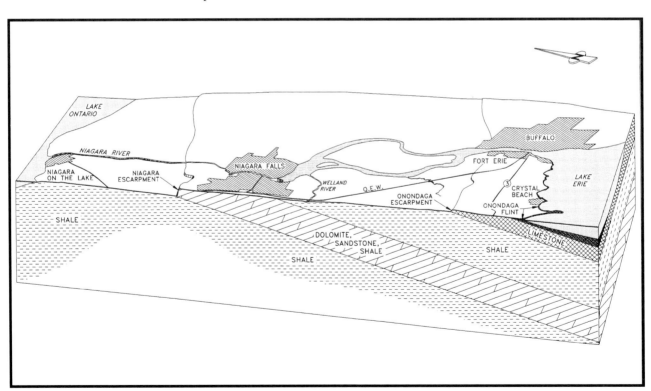

Cut-away bird's-eye view of the Niagara Peninsula, looking east. This figure shows the bedrock formations underlying the Niagara Peninsula. The dolomite, sandstone, and shale layer, which dips down to the south, outcrops approximately 12 kilometres south of Lake Ontario to form the Niagara Escarpment. South of this is the Onondaga Escarpment which is formed from an outcrop of limestone dipping down below Lake Erie. Onondaga flint is found along the north shore of Lake Erie. The vertical scale of this figure has been exaggerated to show these bedrock formations more clearly.

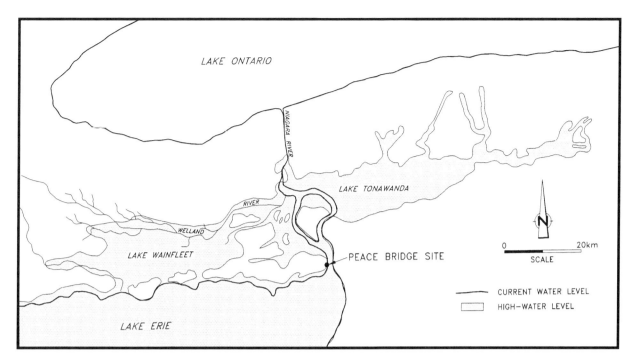

High-level lakes of the Niagara Frontier. Over the last 12 000 years, large areas of the Niagara Frontier were flooded when the level of Lake Erie rose to more than 179 metres above sea level. Major flooding episodes occurred between 11 200 and 10 300 years ago, during the time of glacial Lake Algonquin, and between about 5500 and 4000 years ago, during the Nipissing Rise in the Great Lakes basin. In addition to inundation along the Lake Erie shore and the lowlands of the Niagara River valley, two large shallow lakes were formed, Lake Wainfleet and Lake Tonawanda.

With an understanding of these fluctuations, we would eventually be able to examine the site's stone tools to determine if any gaps in its occupational sequence matched any of the hypothesized rises in lake levels. We could also compare the Peace Bridge site diagnostic stone tool assemblage with those from other sites in southern Ontario, in which stone tools were made predominantly of non-Onondaga flints. These comparisons, however, would have to await completion of our excavations at the site.

In the meantime, we hoped to be able to describe what the environment of the site would have looked like during the various periods when it was possible for the site to have been occupied. We continued to pore over earth sciences reports and maps, shifting our attention from the bedrock to the overlying sediments. These deposits would prove to be of great interest, as they largely determined not only the form of the landscape but also the texture and drainage of the regional soils. The nature of the landscape and soils would have, in turn, greatly influenced the distribution of plants and animals.

Since the retreat of the ice front and the glacial lakes that followed it, the Niagara Frontier has been occupied by a succession of plant communities that have evolved as a result of the glacially deposited soils and climatic change. Initially, when the glacial lake levels were high around 11 000 years ago, the climate was much cooler and the area was a relatively barren, tundra-like environment. Within a century or so, however, boreal forest had colonized the region. It was dominated by spruce but also included pine, fir, hemlock, poplar, and ash.

The dramatic fall in lake levels around 10 300 years ago reduced the moderating effects of the Great Lakes, resulting in relatively warmer summers and colder winters. In response, by about 10 000 years ago, oak began to dominate and together with other representatives of the mixed conifer-northern hardwood forest, especially pine and maple, largely displaced the boreal forest. Lake levels gradually rebounded and climatic warming peaked between about 7000 and 5000 years ago, with annual temperatures as much as two degrees Celsius above modern averages. During this warm period, pine and oak dominated on drier soils, while maple and beech were more prevalent on normal to moist soils. Since then there has been a slight cooling trend that may have slightly expanded the range of maple and beech relative to oak and pine.

Within these long-term climatic trends there were numerous shorter-term fluctuations. For example, the so-called Little Ice Age from about AD 1500 to 1880, was a period characterized by a higher frequency of harsh winters and cool summers. While these may have affected local plant communities, it is currently difficult to gauge the degree and duration of the effects. It also remains to be seen if the current warming trend, perhaps related to El Niño and/or the presence of greenhouse gases in the atmosphere, is a short-term problem or will influence long-term climatic patterns.

With these broad climatic and vegetation trends in mind, we were able to consider what the prehistoric forests of the Niagara Frontier may have looked like, especially in the vicinity of the site. Along the Lake Erie shore, for example, the landscape probably consisted of sand dunes and ridges with cedar, juniper, rushes, and sedges, interspersed with poorly drained wetland basins and marshes with some deciduous swamps.

On the Niagara River floodplain specifically, there likely would have been open meadow along the waterfront and a complex forest just inland with species tolerant of poor drainage and occasional flooding. A little further inland there would have been a variety of upland hardwoods with drought-tolerant oaks, butternut, and shagbark hickory on the dry slopes of the moraine scarp.

In essence, this complex forest community has likely prevailed on the floodplain since the lake levels receded 4000 years ago, just as the other regional forests have remained fairly constant in response to relative climatic stability. This is not to say that the forests have been static, since fire, flood, disease, and severe weather all contribute to the on-going process of forest succession and change. But these events are generally beyond our ability to detect in the past.

We were also able to supply hard evidence to support these forest community reconstructions. While excavating at the Peace Bridge site, we had systematically recovered wood charcoal and charred nuts from cultural features which, in some cases, could be dated. Since it is generally assumed that firewood was not transported great distances but was collected locally, we knew that wood charcoal frequencies could provide some idea about the composition of local forests.

At the Peace Bridge site, wood charcoal suggested that ash, elm, and oak were common, with subordinate representation by white pine, ironwood, and tamarack. Maple was poorly represented. Nut remains were the most abundant class of charred plant food waste at the site, and they included butternut, hickory nut, beech nut, and acorn.

Nuts are considered to have been an important source of storable food throughout prehistory, although yields would have been inconsistent from year to year. While significant energy would have to have been expended on their collection and processing, these activities could often be coordinated with fall hunting excursions, since many prey animals and birds were also attracted to the nuts.

There was also evidence to suggest that oak was more available during the Late Archaic period, while beech was more plentiful during the Late Woodland period.

THE CHANGING NIAGARA ENVIRONMENT

At present, the Niagara region lies at the northern limit of the Deciduous Forest Region, sometimes referred to as the Carolinian Forest. Like the Great Lakes-St. Lawrence Forest Region to the north, the common trees include sugar maple, beech, elm, basswood, red and white ash, white oak, and butternut.

Also relatively common, however, are several tree species which are at their northern limit in this region and are rare in other parts of southern Ontario. These include black walnut, sycamore, swamp white oak, and shagbark hickory.

Other species at the edge of their northern range include: tulip-tree, cucumber tree, pawpaw, red mulberry, Kentucky coffee tree, redbud, black gum, blue ash, sassafras, mockernut hickory, pignut hickory, black oak, and pin oak.

Before the large-scale land clearance of the nineteenth century, the low-lying clay plains, which were once the bottom of glacial Lake Wainfleet, were rather damp and generally populated by swamp white oak and white willow, with occasional white elm and green ash.

The well-drained uplands of the Buffalo/Fort Erie Moraine, on the other hand, supported maple-beech forests, although black ash swamps may also have been present in this area. Where the soils were more marginal, especially near the brow of the Onondaga Escarpment, oak and hickory prevailed, sometimes interspersed with prairie, in a vegetation community known as savannah.

When these regional trends were considered in light of climatic change over time, we can begin to envision how the Niagara forests might have changed over the duration of human occupation. Since a large proportion of the area consisted of inadequately drained clay plain, it seems likely that 12 000 years ago, the time of the earliest evidence for people in Ontario, the uplands would have been virtual islands of boreal forest surrounded by bogs or swamps of tamarack and black spruce.

Through the subsequent several thousand years, with the lakes falling to all-time low levels and then gradually rising again, drought-tolerant oaks and white pine would have replaced the boreal forest in the uplands of the moraines and Onondaga Escarpment, perhaps also extending well throughout the lowlands and Niagara floodplain as the drainage system matured.

Oak savannah likely became established on the thin soils near the crest of the Onondaga Escarpment and may have been quite extensive at the peak of climatic warming around 6000 years ago. Increasingly, though, the oaks and pines would have encountered difficulty competing with the very aggressive maples and beeches on well-drained but still moist soils.

When Lake Erie again crested above modern levels at the beginning of the Late Archaic period, the uplands may once again have been surrounded by wetlands, although now the swamps likely contained red maple, white elm, swamp white oak, black ash, and cedar. It seems likely that the forests of the Niagara floodplain were flooded and all traces of previous human settlement swept away by the raging river.

Throughout prehistory, the availability of fish and game to native people would have changed as the individual species adapted to habitat changes brought on by climatic change and water level fluctuations in the Erie drainage basin. When water levels were at their lowest ebb, the Peace Bridge site may have actually been some distance from any source of water.

Expansion of oak-hickory forest, and possibly oak savannah, as a result of climatic warming, would have been a boon to animals like deer, wapiti, raccoon, and wild turkey, but may have reduced or relocated the habitat of wetland animals like moose, beaver, and muskrat. Nevertheless, by 6000 years ago, the rise of Lake Erie above modern levels would have greatly expanded wetland habitats.

In the latter part of the Late Archaic period, wetlands again contracted as Lake Erie dropped to modern levels, and habitats remained relatively stable through the Woodland period. It is important to remember, however, that for animals and the aboriginal peoples who hunted them, the trends from year to year were of more immediate consequence than the long-term trends. Disease, severe weather, plant food failures, natural population cycles, and competition were among the factors which influenced behaviour and affected survival, although such short-term disruptions in the ecosystems of the past are almost impossible for us to detect.

Overall, the archaeological data were consistent with our understanding of the local forest community during the period that the Peace Bridge site was occupied.

Through the summer and fall, fleshy fruits, including wild cherry, wild plum, wild grape, crab apple, hawthorn, elderberry, currants, black nightshade, strawberries, raspberries, blackberries, blueberries, and cranberries, would have attracted both animals and humans. These plants tend to grow at the edge of the forest, in meadows, around wetlands, or along stream courses where the forest canopy is open. Some, such as black nightshade, wild grape, blackberry, and raspberry also tend to proliferate at the edge of human settlements. Carbonized specimens of many of these fruits were recovered from cultural features at the Peace Bridge site.

In addition to nuts and fleshy fruits, aboriginal foragers used a variety of other plants for fresh greens, potherbs, seeds, teas, dyes, medicines, and smoking. Carbonized seeds recovered from the Peace Bridge site included cleavers, chenopod, knotweed, small grass, purslane, and sumac, all of which had many possible uses.

It was becoming clear to us that, beginning in the Archaic period, the Peace Bridge site had been situated in a diverse environment which offered a bounty of plant resources to hunter-gatherer populations. The fish, birds, and land animals, however, were also a major focus of aboriginal economies throughout the occupation of the site. Over thousands of years, traditional hunters, worldwide, developed local strategies for saving time and energy and ensuring reliable, consistent harvests while hunting and gathering. Anthropologists attempt to understand these strategies through considerations of choice in prey, settlement density, local habitat, and seasonal movement.

With these factors in mind, and with our knowledge of historical and archaeological data concerning aboriginal hunting practices in the Great Lakes region, we considered the availability of various prey species to the prehistoric occupants of the Peace Bridge site.

In very earliest times, caribou and mastodon may have roamed the uplands and swamp edges, although there is currently only one site to link these animals with early hunters in the Niagara region. From Late Palaeo-Indian times onward, the four largest mammals of the Niagara region would have been moose, wapiti, white-tailed deer, and black bear.

Moose are fairly solitary creatures which would have occupied the swamps and marshes in the vicinity of Lake Erie. While their size would have made them an appealing prey, their solitary habits and relatively low densities of about 1 per 130 hectares (320 acres) would have limited their harvesting potential. Black bear were likely in the same category. With density estimates of 1 per 1440 hectares (3560 acres), they would only be worth hunting in chance encounters while seeking other more numerous prey. Wapiti and white-tailed deer, although somewhat smaller animals, would have been very attractive due to their relatively higher population densities and gregarious behaviour.

Wapiti, or elk, are herd animals which form separate male and female bands through most of the year, the latter comprising about 25 animals, including calves. After the fall rut, the bands join to form large herds of a hundred or more individuals which stay together until early spring. Wapiti are primarily grazing animals which tend to prefer open areas such as marshy meadows, river flats, and open savannah. Over winter they may also yard to browse in conifer groves when deep snow restrains their mobility. In the seventeenth century, wapiti are among the animals reported to have been occasionally swept over the Niagara Falls. While they may have ranged throughout the Niagara region, they may have been particularly attracted to the open woodlands or savannah of the Onondaga Escarpment.

White-tailed deer are browsers of tree and shrub leaves and shoots as well as many herbaceous plants. In the fall they are attracted to ripening fruit and especially nuts. While they tend to be solitary for most of the year, except for does and their fawns, in winter they yard in conifer — especially cedar — groves when deep snow hampers their movement.

Deer tend to remain within home territories of between approximately 16 and 120 hectares (40 to 300 acres), and population densities have been calculated as high as 1 per 8 hectares (20 acres). Like Wapiti, white-tailed deer would have been attracted through the spring and summer to forest openings where the understorey growth was most vigorous.

In the fall they would have thrived on oak, hickory, and beech nuts available throughout the region, and in winter they could have been effectively hunted in their yarding areas.

Harvesting of smaller animals, including wolves, foxes, cougars, lynx, bobcats, skunks, river otters, martens, fishers, and weasels, as well as rodents such as squirrels and chipmunks, would probably have been opportunistic. As wide-ranging, low-density animals, none of these would have played a central role in the diet and economy of aboriginal peoples. Rather, they would have been taken as opportunity dictated, although some small animals, such as the weasel, may also have had spiritual significance, as they have been found in burial contexts and in medicine bundles.

Many of these animals may have been hunted for specialty pelts. The name for Lake Erie, for example, is derived from the Huron name for an Iroquoian group — who once lived to the south of the lake — called the Erieehronons, meaning "people of the raccoon," after their robes of raccoon fur. Not having seen a raccoon before, Gabriel Sagard, an early French explorer and Recollet missionary, thought the raccoon to be a type of wild cat; hence the French called the Erie the "Nation du Chat." After his visit to southern Ontario in the winter of 1623–24, he recorded the following:

> There is a district in these wide provinces [the inhabitants of] which we call the

NATURE
The Original Big Box Supermarket

As you cruise through the store aisles of your local shopping mall, you are probably familiar with most of the products on the shelves, whether or not you have occasion to use them yourself. Each of us has a general knowledge of thousands of different products, and various trade specialists have additional knowledge beyond that of the general public.

Now picture yourself strolling through a forest. While you might be able to identify a few or even many of the plants you would find there, depending on your interest in nature, your appreciation of the potential uses of these plants is probably only rudimentary at best.

For example, most of us would be aware that the trees could be used as a source of lumber or fuel, and that certain wild nuts and berries are edible. Some of us would also be able to identify other edible plants and mushrooms. But none of us would be as familiar with the potential uses of wild plants as we are with the uses of products in our favourite shopping mall. Yet it was just this sort of comprehensive knowledge of plants and their uses that helped to sustain aboriginal people for thousands of years.

Most prehistoric aboriginal people had a general knowledge of plants, while some, such as the shaman, would possess specialty knowledge about certain medicinal plants and blended preparations. This knowledge base would include: the season when the plant or plant part was available; locations where the plant could be obtained; appropriate techniques for harvesting; methods of preparation and storage, recipes for a wide variety of food dishes; dosages and application procedures for medicines; antidotes such as emetics and purgatives for various poisons; psychoactive plants that could be smoked or consumed as part of shamanistic rituals; properties of various fuels; sources of plant fibre, ranging from cattail down for babies' diapers to vines and barks for making rope and baskets; and the properties of various woods for tools and structures.

Among the early European colonists were doctors and other academics who took a great interest in aboriginal plant use, particularly the traditional pharmacopoeia, since at that time European medicine was similarly based on natural plant and animal extracts. For example, one doctor in Quebec had a herbarium with 800 indigenous specimens from which he sent samples to his colleagues in France.

It is profoundly regrettable that such a knowledge base — the product of thousands of years of experimentation and refinement — should have been pushed aside this century, although, ironically, modern science has recently begun to appreciate this valuable information resource.

HUNTING ELEPHANTS ON THE NIAGARA

The Evidence of the Hiscock Site

The image of a group of men stalking a large elephant browsing on spruce twigs aside the Niagara River is not an image with which we are familiar. Yet, the archaeological evidence from the Hiscock site, situated in western New York State, suggests just such an event for the Niagara region.

The animal in the depiction is commonly referred to as a mastodon, an animal about the size of a modern elephant and outfitted with a trunk and huge upper tusks. Archaeologists and palaeontologists working with the Buffalo Museum of Science have found the bones and teeth of mastodon at the Hiscock site, along with the remains of California condor, caribou, pied-billed grebe, moose, and giant beaver in late Pleistocene strata, dating to 10 000 to 11 000 years ago.

The remains of both juvenile and adult mastodons have been found along with evidence of their diet in the form of faecal deposits containing jack pine cones and fir and spruce twigs. Some of the bones and teeth appear to have been modified, showing evidence of either cut marks or having their ends worn to rounded points.

The more startling evidence of humans at the site, however, comes in the form of fluted bifaces, fluting being a hallmark of projectile point production during Palaeo-Indian times. Traces of blood found on one of the fluted bifaces has been identified as bovine, indicating that the tool was used on a bison or musk-ox at some other point in the band's seasonal round, since no bovine remains have yet been found at the site. A number of the bifaces had been turned into cutting and scraping tools, suggesting that they were used to process the animals on the site. Whether the mastodons had been killed by humans or their carcasses had been scavenged has not yet been determined.

Richard Laub, in charge of the investigation of the site, has undertaken a number of innovative and multidisciplinary projects in order to gain a better understanding of the origin and structure of the archaeological deposits. He dissected an elephant, for example, in the company of anatomists, to determine the effects of cultural rather than natural disarticulation of a carcass; he has participated in experimental flintknapping relating to the tools found on the site; and he has consulted with zoo-keepers to understand how certain plants come to be in the gastrointestinal contents of elephants.

Perhaps the most exciting element of the site is that only a small portion has been investigated, and that the Museum's research program holds great promise for years to come. It, like the Peace Bridge site, is an international treasure.

Cat Tribe; I think the name was given because of these wild-cats, small wolves or leopards, which are found in their territory. From [the skins of] these wild-cats they make robes or blankets in which they introduce for embellishment a number of animals' tails, sewing them all around the edge and at the top of the back. These wild-cats are scarcely bigger than a large fox, but their coat is quite like that of a full grown wolf, so that a piece of wild-cat skin and a piece of wolf's skin are almost indistinguishable, and I was mistaken once in making a choice.

Although once abundant, many of these small animal species are now rare in the southeastern Niagara Peninsula, due to habitat destruction and overtrapping. In the Fort Erie area, for example, the 1811 Thomas Ridout map illustrates a beaver dam and meadow at the headwaters of a stream flowing into Lake Erie at Cedar Bay. This stream, Beaver Creek, no doubt reflects the former presence of this animal. The streams and wetlands of the southeastern Niagara Peninsula would have provided an ideal habitat for beaver, muskrat, and otter, all of which were probably in abundance thousands of years ago.

Even squirrel populations were significantly greater prior to European forest clearance. According to early ethnographic accounts, the Neutral, who inhabited the Niagara region, were widely known for their squirrel pelt robes, which were admired by the Huron.

Later reports document mass emigrations of up to thousands of squirrels, possibly prompted by mast failure, overpopulation, or parasitic infestation. The naturalist, Ernest Thompson Seton, documented one such migration, when thousands of squirrels swam the Niagara River, from Fort Erie to Buffalo. Reaching the far shore exhausted, they could be easily caught by hand, or knocked off fences and bushes.

With the Mississippi and Atlantic flyways

virtually converging overhead, spring and fall waterfowl migrations would also have brought an annual winged bounty to the cooking pots of Niagara's prehistoric inhabitants, just as it did in early historic times. It was recorded, for example, that the Fort George garrison at Niagara-on-the-Lake was provisioned for a considerable time through the collection of large flocks of swans, geese, ducks, water hens, and teal that had been swept over Niagara Falls.

Earlier, in the seventeenth century, it had been recorded that a local aboriginal group essentially made their living by retrieving birds and game which floated downstream, having been swept over the falls. Similar quantities of waterfowl must have been available for the taking from the river-front and coastal marshes in the vicinity of the Peace Bridge site.

Inland, an equally abundant resource would have descended in the form of enormous flocks of passenger pigeons. The enormity of the flocks was captured by an early account of a visitor to Ontario who, in 1799, while travelling from Niagara to York (Toronto) by boat, witnessed one continuous flock of pigeons flying overhead. Both a migratory visitor and a warm season resident of the Niagara Frontier, passenger pigeons nested in colonies from under one to several thousand hectares in extent. Attracted to their primary food, beech nuts, they also fed on other deciduous tree seeds, including elm, maple, birch, alder, hickory, pine, hemlock, and dogwood, which they would have found in hardwood forests throughout the Niagara Frontier. They were hunted to extinction by the turn of the twentieth century.

Another potentially important game bird would have been the wild turkey. As primarily ground dwelling birds, wild turkeys prefer the edges of nut-producing forests where they have ready access to both food and understorey cover. Over winter they congregate in separate flocks of males and females which separate in early spring to breed and nest. In the Niagara region, the open oak-hickory forest in the vicinity of the Onondaga Escarpment would have provided ideal habitat.

The harvesting calendar would not have been complete without the seasonal catches of fish from the Niagara River and Lake Erie. While fishing was likely an ongoing activity, spawning runs would have significantly increased the potential yield at certain times of year. Indeed, certain deep-water species would only be available when they came into shallow waters to spawn.

The Peace Bridge site was well-placed close to both the river and the lake. In the spring, the shallows or embayments of the river would attract spawning white bass, smallmouth bass, yellow perch, walleye, sauger, and suckers. In the fall and early winter, lake whitefish and cisco would come into the shallows, while burbot would follow them in late winter. Year-round residents of the smaller waterways would include lake sturgeon, channel catfish, smallmouth bass, yellow perch, and freshwater drum; and in shallow, weedy bays, longnose gar, bullhead, bowfin, northern pike, muskellunge, walleye, and sauger.

Just as ecologists do not detail every nuance of a modern ecosystem, neither do archaeologists need to know every detail of the prehistoric environment in order to interpret the archaeological record in meaningful ways. By reviewing the broad ecological trends within the Niagara region, we were able to understand how people might have been influenced by their surroundings, allowing for a more complete and realistic interpretation of the cultural remains.

As it turned out, our archaeological findings would ultimately prove useful in addressing certain environmental questions. This is not surprising since such frameworks are dynamic, being constantly revised whenever and wherever new data become available. For example, much of the foundation for the Peace Bridge site environmental framework had been constructed by ASI archaeologist Martin Cooper

DEER, DOGS, AND DRIVES

The image of the solitary aboriginal hunter silently stalking his quarry through the forest primeval may have more to do with romanticism and Hollywood than reality. While solitary hunting was undoubtedly done, much more efficient communal hunting was likely the norm, especially for pursuing gregarious animals like deer and wapiti. Hunting parties with dogs would have been more successful because of their ability to cover more ground and cooperate in the field dressing and transport of game back to the camp or village. Customs for sharing meat and other animal products among the hunters would also ensure that no individual family went hungry, regardless of the success or failure of any one hunter during a particular hunting expedition.

Throughout much of prehistory, small hunter-gather bands of up to about 50 people likely could only field hunting parties of a dozen or so men, although larger parties would have been occasionally possible when one or more bands came together, as may have occurred during the spring fishery at the Peace Bridge site. During Late Woodland times, however, villages of several hundred people could have mustered much larger parties, and such groups are known to have staged massive hunting expeditions.

In early November of 1615, Samuel de Champlain accompanied the Huron on one such deer-hunting expedition to eastern Ontario. He reports that this party of 25 took less than 10 days to construct a V-shaped stockade that was eight- or nine-feet high and 1500-paces long on each side. At the apex of the stockade was a five-foot-wide opening into a tapered enclosure. Once this structure was completed, they went into the woods about half an hour before daybreak, taking up a position about two kilometres from the open end of the V-shaped fence.

Spreading themselves out about 80 paces from each other, they then began marching towards the structure while striking two sticks together to drive the deer before them. As they approached the apex of the deer drive, they began shouting and howling like wolves, which prompted the deer to stampede into the enclosure where they were brought down in a hail of arrows. Repeating this procedure every second day, the group was able to harvest 120 deer in 38 days. Champlain also reported that parties of several hundred Huron would drive deer onto points of land where, attempting to flee via the water, they would be dispatched by waiting hunters in canoes.

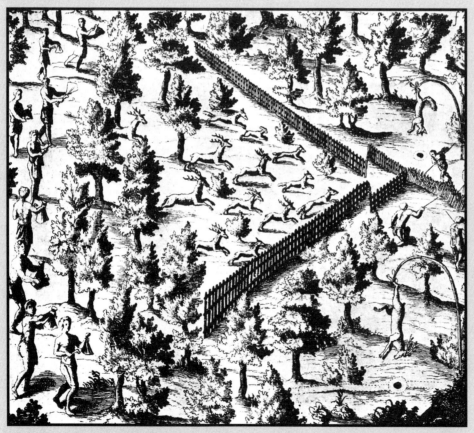

A fanciful illustration of the deer drive constructed in Samuel de Champlain's presence, 1615.

in the course of his doctoral research concerning Late Woodland occupations in the southern Niagara peninsula.

Cooper had also conducted extensive archaeological surveys and documented dozens of new sites through the Town of Fort Erie, employing many local students and volunteers, among them Jim and Sue Pengelly. Jim Pengelly went on to become a volunteer conservation officer for the Ontario government and eventually pursued studies at Brock University, which led him to important new insights concerning water level fluctuations in the Lake Erie basin, some of which he published. Supporting evidence for some of Pengelly's insights would eventually come from excavations at the Peace Bridge site. In this way, it can be seen that both the cultural and natural worlds are subject to continuous and overlapping historical inquiry. The complex relationship between people and their environment in the Niagara Frontier shows the need for such multidisciplinary approaches.

Jim Pengelly at the Orchid site in 1988, holding the small brass pot in his hand and pointing to the layer of human bone.

4   Clues Underfoot

After our initial discoveries at the east end of Walnut Street, we soon discovered that it was not only the Peace Bridge Authority that had ambitious plans for this part of Fort Erie. The public works department of the town had been planning for some time to replace water and sewer lines and provide new servicing to the businesses along Niagara Boulevard between Queen and Forsythe streets. In fact, this section of replacements and installations was only one of many that the town engineers had designed and implemented for the early 1990s. Since news of the startling results of the Walnut Street excavations were released in the media in the fall of 1992, however, the town staff was somewhat nervous about what might lie under the pavement in front of the Surma and Orchid sites.

The town staff were already familiar with archaeological assessments, as they had called on us to undertake a number of studies in the past. It was not surprising, therefore, that they asked us in March of 1993 for a price to assess this particular section of work.

In preparing the costing, we were acutely aware of the results from the 1960s excavations and our own investigations just a block south of the southern starting point for the town work. The big question was whether the paleosol deposit, which usually appeared at a depth of 60–80 centimetres, was still intact below the road and sidewalk surfaces.

After careful consideration, we thought it might remain intact and advised Bill Packer, the engineer responsible for environmental studies, that a post hole auger would be needed to access deeply buried deposits under the road bed. This meant traffic control, service locates, and a host of other hassles, but Bill Packer agreed that it was better to be safe than sorry. The last thing anyone wanted was to encounter an unanticipated archaeological deposit or burial in the process of undertaking the work, resulting in a halt in construction and a delay charge from the contractor.

We didn't have to wait long for justification for our decision. It was only a few weeks after we had submitted our proposal to the town that the Walnut Street burials were discovered under the curb at Walnut and Niagara. The fact that the second burial had been severely impacted by a service line only underscored the decision for the town. While it would be a while before we received authorization to proceed with our field study, everyone had become convinced that it was necessary.

In the meantime, the Peace Bridge Authority had advanced their plans for the new commercial customs building and the related sitework. While they had known for some time that they were going to close Walnut Street and that they needed additional land, they had decided to leave the actual design of the new facilities and truck yard to the successful consultant team. Only days after the discovery of the Walnut Street burials, a request for proposals was sent to eight firms, who had previously been selected from those who had responded to a call for an expression of interest. The

Peace Bridge Authority was looking for a team to provide them with professional architecture, engineering, surveying, and consultative services to help design the new commercial customs facility and overall sitework.

While such an ambitious project involving so large a land holding was unusual for this section of Fort Erie, even more peculiar was the inclusion of a statement on the first page of the call for proposals, indicating that this particular project would require, among other things, "a respect and accommodation for areas of archaeological significance." This was an assertion that the consultant teams had never before seen written into a terms-of-reference, but it accomplished the goal of emphasizing the role of archaeology from the very first moment of the project.

What was clear to all of the consultants was that the Peace Bridge Authority meant business — the protection of archaeological deposits was a priority. In fact, Ron Williamson even gave a slide-illustrated presentation at a mandatory pre-proposal conference. Not only did this allow for his introduction to all of the team leaders, since our firm was common to all of the proposals, but it provided an opportunity to stress that while much work remained to be done to define the extent and nature of the deposit within the study area, it was probably everywhere.

The implication of that conclusion was that each member of the successful consulting team, from the architects, to the landscape designer, to the services and electrical contractors, would have to consider archaeological concerns. The proposals were due by the end of June so that a consultant group could be selected by the end of July.

While there were many strong contenders among the eight short-listed groups, the Peace Bridge Authority chose the team headed by Moriyama and Teshima Architects of Toronto. This firm not only had an excellent international reputation, but had designed many landmarks familiar to Ontario residents, including the Scarborough Civic Centre, the Ontario Science Centre, and the Metropolitan Toronto Reference Library. They were also familiar with the Niagara Region, having undertaken a major planning study for the Niagara Parks Commission. Williamson was also familiar with Moriyama and Teshima, having briefly helped their staff with their research for the Niagara Parks Commission document. The two firms' co-ed slo-pitch softball teams had even managed to play a few games against each other.

Within days of their selection, we were working cooperatively with the Moriyama and Teshima team, successfully forging working relationships. These relationships were important since the archaeology was about to set the agenda for much of the ensuing three years to an extent that neither had expected.

Prior to the selection process, the Peace Bridge Authority had already approached Williamson about what would constitute a logical next step, in an attempt to understand the full extent and nature of the archaeological deposit in the study area. By the end of June, Williamson had designed a program of research aimed primarily at documenting heavily disturbed areas which could be considered unlikely to yield significant deposits, although he warned that subsequent field assessment was probably inevitable. It was just a matter of seeing if the size of the study area could be reduced, thereby minimizing costs.

The middle week of July saw letters of authorization arrive at our head office in Toronto from the Peace Bridge Authority to start the background research, and from the town to conduct a field assessment of the substructure of Niagara Boulevard. In order to stay on schedule, and to have initial results for the selected architects by September, background work for the Authority was to be conducted immediately. The town work, on the other hand, would be undertaken in the middle of August.

We therefore set to work on the Peace Bridge Authority study. The first task was to define the study area and, to our surprise, it covered an area of over 11 hectares. It was bound by portions of Goderich, Queen, Waterloo, and Princess streets, Niagara Boulevard, and the Canada Customs building at the Peace Bridge.

Our main objective was to assess the nature, evolution, and extent of past land disturbance within this area. In order to secure that information, Williamson sent his most knowledgeable historical researcher, Eva MacDonald, to the Public Archives of Ontario. In addition to other records at the archives, she consulted relevant nineteenth- and twentieth-century maps and atlases, including several editions of the fire insurance plans of the town. In addition, she consulted published historical literature, and even conducted interviews with knowledgeable informants from Fort Erie to determine, for difficult cases, the extent of subsurface disturbance associated with former or still-standing structures.

One of the challenges of the study was to determine the full extent of disturbance represented by structures through time and to delineate the exact locations of now demolished buildings. This was especially difficult for buildings dating to the earliest occupations of this part of town, an area with a rich historic past that even extended into the mid-eighteenth century.

Indeed, a garrison had been established at Old Fort Erie in 1764, although it was not until after the American War of Independence (1774–83) that the area around Fort Erie became the focus of domestic settlement. In 1784, Col. John Butler's regiment was disbanded and soldiers who served the Crown were given grants of free land to encourage them to remain in Canada. Butler, himself, was instructed to purchase additional lands in the Niagara peninsula so that all who wished to settle could be accommodated, and a survey of the peninsula was begun.

Ten families received grants in the Fort Erie area and a primitive ferry service began between Black Rock and Fort Erie, bringing across additional loyalists, including Quaker families from Pennsylvania, New York, and New Jersey.

In June of 1796, the Crown awarded lots encompassed within the study area to John Garner, who had served as a private in Butler's Rangers, and received the land as payment for military service. Lot 1, however, already contained a grist mill erected in 1792 by William Dunbar, who had hoped to capitalize on the water power created by the swift set of rapids located nearby. In 1795, Dunbar had petitioned the government to have the mill site granted to him, as he had invested considerable energy in cutting a mill race out of the rocky shore. The mill race remained a feature on the Fort Erie shoreline for over a century, as it was visible in the photograph taken of the ground-breaking ceremony for the Peace Bridge in 1925.

Dunbar's grist mill was the earliest recorded structure to have been present in or near the study area. The boundary of the original 20-acre mill site was shown on an 1854 plan of the village of Fort Erie, drawn by the Royal Engineers, and can be seen to encompass a sizeable portion of the study area, extending as far north as modern-day Queen Street. The mill was a significant early business, and after building lots were placed on sale in Buffalo, in 1803, it even attracted people from the east side of the river.

By 1807, the village of Fort Erie contained 30 houses, all of which, with the exception of the mill, were destroyed by the Americans in the War of 1812. Cultivated land was still confined to a narrow strip along the river and two roads were passable by wagon; one following the river and the other extending between Point Abino and Millers Creek, along the summit of the limestone ridge.

Fortunately for the merchants in the village, the hostilities had not damaged Fort Erie's reputation as an important commercial distribution centre for the western frontier and other settlements on the Great Lakes. Taverns and stores that were rebuilt close to the ferry landings between Garrison Road and Bertie Street did a thriving business, as did the grist mill which, by that time, had been renamed Fort Erie Mills.

While the commercial growth of Fort Erie was notable during the first quarter of the nineteenth century, the village's importance diminished after 1825, perhaps due to the construction of the Erie Canal which made it more convenient for people in Buffalo to trade with the rest of New York State, and the opening of the first Welland Canal, which also drew commercial traffic away from Fort Erie.

The arrival of the Buffalo, Brantford & Goderich Railway in 1853, however, brought about another era of economic expansion. One of the new commercial enterprises was the "car ferry" which shunted railway cars arriving at either the Fort Erie or Buffalo terminus onto a special cross-river ferry known as "The International Steambridge."

There were significant changes to the landscape within a year that the railway was built. An 1853 map includes the proposed railway right of way and several structures west of the mill. Neither Queen nor Walnut streets had been opened, although the rights of way for Niagara Boulevard and Erie Street were shown. By 1854, however, Queen Street had been opened, a depot for the railway had been constructed, and tracks were laid to the ferry wharf adjacent to the terminal building at the foot of Forsythe Street. An engine house, turntable, and repair shop were also built in the yard.

The possibility that these structures represented significant subsurface

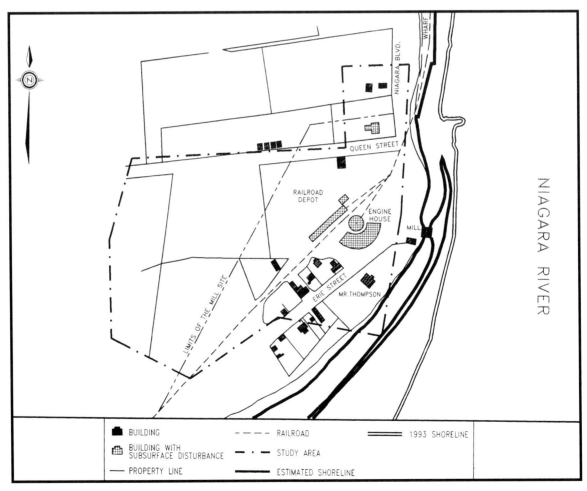

The study area in 1854, based on a plan of the village drawn by the Royal Engineers.

disturbances was later examined when we encountered deep foundations during excavation for catchbasins, south of Walnut Street, in the vicinity of the new commercial customs inspection booths.

Even more changes were evident by 1855. The area east of Goderich Street and south of Princess Street had been completely subdivided into building lots, and Victoria (now Waterloo), Queen, Archange, Erie and Walnut streets were named thoroughfares on the survey. Walnut Street, however, ended at the depot yard. The significant rise in population, from 180 people in 1843 to 706 people at the time of the 1860 census, can also probably be attributed to the industry associated with the coming of the railway, as perhaps can the village's incorporation in 1857.

The year 1857 was also significant in that the governments of Canada West (Ontario) and New York State approved a charter for the construction of a railway bridge that would permanently link the terminus in Fort Erie with Buffalo. It was not until 1873, however, that the International Bridge was completed under the direction of Col. Casimir Gzowski and pronounced an immediate engineering success.

The construction of the International Bridge north of the former car ferry terminus, however, had a devastating impact on the continued economic growth of the village. By the end of the nineteenth century, the village's population had grown very little from the 1860 period. There was also little commercial growth although the landscape continued to change.

At some point after the railway yard was abandoned, the engine house was removed and Walnut Street was extended east of Archange Street to meet Niagara Boulevard. Homes were constructed south of Walnut Street and west of Erie Street, in the area of the old engine house. The railway tracks that were used in the days of the car ferry, however, remained intact and were used by the contractor to bring in building materials for the construction of the Peace Bridge.

The Peace Bridge, named in honour of the international friendship signified by the longest undefended border in the world, was envisioned by a group of Fort Erie and Buffalo businessmen as a solution to some very real local problems. By facilitating the passage of vehicular traffic across the river, a service which at that time was being provided by a ferry, it was anticipated that the Peace Bridge would bring economic prosperity to both communities.

Constructed in the mid- to late 1920s and opened in 1927, the enthusiasm with which people regarded the project was reflected in an article written in 1927 that stated, "The supersession of the ferry by the bridge will, is expected, restore to the old Town of Fort Erie much of its former economic glory."

In order to build the bridge approach in Fort Erie, approximately 10 acres of land with frontage on Walnut, Erie, and Goderich streets were expropriated from approximately 15 property owners. A newspaper account from February 19, 1926, in the *Fort Erie Times*, indicated that all the owners whose buildings were in the way of the proposed bridge were allowed to move their buildings to another location.

The farm properties were rapidly cleared and levelled in order for the "Peace Bridge Plaza" to be constructed. This, in effect, terminated the Goderich Street right of way south of Walnut Street, in order to accommodate traffic passing over the bridge. It is clear that a significant portion of the ridge along which Goderich Street extended was excavated to level grade to form the highway entrance to the Canadian customs facility. Needless to say, there were no archaeological salvage excavations in advance of the construction resulting, no doubt, in the loss of countless archaeological treasures.

After the Peace Bridge was opened in 1927, the main Canada Customs facility was a two-storey concrete office building that stood adjacent to the customs booths until 1992. In that year, the Public Bridge Authority offices were moved to a new facility at 60 Walnut Street. In part, this move reflected a growing need to expand all of the Peace Bridge facilities.

The discussion regarding that expansion had been ongoing since the late 1960s, although it was re-energized by the Free Trade agreement of the late 1980s between Canada and the United States. Since that time, the Peace Bridge has been the fastest growing major commercial crossing between the two nations with traffic on the bridge increasing by almost 50 percent since 1990, accounting for at least $80 million in trade each day.

With its new customs, commercial, and truck-processing facilities, along with the opening of the companion and refurbished bridges by 2004, the Buffalo and Fort Erie Public Bridge Authority will be equipped to face the challenges of the twenty-first century, and beyond.

The locations of early twentieth-century structures in the vicinity of the Peace Bridge were documented on a fire insurance plan for the Town of Fort Erie, found by Eva MacDonald at the Public Archives of Ontario. While it was very difficult for MacDonald to discover whether buildings prior to this time had partial or full basements, she was able to consult with Mr. Norman Rouse, a professional property assessor, who had recollections regarding late nineteenth- and twentieth-century structures within the study area.

According to Mr. Rouse, most of the buildings on the south side of Walnut Street were multi-storey family homes with full basements or foundations. The exception was Shore's printing business located in an old, one-storey frame house on the north side of Erie Street, also shown on the 1854 plan of Fort Erie. Only two buildings within the block, north of Walnut Street and east of Archange Street, lacked full basements or foundations. One was the old firehall on Queen Street which was built on a concrete slab, and the second was a small single family dwelling on Walnut Street.

The Town Hall, built in 1893 on the south side of Queen Street, east of Archange, definitely had a full basement, as was shown on the fire insurance plan. Also on that block was the Antidolar Manufacturing Co., which made dental supplies, some examples of which were found during excavations in this area. Within the block east of Goderich Street and north of Walnut Street, only two structures lacked full foundations or at least a partial basement.

A 1951 fire insurance plan indicated that the Canada Customs complex had been upgraded to include two new commercial warehouse and administration buildings. Other changes to the study area included the demolition of three dwellings on the north side of Walnut Street, east of Goderich Street, and the construction of a large gas station/service centre for the Imperial Oil Company. A second gas station was located on Niagara Boulevard, at Princess Street.

By 1951 the Erie Street right of way had been halted at the Peace Bridge, although the dwellings west of Erie Street and south of Walnut Street were still standing. These homes were demolished sometime in the early 1960s as they were not included in a "Plot Plan of the Truck Yards" drawn in 1966 to show the new truck yard. The homes were still visible in an aerial photograph of the study area taken around 1957.

The task for Eva MacDonald and Williamson was to summarize this historical information and pronounce upon the archaeological potential of the study area. As considerable development and change had occurred over the past 200 years, it was felt that the most effective way was to try to map the data at a 1:2000 scale, resulting in a series of maps which showed the locations of structures during selected time periods. In this way, an overlay could be created that reflected the total accumulated

Coke and dental medicine bottles, early twentieth century.

area of significant subsurface disturbance.

Obviously, the map also illustrated the inverse — areas that had never been disturbed. It was Williamson's plan to consider all undisturbed areas to be of high archaeological potential, given the results of the previous archaeological research nearby.

Indeed, our report concluded that all areas within the study area that had not been significantly disturbed, with foundations to a depth of at least two metres, were to be considered of high archaeological potential. Williamson advised that these areas should be thoroughly tested in advance of any land disturbance of any nature. He also suggested that the zones should be assessed in intervals of not more than three metres, using a power auger so as to access and examine deeply buried soil horizons. The three-metre interval was important because both Williamson and Eva MacDonald were uncomfortable with the degree of accuracy that could be obtained through a mapping exercise using the archival record. At the very least, however, we now had a context in which to review various construction plans with the new consultant team, once they had been retained by the Peace Bridge Authority.

In the meantime, the one thing that everyone agreed on was that the Peace Bridge Authority should avoid any subsurface disturbance within the study area, a position that their superintendent of operations, Bob Smith, had arrived at months earlier. Smith was a friend of Williamson's from Snake Hill days, having worked for the town at the time of the excavation, providing all of the logistical support for that project. He was a veteran of archaeological issues and not only recognized and understood the paleosol for what it was, but sensed instinctively the implications of the excavations at Walnut and Niagara. He had also helped Eva MacDonald document the subsurface impacts of various structures within the study area. It was with some humour then that the Peace Bridge staff received a memorandum from the Niagara Parks Commission regarding the Walnut Street burials, their jurisdiction originating with the fact that the burials were actually located on Parks Commission land. The memo warned the Peace Bridge to avoid any subsurface operations in the vicinity of the burials.

We didn't have to wait long to get into action, although it was the Town of Fort Erie field project that was undertaken first. The town wanted us to proceed with the testing of the Niagara Boulevard so as to leave lots of time for a construction date in 1994. By mid-August we were out in the middle of the Niagara Boulevard with a backhoe and traffic control support, drilling holes into the roadbed and associated sidewalks. The test holes were placed in the areas of proposed lateral reconstructions between Forsythe and Queen streets using a 30-centimetre diameter power auger mounted on the back of a backhoe provided by Jim Flake and operated by his son.

The locations of the laterals were chosen since that ground was supposed to be relatively undisturbed below the roadbed and would provide an effective test of the presence of archaeological deposits. The power auger was required to reach and assess any deeply buried soil horizons overlain by the asphalt, granular, fill, and any alluvial deposits associated with flooding of the Niagara River. The test units were typically excavated to a depth of 100–200 centimetres to the underlying sterile sands, thereby

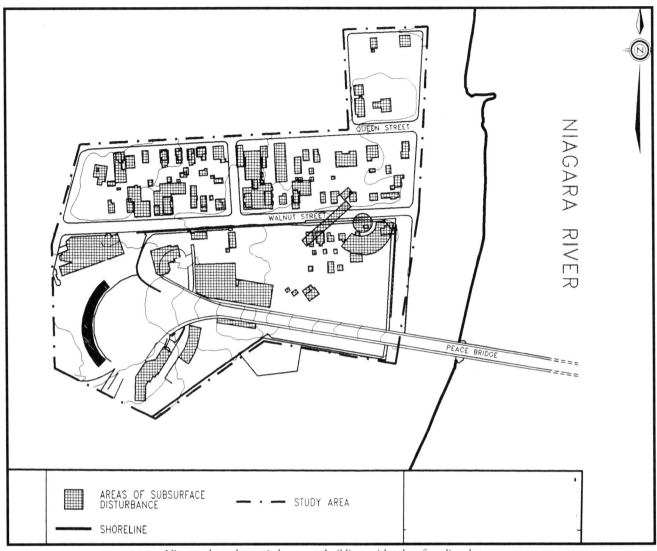

Nineteenth- and twentieth-century buildings with subsurface disturbance.

allowing for an examination of the soil stratification and the detection of the pale-osol. The soils from any of the undisturbed horizons were screened in an effort to determine if artifacts were present in the soil layers.

In total, 30 units were excavated along the route, three of which were negative since they were totally disturbed. To our astonishment, all of the remaining units yielded evidence of the artifact-laden, black organic paleosol at an average depth of about 50 centimetres. This horizon appeared disturbed to varying degrees but, nevertheless, was present directly below the concrete, asphalt, and fill material used to pave the sidewalks and surface of Niagara Boulevard.

A layer of sandy subsoil at a depth of approximately 80 centimetres, underlying the paleosol, also contained artifacts in a number of the test units suggesting that there had been substantial prehistoric occupation in the area. While this may not seem too surprising since these units were situated directly east of the Surma site, that the deposits were intact below the roadbed and sidewalks seemed like a miracle given the degree of disturbance over the years. One of the units even yielded a complete projectile point diagnostic to the Late Archaic period. Known as a Crawford Knoll point and dating to approximately 1200 BC, it was manufactured from the nearby Onondaga flint and fit comfortably within the range of material found previously in

Backhoe-mounted post hole auger being used to place test units on Niagara Boulevard. Note the black paleosol within the auger core.

the area. Another test unit contained, in addition to flakes of Onondaga flint, a ceramic rim sherd diagnostic of the Transitional Woodland period (AD 600–900).

Perhaps even more astonishing, however, was the fact that over 1300 artifacts were collected from the 27 positive test units — units that were only a foot in diameter. This suggested an artifact density similar to that which we had encountered the previous fall at the corner of Walnut and Niagara. The range in time periods represented by the artifacts were also comparable. Clearly there had been substantial occupations in this area and, based on the recovery of numerous bifaces, the site occupants had focused on the manufacturing of flint blanks for further reduction into finished tools, either at other areas of the site or inland at other communities.

Williamson now had to meet with Bill Packer from the town to break the news about our findings. The presence of this horizon directly below the sidewalks and surface of Niagara Boulevard had important implications for Packer's project. There was significant potential that the excavation of any new trenches would impact this archaeological feature. We, therefore, had to recommend that any future servicing or roadwork associated with the project be preceded by mitigation of any potential impacts on the archaeological deposits. This was to involve either protection or salvage excavation. As this was the first time that one of these town studies yielded such dramatic results, Packer needed to consult with his department colleagues and superiors and decide on a cost-effective course of action.

The decision wasn't whether to proceed; clearly the residents and customers in the area needed upgraded water and sewer facilities. Rather, it was how best to mitigate the impacts to the deposits, either by using an engineering method to avoid disturbing them, or excavating them in advance. Mostly, the decision would rest on a cost analysis. Williamson also recommended that re-excavation of the old sewer trenches be monitored by an archaeologist. While that seemed odd to Packer, in that the soils would already have been disturbed during the initial installation of the services, Williamson was worried that the original excavations may have impacted burials; he had already seen a disturbing example in the case of Walnut Street. Justification for his decision would have to await the fieldwork the following fall. In the meantime, we returned to Toronto and started to compile our report on the borehole testing.

It was late September before Peace Bridge officials, members of the new consultant team, and Williamson met to discuss the results of the background research. The consultant team and the Peace Bridge officials had reviewed the study and were quite impressed with the vast amount of black on Williamson and Eva MacDonald's map, representing probable areas of deep subsurface disturbance. Williamson, on the other hand, was overwhelmed by the amount of white, undisturbed space within the study area map, producing visions in his mind of thousands of artifacts and dozens if not hundreds of undisturbed burials.

What was clear was that some form of physical inspection to test the accuracy of the background research was necessary. It would also be essential to gauge the richness of the deposit in undisturbed areas. There were two basic options in terms of approach to the work. The first was to advance the site design to a point that the field tests could be placed strategically around areas to be disturbed, while the second was to test the entire study area and design the building around the results of the assessment.

The team chose a compromise position which was to test first but only those areas within the study area on which the building could conceivably be sited. In the midst of fears about scheduling of design and construction issues, and acknowledging that it was in everyone's interest to meet the ambitious schedule of the Peace Bridge, Williamson advised that the testing should commence immediately. In this way, all of the mitigation issues would be out on the table during the design phase.

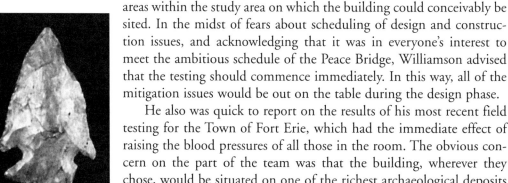

Crawford Knoll projectile point (1200 BC).

He also was quick to report on the results of his most recent field testing for the Town of Fort Erie, which had the immediate effect of raising the blood pressures of all those in the room. The obvious concern on the part of the team was that the building, wherever they chose, would be situated on one of the richest archaeological deposits in northeastern North America.

The Peace Bridge officers and the design team were looking for reassurance that any deposits could be salvage-excavated in advance of construction. Williamson answered that it was premature to provide such assurance until at least the field testing was undertaken. On the other hand, he pointed out that the obvious choices for placing the building were near either the Surma site, where a couple of dozen burials had been excavated in the 1960s, or the Walnut Street site, where we had excavated the richest one-metre test square we had ever seen and had documented two burials.

With those comments, the design team asked us to prepare a cost proposal for the field assessment, although they wanted it focused on two main options for building locations. They also instructed us to contact the leadership at the Friendship Centre, given the risk for encountering human remains in the work. Their position was to remain completely open regarding their objectives and to make it clear to the aboriginal community that they genuinely respected their concerns.

The costing was forwarded within days and the decision to proceed with the field testing was made within one week. The final discussions regarding the field testing program revolved around the need for the work to contribute to the ongoing discussion of the best location and design for the building and for there to be no delays. On October 1 Williamson received a call from Bob Smith asking for the details regarding the assessment. As always with the Peace Bridge Authority, Smith's questions were aimed at helping to get the job done quickly, but effectively.

Williamson and crew, including Pete Flake, were there two weeks later, focusing on the assessment of two alternative building footprints located west of Niagara Boulevard and immediately north and south of Walnut Street. Once again a backhoe-mounted, one-foot diameter power auger was used to drill test pits down to sterile subsoil, and the paleosol and any other cultural strata were screened.

Over 130 test units were excavated in the two potential building zones, 112 of which were excavated between Queen and Walnut streets, west from Niagara Boulevard. Approximately half of these units were excavated at two- to five-metre intervals at the northeast corner of the study area due to the proximity of both the Surma component, immediately across Queen Street to the north, and the Walnut component, immediately south of the potential building zone.

The remaining test units were excavated at 10-metre intervals outside of areas formerly occupied by buildings with deep foundations, as identified in the background research. In general, the artifact yields decreased from east to west with numerous units yielding hundreds of artifacts in the northeast zone. Conversely, many of the units with low yields were situated at the far western portion of the building zone.

The paleosol was again encountered throughout the study area at a depth of 50–70 centimetres. Most artifacts were recovered from the black paleosol, and we noted that substantial artifact yields were encountered in some areas immediately adjacent to units yielding evidence of substantial disturbance. This suggested to us that, while the basement of a former house, for example, may have obliterated the archaeological deposit within the footprint, artifacts in their original contexts survived immediately outside of the construction zone. This was a reflection of a particularly rich deposit.

Ground stone netsinkers recovered from features in the east trench area of the south truck yard. Note the notching on the sides of the stones, to facilitate tying of stones to nets.

Twenty-one test units were also placed at five- to 10-metre intervals in the other potential building zone south of Walnut Street and immediately west of Niagara Boulevard. While those areas formerly occupied by structures thought to have had deep foundations were avoided, there were still many positive test units in the undisturbed areas yielding significant quantities of artifacts and soil stratigraphies similar to those of the other zone.

A startling total of 6100 stone artifacts was collected from 101 positive test units, yielding an average of 60 artifacts per square foot of test unit. On any other site in the Northeast, more work would be required if a unit of similar size yielded only one artifact! The recovered stone artifacts were, of course, almost all flakes of Onondaga flint, although a few pieces of exotic materials from Ohio and other parts of the midwestern United States were also recovered. A brief analysis of the flakes and stone tools suggested that most of the material related to the refinement of large bifaces – probably fashioned at the shoreline outcrop – into smaller, more finished tools.

The finds also indicated a considerable amount of time spent refurbishing or resharpening existing tools. While two projectile points were found during the assessment, neither could be related to a particular time period. A number of ground stone tools were recovered, as well as a few ceramic vessel fragments, some of which could be identified to the Transitional Woodland period (AD 600–900), on the basis of their surviving designs.

Williamson had maintained almost daily contact with the rest of the consultant team so as to constantly inform the design process. It was clear as soon as they had started that there were significant deposits throughout the proposed areas of construction. It was also apparent that artifacts and even intact deposits might survive immediately outside of an already disturbed area. The paleosol itself appeared, in places, to be largely intact despite severe surface alteration, while elsewhere it had been disturbed to varying degrees. Consequently, test units yielding little or no cultural material were frequently recorded alongside test units containing moderate or even high artifact yields.

In general, the work confirmed Williamson's growing suspicions about the paleosol or "sheet midden," as Joseph Granger had called it in the 1960s. It was a continuous deposit from Forsythe Street in the north to just north of the Peace Bridge in the south. It also extended, on the basis of these results, for about 200 metres west of the Niagara River, at least in the area of Queen Street. What had started out only a year previously as a routine assessment at Walnut Street had turned into a 20-hectare (50-acre) archaeological site of incomparable artifact density that also happened to have a number of burial components. Moreover, it was clear that this band of cultural material had been largely sealed and protected by the gradual accumulation of an average of 50–70 centimetres of overburden.

Williamson, therefore, recommended that all construction work in those areas that yielded archaeological deposits be preceded by thorough archaeological excavation, should the Peace Bridge wish to disturb the subsurface. Simply, the Peace Bridge and the Town of Fort Erie had a big problem — bigger than anyone had previously anticipated.

By a strange coincidence, news of these finds exploded onto the front pages of the Niagara Region newspapers the last weekend of October, along with stories of the second World Series success of the Toronto Blue Jays. Williamson had given a presentation at the Ontario Archaeological Society's annual conference that Saturday in Niagara Falls, before rushing home to watch the last game in the World Series and celebrating on Yonge Street that night with tens of thousands of other fans.

In the audience that day had been Richard Douglas, Fort Erie bureau chief for the *Niagara Falls Review*, who had caught wind of the fact that Williamson was giving a professional paper on the Fort Erie site. Douglas had followed our work in Fort Erie since our excavation of the Walnut Street site, and later prepared a series of insightful articles, focusing on various analyses of archaeological material.

The headline of the story, in huge letters, read "Experts wowed by artifacts," and his story explained how he had come to that conclusion. He had recorded the reaction of the other professional archaeologists in the room as Williamson had given his paper — "You know this town is a hotbed of history when a roomful of archaeologists issue a collective gasp when told of the artifacts that have been discovered here, especially the 4000 artifacts from a one-metre square." The following week saw similar stories run by all of the regional newspapers, including the *Buffalo News*.

Just prior to the weekend, Williamson had presented a 15-minute slide presentation on the archaeological work we had undertaken in the Fort Erie area to the full consultant team at Moriyama and Teshima's office in Toronto. He described the assessment methodology that was undertaken and distributed a diagram of the boreholes that were drilled making reference to their artifact yields and his conclusions and recommendations. The discussion that ensued centred on the various scenarios for archaeological salvage excavation of deposits prior to development, often focusing on cost factors since the entire development area was an archaeological site.

It was clear to all present that there was going to be a need to design around the archaeological deposit as much as possible, as it was always better to protect rather than excavate an archaeological deposit.

Moriyama and Teshima were ahead of the game, however, as they demonstrated to the team that same day. Having discussed the findings with Williamson while we were still in the field, and having been sensitive to the archaeological issue from the time of the proposal conference presentation, they had prepared an optional design for the new customs facility to rest on caissons and a grade beam rather than a full, excavated foundation with basement. Their reasoning was simple: it would dramatically reduce the need for archaeological excavation.

While they were still considering a number of options for the placement and design of the building, based on meetings with the potential user groups and the Peace Bridge staff, the caisson design even presented an advantage — that being the coordination of truck bay heights with grade levels. There would still be a need for archaeological mitigation, and discussion ensued about the extent and cost of such work, but it was acknowledged by everyone that the caisson design involved significantly less archaeological mitigation costs than those associated with a full foundation.

A number of subsequent discussions, held during the month of November, centred on Willamson's understanding of the archaeological deposit and the costs associated with excavating various areas of the site in relation to the depths and sizes of various planned subsurface impacts.

Meanwhile, the Board and officers of the Peace Bridge Authority were becoming concerned about the ever-increasing amount of archaeology they were undertaking. They certainly had no intention of running a museum and were worried about their responsibilities under provincial legislation. In a mid-November letter to Williamson, Stephen Mayer, the operations manager of the Peace Bridge Authority, inquired after matters pertaining to the relevant legislative requirements for artifact ownership and curation, at the same time as he requested a first cut at the costs associated with mitigative excavations of the caissons, grade beams, and associated services into the building.

In his response to Mayer, Williamson outlined the legislation under which Archaeological Services Inc. was licensed to carry out archaeological activities. The Ontario Heritage Act stipulates that the minister may direct that any object taken under the authority of a licence or a permit be deposited in a public institution of his choice to be held in trust for the people of Ontario. It is also a term and condition of a licence that the licensee keep in safekeeping all objects of archaeological significance that are found under the authority of the licence along with the field records, unless otherwise directed by Her Majesty the Queen. Having yet to hear from the Queen, Williamson pointed out that the application of this section of the act and this regulation typically involves the curation of recovered artifacts by the archaeological consultant until such time that the analyses are complete and that a place for ultimate disposition can be arranged, usually a public repository such as the Royal Ontario Museum.

He also noted that archaeologists usually consult with the landowner and/or client to decide upon the location for the ultimate disposition of artifacts. He concluded by indicating that, while the Peace Bridge had no legal responsibilities for the storage or ultimate disposition of any of the recovered artifacts, he would welcome any input they might wish to make.

With respect to the next phase of archaeological exploration, his first costing was based on his current understanding of what the work was going to entail, knowing full well that the salvage program would likely change before we made it back into the field, likely the following spring.

First, however, Williamson was becoming very concerned with the huge number of artifacts that he was uncovering in these small assessments. He would be excavating much larger areas in the near future and, by comparison, the count would go through the roof. Since most of the artifacts were small flint flakes and since everywhere he had excavated he had found that the paleosol represented the accumulated refuse of thousands of years of occupation, he wondered about the utility of analyzing all of the flint chips when they couldn't be associated with any particular time period, and since they all reflected some form of quarry use.

He reviewed the situation with Robert MacDonald, Martin Cooper, and Debbie Steiss, his staff members that were most familiar with lithic analysis and Fort Erie archaeology, and they together concluded that a better idea would be to recover a sample of the flakes from the paleosol from across the site while still recovering all of the other artifacts.

Such a plan would still have to be reviewed with the Ministry before he could analyze the implications of such a decision for time and cost. He reviewed the plan the following week with Neal Ferris of the Archaeology and Heritage Planning Group of the Cultural Programs Branch of the Ontario Ministry of Citizenship, Culture, and Recreation while discussing with him the results of our field-testing program.

Ferris was the individual in the Ministry responsible for monitoring such undertakings in the southwestern region of the Province. Ferris was also a long-time friend and associate of Williamson, having worked as a field supervisor for him when Williamson was undertaking his PhD research in the early 1980s. Given the special nature of this rich and complex archaeological site, the two archaeologists agreed that the millions of flint chips could be sampled and that an inventory of the recovered flakes was reasonable rather than a detailed analysis, a decision that was applicable to both the testing program and the subsequent phases of work.

We spent the rest of 1993 back at headquarters in Toronto, processing the recovered materials, preparing reports, and writing proposals for the full-scale mitigative excavations that were going to occur in 1994 on behalf of both the town and the Peace Bridge Authority. The first costing for the Niagara Boulevard mitigative excavations was filed in early February and meetings were held in March to discuss ways of altering the design plans to reduce impacts and costs. By mid-April, a revised costing had been submitted based on the final plans.

Williamson also sent a revised costing to the Peace Bridge Authority for salvage excavating deposits associated with all of the planned sitework, including building caissons, gradebeam, landscaping, electrical, truck pads and yard areas, and water and sewer services. This was the first proposal for all of the anticipated archaeological work, although in the end it fell far short of predicting all of the work that would need to be undertaken over the ensuing three years.

By the middle of May, the Peace Bridge Authority's consultant team had reassembled at the offices of Moriyama and Teshima for another thorough discussion of the requisite archaeological work, given the current design and overall project schedule. Even with the new designs, the implications were clear—there was a huge amount of archaeology that had to be done. While it wasn't quite back to the drawing board, there was a need for more effective avoidance strategies to reduce the amount of potential delay that the archaeology represented.

Soon after the meeting, Williamson submitted his final revised costs for conducting excavations for the customs facility building caissons and electrical and servicing lines and trenches for the north employee parking lot. The latter area was situated directly on top of the Surma site on the north side of Queen Street and represented to Williamson an extremely high potential area about which he was worried. He had been reassured by the team, however, that for the most part, all operations would be above the grade of the paleosol. He also received good news — the customs building's first-floor structure had been redesigned to eliminate the need for the grade beam, which had represented a great deal of archaeology. Clearly, the efforts to identify the extent of the deposits were paying off. Not only was there a reduction in the time and costs for the archaeological component, but more importantly, there was a significant reduction in the impacts to the archaeological resources. Within days he was informed of similar changes to the landscape plans. Nothing could have pleased Williamson more.

That did not mean, however, that there was not a considerable amount of field archaeology to be done — and done soon. We received the first call of the 1994 field season in the last week of May, indicating that we needed to clear the borehole locations for the geotechnical investigations planned for the following week. How fast could we arrange for that work to be completed? Thus began one of the most exciting, prolonged periods of archaeological exploration with which our team had ever been involved, and it all started the following week.

Genesee feature under the sidewalk on the north side of Queen Street.

5   Clearing the Way

It was a warm, early June day and we were barrelling down the QEW on the way to Fort Erie from Toronto. It wasn't the first day of the field season but it was the first day on the Peace Bridge site in Fort Erie, and we were excited at the prospect of recovering material from the Surma site. On the other hand, we were only investigating a couple of small areas and we were prepared to deal with whatever lay ahead, big or small.

Our task was to examine the locations of six geotechnical boreholes in the area of the north employee parking lot, which was designed for the area between Queen and Princess streets, on the west side of Niagara Boulevard. Given the results of our fieldwork the previous fall, the Peace Bridge Authority had determined that there would be no subsurface disturbance of any nature, anywhere on the site, that we had not first cleared. The rule even applied to boreholes being placed on the site by other team consultants to gather data for the design process. Even surficial disturbances and demolitions of structures were to be monitored by one of our staff.

We rolled into the lot to find Peter Flake feigning sleep inside his backhoe. Since we usually drove in from Toronto, we rarely beat Flake to the site, and he usually liked to remind us of the fact. Flake was back since we again needed the use of his backhoe-mounted power auger to drill test pits down to sterile soil in the immediate vicinity of the geotechnical boreholes. We had also brought hand screens to sift any intact paleosol that we might encounter.

Fourteen test holes were drilled in the vicinity of the planned locations for the geotechnical boreholes to ensure that they would not disturb intact archaeological deposits. One of the boreholes was situated within the former foundation of the Queens Hotel and only rubble fill was encountered in the surrounding test units. Nine more test units were placed adjacent to a few boreholes, situated around the perimeter of the former hotel. These units all yielded evidence of the paleosol at a depth of 50–70 centimetres below surface.

While only finished tools were collected from most of the units, all of the artifacts were recovered from at least one, in keeping with the new Ministry protocol. The other two boreholes were located away from the former hotel site closer to Princess Street and were in completely disturbed areas.

In total, 929 lithic artifacts were collected from the test units, again consisting mainly of small chips of Onondaga flint indicative of tool production. A projectile point tip and a few other tools were also found, although none was diagnostic of a particular period. Five ceramic vessel sherds were also recovered, all apparently dating to the Transitional Woodland period (AD 600–900).

While it was concluded that there were cultural deposits below the surface in at least the southeastern portion of the parking lot, no human remains or intact cultural features were encountered, and it was recommended that the boreholes could be placed in the planned locations.

Although brief, the work represented an effective introduction to the north employee parking lot area since we anticipated that we would be back carrying out further studies within a week or two. We were not wrong, and within two weeks a team led by Williamson had returned to Fort Erie, only this time to stay for a few days. Our task was to investigate the proposed locations of all light standards, electrical control boxes and conduit, catchbasins, and storm sewer lines associated with the parking lot. All of these areas had been marked on the ground surface along with all of the locations for active services.

The plan was to excavate in these areas with Peter Flake's backhoe, only this time using a smooth-edged bucket to remove the upper pavement and fill layers to within a few centimetres of the paleosol. While archaeologists are typically depicted excavating with shovels, mason's trowels, paint brushes, and dental picks, when large amounts of overburden have to be removed, we bring in the big guns: earth-moving machinery.

For us the tool of choice was a Gradall, a truck-mounted excavator with a telescoping and rotating arm. Usually equipped with a smooth-edged bucket, they are a familiar sight along the edges of highways where they are used to excavate ditches. In the hands of a skilled operator, such as the one that we regularly employed, the Gradall could provide control to the centimetre when excavating in sensitive areas. A backhoe, with its arm swinging through an arc rather than a straight line, is much more difficult to control while maintaining a consistent, smooth grade. Williamson was not worried, however, as he had come to recognize that Flake, although young, was one of the best operators in the region.

For the first few units, Williamson guided Flake through the unfamiliar task of stripping away the overburden — centimetres at a time. Within an hour, the lesson was over and Flake was anticipating our needs. Once the paleosol was encountered, it was screened in one-metre test units, in accordance with our grid that was tied into one of the surveyor's data points. If any pit features were encountered, they were carefully recorded, photographed, and excavated.

While many of our initial test units were in completely disturbed areas, we did not have to wait long to encounter the same kind of deposit that we had seen at the Walnut site in the fall of 1992. Indeed, in a trench excavated to accommodate a storm sewer service, originating at a proposed catchbasin just inside the south wall of the former Queens Hotel and extending southward to meet the existing sewer line in the middle of Queen Street, not only was the paleosol encountered but three pit features were found emerging from beneath the layer.

The mostly undisturbed paleosol was excavated in one-metre squares yielding, in addition to thousands of flint chips, numerous complete and fragmentary bifaces and diagnostic tools. The finds were coming at such a furious pace that Flake couldn't resist and jumped down from his backhoe to grab a screen, a sight that was to become familiar over the ensuing years.

The vast majority (in fact, almost 80%) of the diagnostic tools found in this area were Late Archaic Genesee (1800 BC) in origin, although Late Archaic Crawford Knoll (1200 BC), Early Woodland Meadowood (800–300 BC), and Transitional Woodland Princess Point (AD 600–900) tools were also found. While no ceramic vessel fragments were found in the features, the paleosol yielded many fragmentary neck and body sherds of both Transitional and Late Woodland origin.

Portions of two of the features situated within the trench were completely excavated and found to contain little more than a few hundred flint chips. The other feature was partially exposed below the north Queen Street sidewalk. As a human finger was found in a concentration of bone near the bottom of the pit, it was decided to adjust the trench slightly so as to avoid further impacting the feature. It also contained a complete Genesee projectile point, along with a biface fragment and a large quantity of flint chips indicating that, if the finger did point to the presence of a burial, it likely dated to 4000 years ago. Also interesting was the fact that this area of investigation was close to the area excavated in 1965, although there was no way of determining if the feature we found was the same one encountered in 1965 under the sidewalk.

Although excavations continued throughout the parking lot for several days, no other large expanse was exposed. On the other hand, several units excavated to clear the way for light standards yielded layers of undisturbed paleosol containing Late Archaic Genesee and Late Woodland projectile points as well as other tool fragments and thousands of flint chips. In one disturbed unit, eight bifaces, four netsinkers, and a fragmentary ceramic vessel sherd were recovered along with several twentieth-century brick fragments underscoring the necessity of screening even disturbed soil horizons in some cases.

One of the last units to be excavated, situated within the former footprint of the hotel, yielded artifacts and stratigraphy that alone seemed to tell the 4000-year history of that particular locale. A 13-centimetre thick layer of paleosol, documented in the unit at a depth of just over one metre, yielded a Late Archaic Genesee tool. The west face of the unit revealed a series of rubble and fill layers relating to the demolition of the hotel but also a fired soil layer at a depth of 102 centimetres, just above the remaining intact paleosol. The fired soil probably related to the destruction of the hotel by fire in 1986. In that one unit, the trained eye could reconstruct the history of the building and determine that it had been originally constructed on a 4000-year-old aboriginal site.

In the end, dozens of diagnostic stone tools and bifaces as well as tens of thousands of flint chips and ceramic vessel fragments were recovered, justifying the field efforts at clearing the locations where subsurface disturbances could not be avoided. What was distressing, however, was that we had just spent three days on the site and had returned to Toronto with an immense number of artifacts.

We were anticipating a call from the Peace Bridge Authority any day to return to Fort Erie and get on with the clearing of the caissons for the customs facility building. While we were excited at the prospect of discovering what might be found in a generally unexplored area of the site, the results of the parking lot mitigation suggested that the Toronto office would soon be full to the brim with artifacts from Fort Erie. Our only hope was establishing a routine for the laboratory staff to ensure that material was processed soon after it came into the building. In that way, it wouldn't overwhelm us even if our expectations were exceeded.

By the end of June, we had received two more memorandums, one from the Peace Bridge Authority authorizing us to go ahead with the caisson investigations and another from Moriyama and Teshima outlining the remaining issues to be addressed prior to fieldwork. Most of those issues revolved around the final number and locations for the caissons. Williamson was most concerned that they be marked in the field by the Peace Bridge Authority surveyors and that their full extents be clearly delineated. What he wanted to avoid was investigating too small an area for any of the caissons, especially since they varied in size. The latter memorandum also informed us that the decision had been made to include a discussion of archaeological issues in the call for proposal for contractors for the construction of the building. Few contractors had experience with archaeology to the extent that was anticipated in this case and there were likely to be some unavoidable delays regardless of how much planning was undertaken.

Within a week, designs for the building arrived at our office, as well as large-scale maps showing the exact location and size of each caisson, and within days the caissons were marked in the field. On July 12, we moved to Fort Erie for almost a month.

Rather than stay in a hotel, however, the crew was delighted when Williamson announced he had struck a deal with local journalist Harry Rosettani to use his house as home base during the field operations.

While they had all met Rosettani and had spent many an evening consuming vast quantities of chicken wings, pizza, and beer with him (and not necessarily in that order), they were particularly pleased with the fact that Rosettani had a lovely swimming pool that was only moments from the hot site. The Peace Bridge Authority also came out ahead since the fee we paid Rosettani was much less than we would have paid for hotel rooms. It also meant that the crew could cook their own meals rather than dine out every night. Even better, however, were the nights that 84-year-old Mama Rosettani cooked up a storm and we had genuine Italian fare delivered to our door!

The crew for the project consisted of Williamson, Debbie Steiss, a senior archaeologist from Toronto, Jane Cottrill, an archaeologist from the Stratford office, and Paul McEachen and April DeLaurier, two student archaeologists who had worked for us for several years during the field seasons. They had all been briefed and were ready to go. Arriving at the site, they found Peter Flake ready to go as well. In the following weeks, all of the caisson locations were excavated using Flake's smooth bucket backhoe and the same field techniques as in the north employee parking lot.

Genesee projectile point (2000–1500 BC).

All of the caisson excavations revealed generally similar stratigraphic profiles to those outlined during the borehole assessment of the area — asphalt and granular overlying clay fills overlying disturbed and/or undisturbed black paleosol, which was encountered at a depth of 35–80 centimetres, overlying sand or lake clay. All of the units with paleosol yielded artifacts, usually in large quantities, especially those in which pit features were found. In many of the units, complete, large, circular features were exposed, while in others only portions of the features were present. In still others, features were only detectable from profile stains in the walls of the units. In summary, by the middle of August, we had documented 49 pit features, recovered approximately 141 kilograms (well over 300 pounds) of flint chips from the paleosol overlying the features, and tens of thousands of more flakes and tools from the features themselves, in addition to substantial quantities of animal bone.

Since we were excavating large portions of prehistoric pit features for the first time on the site, we also began to take 4- to 10-litre samples of soil from each feature, placing the soil within green garbage bags. The samples were then returned to Toronto and subjected to a process called flotation, which uses water to isolate carbonized plant remains. These remains are later examined microscopically to identify specific plant species and to reconstruct the plant component of the site inhabitants' diet. It is not unusual for an excavation area to have dozens of half-full green garbage bags littering its perimeter by the end of an excavation and the Peace Bridge caisson site was no exception.

A few of the features yielded huge quantities of lithic debris and tools. One

Trenching for new service lines in the north employee parking lot. Note the abandoned buried service lines within the trench. ASI archaeologist Bruce Welsh monitors the excavation.

feature, for example, was situated in a caisson in approximately the centre of the building. It was a deep feature, about a metre in diameter, that yielded over eight thousand pieces of flake debris, the base of a Late Archaic Genesee projectile point (1800 BC), the base of a Genesee preform, the base of a Crawford Knoll projectile point (1500 BC), and more than two dozen other stone scraping and cutting tools. Once the flotation samples from the feature had been analyzed, it was found that it also contained a small quantity of nut remains along with the seeds of black nightshade, raspberry, elderberry, and goosefoot.

Another incompletely exposed feature contained lenses of fired soil and a large quantity of fire-cracked rock, suggesting its prehistoric use as a hearth. The feature yielded at least two Genesee (1800 BC) tools, among many others that couldn't be identified to a particular time period, as well as over 2.5 kilograms of flake debris. A complete and very unique limestone pestle was found in the paleosol above the feature. Since these features were excavated through the paleosol into the subsoil at the time that the site was occupied, we carefully examined the soils immediately above the features. In this case, the paleosol above the feature yielded, in addition to the pestle, three flint tools, a few ceramic vessel sherds, and almost two more kilograms of flake debris.

Sometimes it was necessary for us to vary our field techniques on the basis of initial observations about a feature. In one case, for example, screening of the paleosol above a feature yielded several Genesee projectile points and tools and over eight

Partially constructed steel framework for the Peace Bridge commercial customs facility. Note the poured concrete caissons in the foreground.

(John Snell, Moriyama and Teshima Architects)

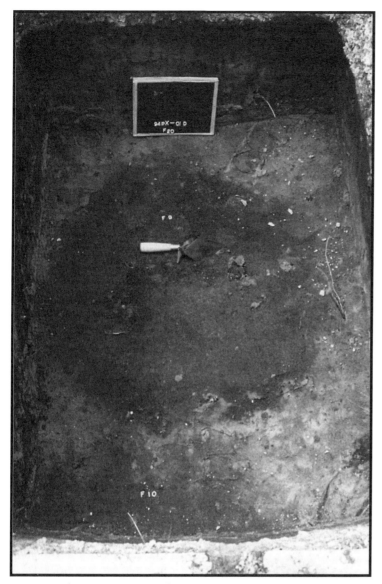

Exposures of an entire and partial feature in one of the caisson excavations. Note the paleosol in the walls of the excavation unit under the layer of granular.

kilograms of flake debris. Noting that many of the flakes were quite small, some no more than a few millimetres across, we decided to sift the feature fill using window screen rather than the usual six-millimetre mesh. The feature contained two tools and hundreds of flint flakes, many of which were minuscule. While the feature also contained 37 fish bones, most of which were bullhead, sucker, and pickerel, as well as a small amount of acorn, walnut, and other unidentified nut meat, the recovery of a concentration of small flakes hinted at a scene of a man sitting over the feature 4000 years ago, sharpening a projectile point or some other tool.

Other features appeared to have been used for very special ceremonies. One pit, for example, situated in Caisson A6 near the northwest corner of the building, was incompletely exposed within the unit yet yielded evidence of a ritual never before documented in Ontario. The feature was found to contain a pocket of calcined bone and a layer of fired soil at a depth of 30–40 centimetres below the top of the feature. In addition to the calcined bone, a small quantity of flint tools and flakes, some burnt, were recovered. A soil sample taken from the feature and later subjected to flotation also yielded nut remains, raspberry seeds, knotweed, and a small number of grass seeds.

The pocket of bone consisted of 343 grams of very small calcined fragments. These were all carefully excavated and collected and returned to Toronto to the laboratory on one of our trips back to headquarters. Once they had been processed, Williamson examined them and called Stephen Cox Thomas, a friend and colleague, who regularly identifies and analyzes our animal bone samples. He asked Thomas to examine the bone assemblage and to offer an opinion on what had been found.

Thomas determined that the bones had been subjected to very high heat as most of the bones had warped, shrunk, and suffered severe internal fracturing. This was particularly true of the long bones. During his preliminary work, the cortical texture of many of the long bone fragments suggested to Thomas the presence of either human or bear. He recommended to Williamson that more detailed examination be undertaken.

Within a few days the story behind the feature started to emerge. Thomas was able to positively identify a small midline fragment of a lower human jaw and other human skull fragments. Although the fragments were very small, he was able to identify them as human since the side and upper portions of the human cranium are distinctive, compared to other large mammals indigenous to Ontario. They have a different curvature and the appearance of the inner surface of the skull is generally smoother in humans. Also, the configuration of the cranial sutures are useful differentiating features. These are the lines that are formed when the sections of the skull, which at birth are unfused, consolidate to form the adult skull. Besides jaw and skull-case fragments, Thomas also identified human facial (brow ridge and cheek) and leg bone fragments, as well as a few pieces of vertebrae.

As Thomas's work proceeded, it became obvious that non-human bone was also present in the sample. As the collection was small and difficult to identify without a reference collection, he took the material to the Howard Savage Osteoarchaeological Collection housed in a laboratory at the Department of Anthropology at the University of Toronto. There he was able to compare the recovered specimens with literally thousands of other animal bones from species of known gender and age. He identified three non-human species, including a portion of a wing of a Canada goose and leg bone fragments of a bobcat and white-tailed deer. Several pieces of worked deer antler were also recovered that appeared to him to be fragments from an awl-like tool. Other thoroughly calcined tool fragments had been identified in the field, including bead sections, parts of a perforated needle, and pointed antler tine tips, which may have been blanks for harpoon points or antler flaking tools.

Thomas concluded that the sample was an odd mix of elements and tool pieces. Most of the identified material was human, probably belonging to an adult male. Given the evidence, he suggested that the

Limestone pestle found above a Genesee feature (1800 BC).

concentration of bone represented an intentional human cremation. Since some of the bones had deep internal cracking and had warping, which is consistent with a cremation soon after death, he suggested that the cremation occurred when the bone was in a fresh state.

If Thomas was correct about the cremation, it would not only explain the presence of an extensive layer of fired soil in the feature but also the absence of more vertebral and rib fragments or small hand and foot bones from the burial, since they consist primarily of spongy bone with very thin layers of cortex. Calcination requires exposure to high temperatures for a prolonged period of time and while it is possible that only selected portions of the individual were subject to cremation, the calcination process is intensely destructive and elements surviving calcination are greatly weakened and more vulnerable to further disintegration. On the other hand, it is also possible that the remains were removed from some other cremation site resulting in the loss of some of the smaller elements of the body.

Thomas, in his report to Williamson, also wondered whether the general animal remains and bone and antler tool fragments represented intentional grave inclusions to accompany the individual to the afterlife. Williamson accepted Thomas's conclusion and interpretation of the feature and instructed his staff to keep an eye out for similar evidence as they continued with their work at the site. It was only in 1997, however, that the evidence from the feature was examined very carefully in light of data from other northeastern sites. As a result of that research, Williamson was delighted to learn that they had found, locally, an example of a mid-Atlantic burial

Plate 1: Media and general public watch (left to right) Ron Williamson, Martin Cooper, and Debbie Steiss excavate the Walnut Street burials.

(Harry Rosettani)

Plate 2: Tobacco ceremony performed by Six Nations faithkeeper prior to covering the burial area.

(Harry Rosettani)

Plate 3: Old Fort Erie with migration of passenger pigeons in spring. Water-colour by E. Walsh, 1804.
(Royal Ontario Museum)

Plate 4: Water-colour by H.H. Green showing the proposed location and design of the Peace Bridge. "When the bridge is opened," a commentary of the day on Green's drawing observed, "the ancient Fort Erie ferry and all the problems of traffic which are now connected with it will bother no one." All this came to pass when the bridge opened in 1927.

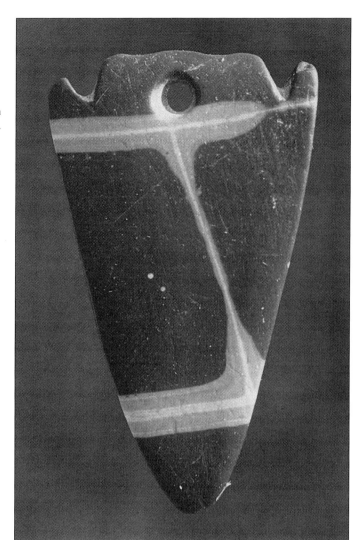

Plate 5: Arrowhead pendant made from banded slate and found on a copper necklace. The coloured banding is natural.

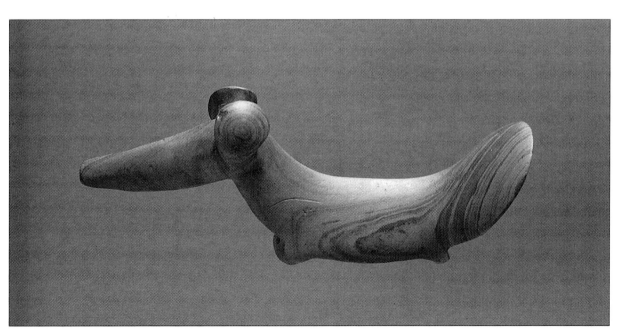

Plate 6: Pop-eyed birdstone made from banded slate. Wilfrid Jury Collection.

Plate 7: The crew excavates the east half of the trench at Forsythe Street and Niagara Boulevard. Debbie Steiss (left) and Jane Cottrill (right) wait for Rob MacDonald (centre) to provide them with soil to screen. Note the small black stains with flags representing the locations of former posts and the larger black stains representing the locations of cultural features, all suggesting the presence of an ancient house structure.

(Harry Rosettani)

tradition dating to the Late Archaic period. While it was a first for Ontario, it was perfectly consistent with the major occupational period at the site.

Two other human burials were encountered during the caisson excavations on the south side of the building near a planned staircase. The feature in which the burials were located was incompletely exposed, although it was clear that the general area had been very significantly disturbed by the placement of a water-line and a number of other service pipes at some time in the past. During the excavation through the construction trench for the water pipe, fragments of human bone were encountered, reminding us of the Walnut situation in the spring of 1993. The preservation of the fragments was extremely poor with no complete elements, although two left identical skull fragments indicated that the bones represented at least two individuals.

When the bones were first encountered, Williamson called on Christopher Dudar, a former student of his Snake Hill colleague Susan Pfeiffer, to come to Fort Erie and help define the situation. With his background in human biological anthropology, Dudar was in increasing demand for situations where it was necessary to record forensic data concerning skeletal remains in the field. This is the usual course of action when bone is in a very fragile, weathered state or when human burials are going to be left in the ground. Both circumstances applied in this situation.

One of the individuals was only identifiable from fragments recovered from the backfill of the trenches, including part of the left ear bone, various unidentifiable skull fragments, one permanent upper jaw incisor, and two small (three to four centimetres) pieces of leg bone. The incisor exhibited extreme tooth wear with only a tiny bit of enamel remaining below the root dentine. The wear on the tooth indicated to Dudar and Williamson that the individual was adult at the time of death. No other indicators of age were present. Dudar guessed that the individual was female based on an observation on one of the skull fragments. He also noted that one of the skull fragments from the area of the ear had possible bone growth that was perhaps related to otitis media, a middle-ear bacterial infection common to prehistoric aboriginal peoples. The diagnosis, however, could only have been confirmed with X-ray evidence.

The other individual was discovered in a largely undisturbed state in the southeast corner of Caisson J9 within a feature at a depth of 80–90 centimetres. The apparent absence of vertebrae, ribs, and hip bones, and the parallel arrangement of the long bones with the skull on top suggested to Dudar and Williamson that they were dealing with a bundle burial. While no pathologies were noted on any portions of the exposed bones, there was significant tooth loss in the jaw and the remaining teeth were extremely worn, both suggesting an adult of advanced age. In the absence of any other sex estimation landmarks, the presence of pronounced supraorbital ridges suggested male sex to Dudar.

The presence of a ceramic neck sherd that had been decorated with a cord-wrapped stick, next to the skull, suggested to us that the burial likely dated to the Transitional Woodland period, as did the Walnut Street burials and some of the Surma site burials. In keeping with the protocol developed subsequent to the discovery of remains at the Walnut Street site, the location of the caisson was moved slightly and the stairs into the customs facility building were redesigned so that the burial could remain in place.

Humans, however, were not the only animals to have been buried in the area. We were quite surprised while working through an historic layer in one of the caissons to find the front end of an animal burial. An examination of the bone by Stephen Cox Thomas established that the remains were those of a domestic dog. His examination of the teeth and long bones of the animal indicated an age at death of over seven to eight months and probably beyond the one-year mark.

The most interesting feature of the dog was the degree of dental crowding with major overlapping noted throughout the premolar row and outward bowing of the tooth rows. The result of these traits was a markedly reduced muzzle length, consistent with historic period dogs. Despite this rather unique historic feature, the disturbed paleosol also yielded prehistoric materials including a Genesee projectile point and tools (1800 BC), a Late Archaic Hind projectile point (900 BC), and a modest quantity of flake debris.

In general, the mixing of deposits, both within and between the prehistoric and historic periods, was a pattern in all of the examined caissons. A large, incompletely exposed feature in Caisson G14, for example, contained a Genesee projectile point (1800 BC), an Early Woodland Meadowood biface base (800–300 BC), seven complete or fragmentary bifaces, a number of expedient tools, 13 fragmentary ceramic sherds, and a large quantity of flake debris. Moreover, the disturbed paleosol above the feature yielded 10 complete or fragmentary bifaces, several of which were likely Late Woodland in affiliation, along with two definite Late Woodland projectile point fragments.

These artifacts along with the ceramics found in the feature suggested that the feature was actually a Late Woodland pit with earlier material having been added at the time of in-filling with the surrounding artifact-laden topsoil. This was commonly encountered across the site resulting from repeated use of the quarry in prehistoric times and use and reuse of the same lands during the historic period.

Another one of the caisson units was illustrative not so much of the mixing but of the general richness of the paleosol on the east side of the study area adjacent to Niagara Boulevard. Despite the fact that Unit C17–18 contained no features, the paleosol in the area was very rich. It extended from a depth of 45 centimetres below asphalt, granular, and fill to 65–70 centimetres. The yield from this single area consisted of almost 100 ceramic vessel sherds, many attributable to the Transitional Woodland period, dozens of refined tools and approximately 16 kilograms (35 pounds) of flake debris.

Stephen Cox Thomas examining a small animal bone in a laboratory at the University of Toronto.

(Richard Douglas)

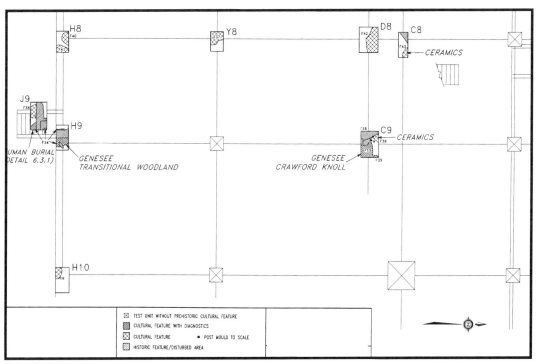

The results of excavations in the caissons in the south central portion of the commercial customs building. Note the location of the human burials.

The richness of the deposit was further apparent on August 8, when we returned to Toronto in an appreciably sluggish van, which we attributed to the weight of our stone cargo. It was a good feeling to have finished the work, although we knew we would have to return later in the fall to monitor the removal of rubble from a few of the caissons, to be sure that there were no artifacts or remains hiding below the disturbed layers. On the way home, Williamson was preoccupied, not with plans for this future work, but with recollections of the past four weeks and what had been found, especially the enormous load of artifacts with which they were returning. In the context of the considerable amount of fieldwork left to accomplish that summer and fall for the Town of Fort Erie along the Niagara Boulevard, he reminded himself to ensure that the laboratory staff were adhering to the schedule that had been established.

The following day he officially reported to the Peace Bridge Authority that he had completed the assignment, and summarized the field accomplishments — 151 square metres of excavation over the four week period. Those figures would provide Williamson with an effective guide over the ensuing two years in predicting the staff he would require for various assignments on the project. They also provided a benchmark against which to predict the numbers of artifacts that would be coming into our labs.

At about the same time that we were contemplating the immensity of the analysis tasks ahead of us, based upon the fieldwork that had been conducted to that point in time, Bill Packer called to set up a meeting for August 31 regarding the final phase of Niagara Boulevard work. He told Williamson that the town had retained the local contracting firm of Alfred Beam Excavating Limited. Packer wanted to have a pre-construction meeting with Williamson, Alf Beam, and the project engineer, Doug Ingram, of Kerry T. Howe Ltd., to ensure that everyone was working off the same page.

At stake from Alf Beam's perspective was a budget and timetable that had been established through the usual bidding process. Williamson was very mindful of

Beam's concern and, since many would view this as a precedent-setting collaboration between archaeologists and the construction trade, at least in Fort Erie, he wanted everything to go as smoothly as possible. At the same time, however, he had an over-riding concern that nothing compromise the integrity of any archaeological deposits that had survived the decades of urban development, nor impede the team's ability to properly record and salvage these deposits. For his part, Packer wanted the sanitary sewer, storm sewer, and water-main upgrades to go quickly and smoothly, to mini-mize the inconvenience to local ratepayers, and he did not want any major snags from either the archaeological or construction contractors.

With reputations at stake, everyone had a vested interest in ensuring a positive outcome. The decision was made to do the large storm sewer crossings first and Williamson outlined the field procedures for everyone. Most importantly, the con-tractor was warned of possible delays and Williamson and Beam agreed it would probably be a good idea to meet with his big machine operators in advance.

The start date for the work was set for mid-September and Williamson returned to Toronto to set up another crew for Fort Erie. Due to the demands of other ASI projects that fall, he was unable to direct the fieldwork and turned instead to Rob MacDonald, his friend and colleague from the Stratford office. With some staff members from the Stratford office and some from the Toronto office, MacDonald had an experienced crew with which to work.

It was a sunny morning when we assembled in the gravel parking lot at the cor-ner of Forsythe Street and Niagara Boulevard. Coffee cups in hand, colleagues from the two offices who may not have worked together for weeks or months exchanged greetings while they unloaded equipment. Alfred Beam's construction crew was already hard at work preparing to remove the asphalt at the southwest corner of the intersection. Len Grenville, the construction inspector, was there too, making sure that the work was done to the required specifications, as was Bill Packer for the Town of Fort Erie. As introductions were made between the various team leaders, each knew that the project was going to be a new experience and each hoped it would be a good one.

In spite of understandable apprehensions, the initial mood seemed rather upbeat. While this was partly because of the professionalism and positive outlook of the peo-ple involved, the Town of Fort Erie had created the proper environment for a con-structive collaboration by anticipating the role of archaeology and incorporating it into the project design. What the participants couldn't know was that the first major test of this positive mood would come within a few hours.

With the flag crew diverting traffic to the east side of Niagara Boulevard, Beam fired up the big excavator and began peeling back the asphalt. A private pilot in his spare time, Beam was a deft hand with machinery. Sitting in the cab with his black aviator sun-glasses shielding his eyes from the mid-morning glare, it was impossible to gauge his reaction when moments later MacDonald signalled for him to stop exca-vating. He and the rest of our team had been monitoring the work from a safe dis-tance when they had spotted the tell-tale blackness of the paleosol showing through the crushed stone — "granular A" or "granular" in the trade jargon — which overlay the asphalt. After a quick consultation, it was agreed that the big excavator would complete the task of removing the asphalt, but the granular would be removed sepa-rately.

Once the asphalt was up, Beam's foreman, Mark, brought in the smaller backhoe with a smooth-edged bucket that we had specially requested. Given the context of this job, it wasn't possible for us to work with Pete Flake. We, therefore, found our-selves guiding yet another operator through the unfamiliar task of stripping away soils very carefully—in this case, granular—two centimetres at a time.

Mark also proved to be a quick study, and soon the two-metre-wide trench was exposed from the curb to the centre of Niagara Boulevard. The effectiveness of the smooth-edged bucket was immediately apparent. While most construction excavation is done with a toothed bucket, which facilitates penetration into compacted soils, it cannot shave the soil to provide a clean exposure. Even with the bucket laid so that the teeth are parallel to the ground, the bottom of the bucket smears the soil as it is drawn forward, thereby obliterating important differences in soil colour and texture. In contrast, the edge of a toothless bucket can be drawn forward like a razor, peeling off a few centimetres of soil at a time and leaving a perfectly clean exposure. When viewing such an exposure, the trained eye of the archaeologist can read the entire history of ground disturbance at a glance. What we saw in the west half of this first trench was a large, 13-square-metre patch of undisturbed paleosol carved up by a network of intersecting twentieth-century utility trenches.

This was rather more than we had counted on. Since the construction project mostly involved replacement of existing sanitary sewer and water-main pipes that were already ensconced in their respective trenches, we had expected that most of the archaeological salvage work would focus on residual deposits that had been disturbed by earlier trenching and road construction. While the advance borehole testing had detected the widespread presence of paleosol beneath the street, it had seemed too much to hope that very much of the paleosol had remained undisturbed through decades of urban development. Yet here, less than half a metre under the surface of Niagara Boulevard, was the largely intact ground surface on which aboriginal people had trod for thousands of years. For those of us who had worked on the previous Fort Erie projects, this was quite a moment. Never before had so large an area been exposed and we looked forward to exploring the area.

As it had turned out, Williamson was in Fort Erie himself on that day to make a slide presentation at a pre-proposal conference at the Peace Bridge Authority for contractors interested in bidding on the customs building and sitework job. When he finally made it over to the job site later in the day, he, too, was astonished to see such a large area of intact paleosol under the roadbed. With the background growl of heavy equipment as a constant reminder, however, there was little time to marvel over the discovery. Immediately, some of us began gridding off the area to map and photograph the exposure, while others grabbed screens, shovels, and trowels, and began labelling artifact bags. As the recording team moved from one metre-square to another they were quickly followed by a skilled excavator who carefully shovelled paleosol to waiting crew members with bi-pod screens.

Each bi-pod screen consisted of a 60-centimetre (two-foot)-square frame constructed like an open box with three-inch high sides of one-by-three lumber. Quarter-inch steel mesh was attached to the bottom of the box, and a pair of handles, formed from the extension of the two sides, projected from one end. At the other end were a pair of one-metre (three-foot), cross-braced legs which were affixed with bolts that allowed the legs to fold flat against the bottom of the screen. When the screen was picked up by the handles, allowing the legs to stand on the ground, soil could be shovelled into the mesh-lined box and sifted with a vigorous back-and-forth motion. Under ideal conditions, a four-person crew could process up to a cubic metre of soil per hour. Here, although the soil was coarse-grained sand, the sheer number of artifacts in each shovelful meant that the screen operators had to stop frequently to sort and bag them.

By the end of the day it was becoming clear that reinforcements would be needed in order to avoid seriously delaying the construction crew. Fortunately, while we had been furiously engaged in salvaging the contents of Trench 1, Beam and his crew had been able to re-deploy to other aspects of the project. But Trench 1 was the starting point, so the redeployment couldn't continue indefinitely. With this in mind a call was made to Martin Cooper back at ASI headquarters to temporarily reassign people to Fort Erie until the crisis was past.

The next morning work began early, as our expanded team synchronized their work schedule with that of the construction crew. As the paleosol was removed and the buff-coloured subsoil exposed, black stains of various sizes were revealed. We immediately recognized the largest of these stains as pit features that had been excavated by the inhabitants of the site to discard refuse or to serve some other function. At the same time, we began to notice several smaller stains, approximately five to 15 centimetres in diameter. These we recognized as post moulds, the dark remnants of wooden posts that had been driven into the ground as part of some sort of structure. Just as dark topsoil had replaced subsoil to leave a stain where pits had been dug, any post hole which had penetrated the subsoil was likewise replaced with topsoil after the post was either pulled out or left to rot away.

The size of the post moulds was consistent with many we had seen on Late Woodland sites in association with house structures, and some seemed to be aligned in segments reminiscent of walls. As the paleosol had yielded many fragments of Transitional Woodland (AD 600–900) ceramic vessels, we wondered whether the posts might be a part of a house from that period. On the other hand, given the proximity of the historic Neutral Orchid component across the street, it seemed reasonable to speculate that this may have been a portion of an Iroquoian longhouse or related village structure, perhaps a palisade. Unfortunately, though, the exposure was too limited in area to determine its function; and the mixing of deposits, as in other parts of the site, also made its cultural affiliation difficult to determine.

As we continued exposing, recording, and excavating prehistoric cultural features within Trench 1, we suddenly made an astonishing discovery. Immediately beneath a gas pipe was the bottom half of a pit containing what appeared to be a nearly intact pottery vessel from the Early Woodland period. This type of pottery, called Vinette 1 ware, represented the very earliest pottery made in the Great Lakes region over 2000 years ago. Although it was rare enough to find a few sherds of this early pottery, to find a nearly intact vessel was indeed remarkable. Unfortunately, the trench for the gas pipe had sheared off the top of the feature, and with it the rim and neck of the pot.

As disturbance and soil compaction had fractured the vessel, it was now being completely supported by the matrix of soil which surrounded it inside and out. In order to preserve its integrity as much as possible, we carefully carved away the surrounding dirt leaving the vessel embedded in a cube of soil. The cube was then cut away from the underlying soil and gingerly transferred to a cardboard box for transport back to the laboratory where it could be restored and analyzed.

By the end of the day we had finished removing and screening the paleosol from 13 one-metre squares and had nearly finished mapping, photographing, and excavating nine cultural features and 18 post moulds. We had also mapped the utility trenches which criss-crossed the area in order to provide a complete picture of the archaeological features, both historic and prehistoric, that we had encountered. As soon as we had finished working in the part of the trench where the new water main was going, the construction team began their installation.

The next morning, even as the big loader began backfilling the trench with granular, we completed our removal of the last few features. Once the trench was filled and packed, the flag crew diverted traffic to the west side of Niagara Boulevard and

Beam brought in the big excavator to remove the asphalt on the east side. Mark followed with the backhoe to strip off the granular and reveal the underlying paleosol. Soon we were back at work gridding off the trench and screening paleosol. Once the paleosol had been removed and the area carefully trowelled to provide the cleanest possible exposure, 10 more features were revealed, as well as a much higher density of post moulds. Work would continue in the east half of Trench 1 until the end of the following day.

As we toiled away in the late summer sun, the passers-by began to notice that there was something unusual about this project. The activities which attract the curious to construction sites now included people with hard hats sifting dirt, taking photographs, and making copious notes. As curious residents became aware that this was both a construction site and an archaeological dig, the daily stream of "sidewalk superintendents" began to include people clutching shoeboxes full of arrowheads for the archaeologists to identify.

The knowledge and artifact collections of avocational archaeologists and private collectors can be invaluable, since they can often pinpoint site locations which are not yet registered or which have been destroyed by development. Recognizing this potential source of local information, and the importance of public relations to this project, we sacrificed lunch breaks in order to share knowledge and information with local residents. The same courtesy was extended to members of the news media from Fort Erie and Buffalo, who quickly put archaeology back into the local headlines. Soon, town councillors, and even Mayor Teal, dropped by to see what the fuss was all about.

On first glance the view from the sidewalk was not that impressive: a metre-deep trench, two metres wide by five metres long. Here and there in the buff-coloured soil in the bottom were large, black stains, some extending beneath the road, others intersecting each other. Peppered around the large stains were small blotches, most no bigger than the palm of your hand and many becoming faint as the sun parched the damp sand. As we explained the origin of the stains, however, a revelation came to the curious onlookers. First, they could envision six-metre (20-foot) saplings rising from the larger post moulds. These gradually resolved themselves into a bark-covered house structure six metres (20 feet) wide and 20 metres (65 feet) long. Then, a group of such structures took shape, accompanied by a series of fences and racks, many with drying fish and skins.

Suddenly the vision was populated by dozens of native people, some heading out into the river in canoes, nets in tow, others leading groups of laughing children down to the river to swim, and still others heading out to hunt, accompanied by small, lean dogs. Over there was a group of old men, sitting and talking while they deftly fashioned tools from the blocks of flint which lay piled beside them. Every so often they would toss a useless chunk into the nearby garbage pit, which they had dug to dispose of the sharp flakes so that the children would not cut their feet. An old woman, who had been tending a pot of soup nearby, came over to chat with them. With her she brought other contributions to the garbage pit; the remains of a broken pot and the leached bones she had retrieved from the soup pot.

As the post moulds faded in the summer sun, this momentary glimpse of an earlier time faded with them, returning the onlookers to this trench in the middle of Niagara Boulevard. But now this trench had new meaning. It was an aperture through which they had viewed another town, extending in all directions beneath their very feet. In future, as they walked these familiar streets, they would always harken back to that other time, and wonder what it was really like.

We wondered too, for although we had found pottery and stone tools in our

Reliving the past: (top) women cooking over an exterior hearth. Note the fish-smoking rack in the background; (bottom) men sitting in an encampment. Note the house structure in the background.

excavations, which gave us a sense of what had happened in this trench, it would be many months before laboratory analysis and interpretation would allow it to give up its secrets. For now, though, we had to focus our attention on the next phase of construction. This involved the removal and replacement of the watermain and sanitary sewers which ran up the west side of Niagara Boulevard from Forsythe Street to Queen Street, as well as the storm sewer which ran up the east side.

The procedure was fairly straightforward. Beam would move the big excavator along the edge of the road pulling up the asphalt in a strip that extended from the curb out about three metres (10 feet). He would then dig down through the granular into the sand, which filled the existing sewer or water-main trench until he hit the pipe. The asphalt, trench fill, and disused pipe were all loaded into dump trucks to be hauled away to be reclaimed.

The water-main was about 1.5 metres below the surface of the street, while the sanitary sewer was about three metres down. The bucket of the excavator was only slightly smaller than the width of the original trenches, and since a laser was being used to guide the placement of the sewer pipe, Beam had no trouble staying within the existing trench walls. As he proceeded, our crew, which by now had been scaled back to two people, monitored the excavation to ensure that no damage was done to undisturbed archaeological deposits adjacent to the trenches.

From the pit profiles visible in the edges of the trenches, we could see that the original excavators had sliced through or almost completely destroyed numerous prehistoric features. Once Beam had cleaned out the trenches, he lowered a construction box into the deeper one to allow his crew to safely install the pipe without fear of the sand caving in.

While they were busy with pipe installation, we would jump into the shallower water-main trench to photograph and record any residual feature profiles. Occasionally, a small slab of trench wall would shear off due to vibration and collapse into the trench, sometimes bringing with it some paleosol or part of a pit. The cultural fill would be screened to recover any artifacts and soil samples collected for flotation processing. Generally, though, pit remnants observed in the profile could not be excavated because they were capped by paleosol, roadbed, and asphalt.

As the operation proceeded southward along Niagara Boulevard, Mark used the big loader to backfill the trench with granular in order to maintain public safety and ensure that the unstable trench walls did not collapse. As they installed the new pipes, the construction crew had to reattach the utility hook-ups for the storefronts along the street. Where these lateral connections had to cross the road, they used a boring machine to tunnel across under the road. This was not only more efficient than open-trenching, but it also minimized traffic disruption and avoided the archaeological deposits which were above.

Three times, though, we encountered unseen obstacles which necessitated the use of an open trench. As with Trench 1, lateral trenching ran the risk of exposing extensive undisturbed archaeological deposits. Fortunately this only happened once, in a three-metre wide by four-metre long lateral trench between Princess and John streets. When the trench was opened up towards the end of one day, nine cultural features and eight post moulds were exposed, although the paleosol had been disturbed by the roadbed construction. A call to ASI headquarters brought reinforcements early the next morning, and by the end of that day the entire trench had been salvaged.

Only once did all construction grind to a halt. Fairly close to Queen Street, we noticed a pit remnant, which contained human remains. The skeleton appeared to be in a flexed position, with the knees drawn up to the chest, with the head to the south and the feet to the north. As it was not further exposed, we could not tell to what extent the remains had been disturbed by the trench. As the burial appeared to be safe from any further impact, we proceeded in accordance with the protocol established with the Fort Erie Native Friendship Centre. The burial was left in place, and we ensured that it was not further disturbed after construction activities resumed.

On reaching Queen Street, the designated end of the water-main and sanitary sewer replacement contract, the crews crossed to the east side of Niagara Boulevard at Princess Street to continue the process with the three-metre-deep storm sewer. As they slowly worked their way northward to the starting point at Forsythe Street, we noticed a higher degree of disturbance and far fewer cultural features in the profile. It was apparent that, like the sanitary sewer trench to the west, the deep storm sewer trench had been prone to collapse when it was originally dug. As a result, the walls of the original trench flared out towards the top, leaving little or no evidence of any archaeological deposits that might once have been present.

Although the beginning of the project had made a big splash, inspiring an odd mixture of excitement and dread in all the participants, it had quickly settled down into what had become several weeks of something approaching routine work. Now, in late October, as the final loads of granular were being poured into the trench, we packed up our equipment and said our farewells to Beam and his crew. During the project, both teams had come to appreciate the work and expertise of the other, thereby acquiring a great deal of mutual respect as a result. Moreover, we together clearly demonstrated that archaeological conservation and construction need not be mutually exclusive enterprises.

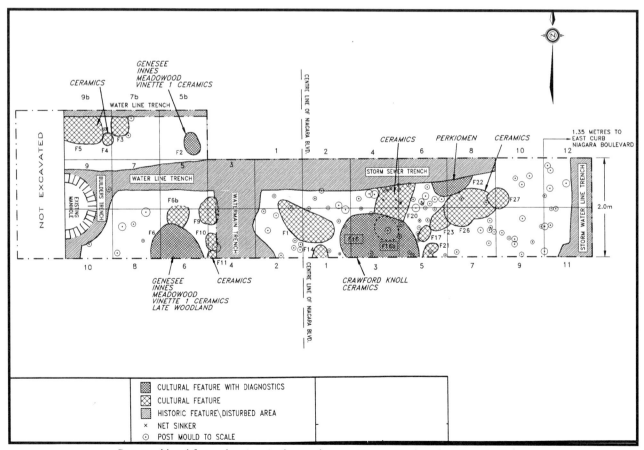

Post mould and feature locations in the trench across Niagara Boulevard, at Forsythe Street.

Barry Lillis and John Wichrowski of Buffalo Channel 2 interviewing Debbie Steiss and Eva MacDonald at the site.

Driving back to Toronto, we were again escorting vast quantities of artifacts. We had so many, that we at times wondered if there could be any left at the site. Only a few months later, we were back in Fort Erie facing the folly of such an idle speculation.

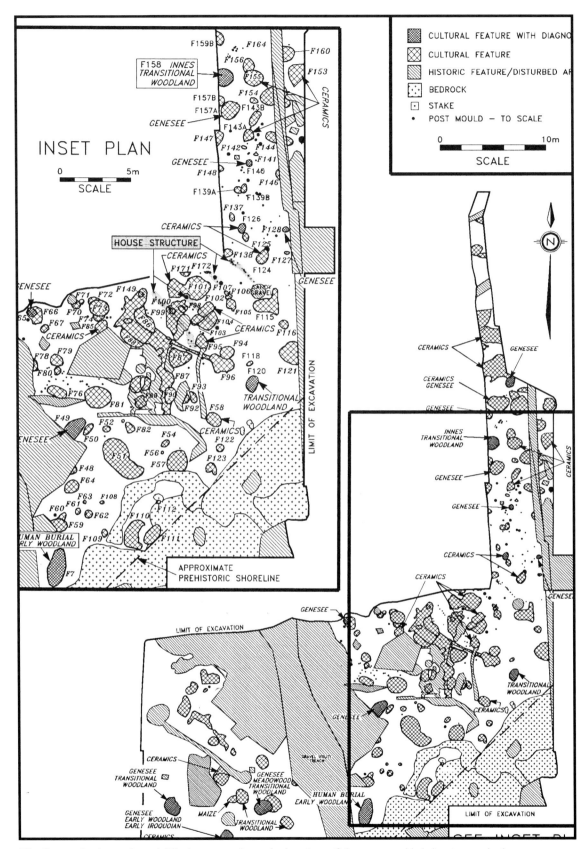

The features in the truck yard. The inset map shows the locations of the post moulds belonging to the house structure. Feature 158, which yielded the remains of the complete seventh-century vessel, is north of the house structure.

6 The Site Revealed

Rob MacDonald stared intently at the computer screen. Beside him, the desk was piled high with books, maps, reports, and other assorted papers. Even on winter days such as this, with thoughts of excavations furthest from his mind, his years of experience interpreting complex stratification were put to good use, if only to keep track of the layers of documents on his desk. On this Monday afternoon in late March, however, the papers had been pushed aside to accommodate several zip-lock bags, each containing a paper label and a handful of flint chips.

For the past few weeks, MacDonald and his colleagues, Deb Pihl and Jane Cottrill, had been conducting an analysis of stone tools from the Parson site, a fifteenth-century Iroquoian village excavation that we had completed in Toronto a few years earlier. It was common practice for us to save this sort of analysis work for the winter months, when we could take a break from the hectic fieldwork schedule and devote our time to major project reports.

Engrossed in thought, he ignored the telephone when it rang. Moments later, Cottrill was at his door to say that Ron Williamson was on the line. This was no surprise, as the two friends and colleagues often spoke to each other by phone several times in a day. This time, though, he was calling from Fort Erie, where he and a crew from the Toronto office had been monitoring construction at the Peace Bridge site, and he had some rather startling news. "I hope you're ready to do some Arctic archaeology," he said jokingly, "because this morning we started hitting some pretty big features under the middle of the truck-yard parking lot! We need you guys down here first thing in the morning to help us out." Hanging up the phone, MacDonald walked to the outer office to break the news to the other staff, reminding them it was Fort Erie and that they had better pack for winter weather.

In his 13 years with ASI, MacDonald had come to expect the unexpected, but this was certainly a first. Normally, the excavation season didn't begin until after the frost had come out of the ground, usually in late April or early May. But thanks to the early onset of spring, the Peace Bridge Authority's construction contractor had decided to take advantage of conditions and forge ahead. Having been warned the previous November of a very tight construction schedule, Williamson had been ready with a small monitoring crew. He had been apprised of the truck-yard work, but the finished grades hadn't been worked out so he had no idea how close the truck-yard work was going to get to the paleosol.

Early the next morning MacDonald wheeled onto the construction site at the east end of Walnut Street. Casting around the site he spotted ASI's van parked near a gaping 25 by 40 metre hole which had once been an asphalt parking lot. Pulling up behind the van, MacDonald and his crew could see the Toronto team hard at work. Williamson came over to greet the new arrivals and brief MacDonald on the situation. Although sunny, there was a bitterly cold wind blowing off of Lake Erie as the two archaeologists stepped down into the excavation area to begin surveying the freshly exposed subsoil.

Williamson explained to MacDonald that the first phase of the construction project involved upgrades to the large truck-yard area. This was to be a staging area where commercial carriers would pull up their vans and semi-trailers while they waited for their turn at the customs booths. In order to accommodate this heavy traffic, the new design called for a thicker roadbed. The plan was to remove the asphalt, remove and stockpile the granular, excavate the underlying soil to a lower grade, replace the granular adding new material to bring it up to the new grade, and cap it all with a new asphalt surface.

Even as we watched, a large excavator was removing the last of the granular, while nearby a backhoe was working to carefully expose the underlying subsoil under the supervision of one of our ASI crew members. MacDonald noticed that between the subsoil and the granular was a thin layer of reddish clay, but no evidence of the pale osol topsoil that we had seen so often while monitoring the sewer replacements the previous fall. Williamson explained that the paleosol topsoil and an unknown depth of subsoil had apparently been removed earlier, likely when the existing parking lot had been built.

He also pointed out that there had once been houses and a railway round-house in this general area, so the potential existence of nineteenth- and twentieth-century disturbance to prehistoric deposits was high. Nevertheless, as the backhoe continued

Features being documented and excavated in the south truck yard. Note the framework for the commercial customs facility building in the background.

to remove the clay fill and shave the subsoil clean, we could see that the area was dotted with prehistoric cultural features.

It was clear that all of the archaeological deposits would need to be salvaged before the truck-yard construction could proceed. Recognizing the mounting urgency of the situation, Williamson and MacDonald joined their colleagues as they prepared to map and excavate the features. Williamson resumed the task of monitoring the backhoe stripping. The subcontractors, Stephens and Rankin Inc., had attached a custom-made, five-foot-long bucket to the backhoe, which was proving to be nearly as effective as a Gradall. The reddish clay fill, which had been laid down on top of the subsoil, peeled off in great, long strips which resembled plasticine in consistency.

Beginning on the north edge of the excavation, the operator would peel off the clay, then thinly shave the subsoil by a few centimetres to provide maximum visibility. He would then back the machine up a few metres and repeat the procedure. This way he would not have to drive over the soil he had just cleaned off. On reaching the south edge of the excavation, he would move the machine to the east and begin the process again.

In the already cleared area, the crew was installing a recording grid to map the features. Using a transit and a tape measure, the crew hammered in 18-inch-long, two-by-two-inch wooden stakes at five-metre intervals throughout the truck yard. Oriented on a north-south axis, the grid was tied into the nearby concrete bridge pier as a fixed point of reference. By affixing measuring tapes to the nails projecting from the top of adjacent stakes, we would be able to triangulate the coordinates of each cultural feature. Back in the laboratory, these coordinates would be input to a computer assisted drafting (CAD) program to allow precise mapping of each feature.

As Williamson followed the backhoe, he noticed that the clay fill was becoming thicker the farther east we went. Then, in the southeast corner of the truck yard, the underlying sand disappeared. In its place was the flinty bedrock, with thin pockets of sand in a few hollows and reddish clay fill lying directly on top. Williamson called MacDonald over to get his opinion on the significance of this discovery.

While MacDonald examined the area, Williamson glanced at his watch. He was glad to see that it was lunch time, as he was looking forward to a hot bowl of soup and a break from the biting wind which swept across the site. He called to the rest of the crew to pack up their gear and head to the van. A Tim Horton's doughnut shop was a short drive away. We often joked that every Tim Horton's was a regional office of ASI, since these places were a favourite venue for our field meetings and lunch breaks and, no matter where we were working in the province, we always seemed to be able to find one.

Over lunch, MacDonald pulled out a pen and began sketching on a napkin. When he finished, he swivelled it around so Williamson could see it from his side of the table. Williamson examined the stratigraphic profile and nodded in agreement. This would explain the disappearance of the sand and the exposed bedrock. Our hunch was that the transition between sand and bedrock represented the location of the original shoreline. The bedrock was very clean, as if it had been washed. We reasoned that if the sand had been removed by machinery, there would be much more soil residue in the cracks and hollows.

We also suspected that clay fill had been laid down in progressively thicker amounts in order to maintain a level grade all the way to the river. The final clue would be revealed the following day when the stripping was completed in that area: the transition line was oriented roughly northeast-southwest, in exactly the location and alignment that the original shoreline was depicted on historic maps.

On returning to the site, we began shovel-shining five-metre squares and trowelling down features to improve the clarity of their definition. Shovel-shining is similar to the centimetre-by-centimetre shaving of the soil that is done by the backhoe, except that it is done by hand, slicing millimetre by millimetre, using a contractor's spade with a specially sharpened blade. With years of practice, the shovel can become a precision instrument in the hands of an archaeologist, capable of highlighting subtle changes in soil colour, texture, and density, while trimming off the merest shaving of soil. It is only exceeded in its fine control by the mason's pointing trowel, the five- or six-inch Marshalltown being the weapon of choice for most archaeologists. Wielded in a scraping motion, the blade perpendicular or slightly angled to the ground, the trowel is usually reserved for defining and excavating cultural features and post moulds, where the least amount of soil-removal is required.

By mid-afternoon we had completed enough work to allow us to appreciate the situation in the truck yard. It was not a situation with which the Peace Bridge Authority and their construction contractors were going to be pleased, especially when we explained the implications of the finds. There were literally dozens of overlapping prehistoric features distributed throughout the entire excavated area representing days of excavation time.

The sensitivity of the find instantly heightened when Shaun Austin and Debbie Steiss exposed a human skeleton within one of the features. The individual had been placed on the right side with the legs drawn up tightly to the chest and the head to the south, facing east. The molars and premolars were extremely ground to the point of exposure of dentine. No sexing, aging, or other observations were possible. Clearly, however, from the nature of the teeth and the size of the hip bones and leg bones, the individual was adult. The grave had originally been excavated down to the bedrock, and the bones were lying right on the flint. It was a miracle that the burial was still intact. With nothing but bare bedrock to the east, it must have been lying at the very edge of the Niagara River. It was also astonishing that it had not been severely impacted when the parking lot grading and filling was done.

As Austin and Steiss meticulously brushed away the sand, Williamson came over to take orders for coffee. Although a mid-afternoon run to Tim Horton's was not uncommon, particularly when working in the cold, Williamson had a special errand in mind. It was Austin's fortieth birthday and he would be picking up a cake for an impromptu dig-side celebration, a long-standing ASI ritual on such occasions. As they gave Williamson their orders, Steiss and Austin didn't even look up, so engrossed were they in their task.

MacDonald was busy supervising the backhoe when Austin called him over to the gravesite. "What do you make of this," he asked, pointing to a light grey cylinder lying partly exposed against the skeleton's upper arm bone. Crouching down to get a better look, MacDonald's eyes nearly popped out of his head. He instantly recognized it as a stone, blocked-end tube pipe, a type of artifact that, like most archaeologists, he had only seen pictured in books or lying behind glass in museum cases.

Dating to the Early Woodland period, this 2000-year-old smoking pipe was carved out of an Ohio limestone. Measuring about 19 centimetres long and three centimetres in diameter, the interior was ingeniously tapered at the mouthpiece to allow the insertion of a small, facetted pebble. While holding the pipe at an angle, the smoker could draw on the mouthpiece and the pebble would allow the smoke to pass while keeping the smoking materials in the pipe.

As Austin carefully released the pipe from the remaining sand, we noticed that below it was a beautifully made T-shaped drill bit of Onondaga flint. Measuring about 7.5 centimetres long and 2.5 centimetres wide at the base, it was obviously

Plate 8: Rob MacDonald and Deb Pihl excavating in the rain, in the three-by-three metre square at the east end of the catchbasin trench. Note the stratification in the wall of the test area; in particular the presence of the paleosol under the granular.

Plate 9: The crew excavates at the intersection of Forsythe Street and Niagara Boulevard. Note the bi-pod screens.

(Harry Rosettani)

Plate 10: Bruce Welsh preparing a section of the east truck pad for photography. The section matches the area shown by the inset plan of the map of the east truck pad, (page 97), revealing the complexity of the soil-staining and of the mapping process. In this photograph a portion of Feature 102 has been excavated, and Feature 105 is immediately above Bruce Welsh's shovel.

Plate 11: In a Huron creation story, Iouskeha and Tawiscaron do battle – Iouskeha with the antlers of a stag, and Tawiscaron with the branch of a wild rosebush. Tawiscaron's blood flows to become the stone known as tawiscara or, as it is known in English, flint.

(Tawiscaron Indian Village, Frontier Landing Recreational Park Inc.)

Plate 12: A variety of Genesee projectile points (2000–1500 BC).

Plate 13: A variety of Genesee preforms (2000–1500 BC).

Plate 14: Ron Williamson at the unveiling of the reconstructed vessel from Feature 158 – and the recreation of the "Ten-Fish Soup" found in the vessel.

(Richard Douglas)

Blocked-end limestone tube pipe.

Pebble in the mouth at narrow end of the pipe.

another cherished tool that had accompanied this individual on his final journey. Noticing that Williamson had just returned with the cake, MacDonald motioned him over to share in the discovery. Later, having carefully covered the burial, we sat around on tool-boxes by the vehicles enjoying cake and hot coffee, and joking with Austin about his unique birthday surprise.

Williamson and Mac-Donald were starting to appreciate the enormity of the task which lay before them, as more and more features had been exposed every hour by the backhoe. With mounting urgency, the crew continued with their excavation of cultural features.

As they began to cross-section one large pit, Deb Pihl and Debbie Steiss began to encounter delicate bones which still seemed to be in their correct anatomical position. Immediately, they switched to excavating with wooden meat skewers and paint-brushes, in order to avoid disturbing the articulations of the small skeleton.

Both archaeologists had expertise in analyzing animal bone, and they quickly identified these as the remains of a small dog. Continuing to excavate, they were puzzled, however, as an extra limb was uncovered. Carefully scraping and brushing, they gradually solved the mystery. There were two dogs in the burial, one on top of the other. With help from Jane Cottrill, they spent the better part of the day gingerly exposing and recording the feature, which they interpreted as a tender veneration of two faithful companions; one a young pup about six months old, and the other a mature dog. Both dogs had been placed on their left sides in a flexed position with their heads to the west in a feature that was only of sufficient depth to bury them.

While they were found in a poor state of preservation, most portions of the body were present and it was possible to determine that the older and apparently larger dog had been placed over the younger and smaller one. A small number of flint flakes and fish bones were also recovered from the feature. While it is possible that the artifacts originated with the soils used to fill in the features, some of the larger flakes were found resting on the skeletal remains, and the fish bones may have been stomach contents or some food left to accompany the dogs on their journey. The older dog had apparently had a broken front leg that had healed before it died.

Later on, we would unearth another young dog, just over a year old, in a burial pit beside the first. It, too, had been placed on its left side with its head to the west, facing north. It also had large chert flakes and shatter around the skeletal remains, with the head actually resting on a large chunk of chert. A large deer rib had been placed across the lower limbs of the animal and a few muskrat and fish elements were also recovered, perhaps together representing a food offering.

Williamson decided it was necessary to speak with Doug Campbell, the site foreman for Stephens and Rankin, about the evolving situation. As Williamson approached, Campbell was squinting through the eyepiece of the total station instrument, calling out orders on the walkie-talkie to his assistant with the prism pole, Rob Bivollotto. His years of experience surveying

Flint drill found with the stone tube pipe.

mines in Nova Scotia and overseeing construction projects for Stephens and Rankin had prepared him for many things, but worrying about archaeological deposits in the middle of a construction site was not one of them. Campbell was a professional, though, and he was learning to deal with it in his usual, laconic, unflappable manner.

The crux of the problem in the truck yard was the need to excavate about 30 centimetres below the exposed subsoil in order to provide a more robust bed of granular below the new asphalt. Checking the level throughout the area exposed so far, Campbell confirmed to Williamson that all of the archaeological features would have to be excavated. With the number of features steadily rising towards 100, Williamson did some rough calculations in his head and then announced that they needed to

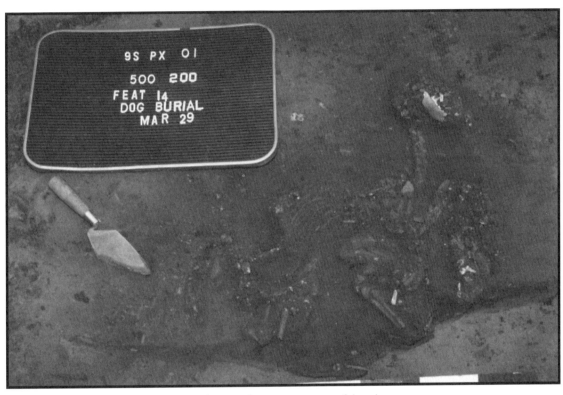

Two dogs in a feature, one on top of the other.

meet with Campbell's group and representatives of the Peace Bridge Authority. If they were to proceed with the excavation, it was going to take a lot longer and cost a lot more than anybody had anticipated.

Later that afternoon, a group of men wearing gleaming white construction hard hats approached the truck yard. Among them were Clifford Elwood, capital projects manager for the Peace Bridge Authority, Bob Smith, John Brucato, project manager for Merit Contractors (the general contractor), and Sto Tritchew, project supervisor for Stephens and Rankin. Leaving MacDonald in charge of supervising the backhoe, Williamson led the group around the site, showing them the human and animal burials, and outlining the various options and costs for mitigating the features.

As they began to resolve the scale of the problem in their minds, they realized that some creative thinking would be required to avoid serious construction delays or budget overruns. Fortunately, by considering archaeological deposits from the earliest planning phase of the project, the Peace Bridge Authority was more or less prepared for such a contingency.

As they packed up the vehicles for the day, Williamson and MacDonald mapped out the game plan for the rest of the week. MacDonald was to finish up the remaining backhoe work while supervising the rest of the crew as they forged ahead with salvaging the exposed features. In the meantime, Williamson would be heading back to Toronto to deal with other business and to marshal extra personnel for a full-scale offensive on the truck yard, starting on Monday. He would also be pursuing discussions with the Peace Bridge Authority to explore their options for dealing with the problem.

The next morning, back in his office, Williamson started to cost the remaining work in the truck yard. By the end of the previous day they had exposed approximately 150 cultural features. With a crew of eight, salvaging approximately eight features per day, he estimated it would take about 144 person days or nearly four weeks to complete the mitigation of just that portion of the yard. He then considered the costs involved in analyzing all the material that would be recovered from such an excavation. There is a maxim in archaeology that for every day spent in the field, another day is spent in the laboratory. In the case of the Peace Bridge site, however, it had turned out to be two days in the lab. Given his experience and acknowledging the economies of scale, Williamson estimated additional analysis time that was almost twice the excavation time.

In a letter to Stephen Mayer, operations manager of the Peace Bridge Authority, he recapped the fieldwork of the last few days and then outlined what was required to salvage all the cultural features in the truck yard as well as the costs and estimated time. He also noted that, should human burials be encountered, additional time and monies would be required, as burial excavation is a much more delicate and time-consuming activity. Finally, Williamson pointed out that the original design for the truck yard had not necessitated cutting below the level of the archaeological deposits, and urged careful re-consideration of the need to do so throughout the remainder of the truck yard. Having faxed the finished letter to Mayer, he turned his attention to clearing his agenda.

Meanwhile, back at the site, MacDonald and Austin were supervising the backhoe as it worked its way northward along a subdrain trench which connected to the truck-yard excavation in the northeast corner. This would be the last part of the truck yard to be exposed, and as they watched they noticed a much higher density of post moulds than they had encountered elsewhere in the excavation. The rest of the crew was over in the southwest corner of the truck yard finishing up the excavation of the first dog burial and charging ahead with the recording and salvaging of other features.

At the end of the day, MacDonald walked over to where Pihl and Cottrill were carefully covering the second dog burial with plastic, to protect the exposed bones overnight. As he took stock of the day's progress he felt an anxious chill, which was heightened by the fading light and relentless icy wind from the lake. These ancient pits were turning out to be unusually large and complex, and they were taking longer to salvage than anticipated. Staring out over the frigid, churning torrent of the Niagara River, he hoped that Williamson and the Peace Bridge Authority had come up with a viable plan.

The following day, a cloudy sky helped as we shovel-shined and mapped several five-metre squares, since the flat light made colour changes in the soil easier to see than the glare of full or partial sun. As Doug Campbell had requested someone to monitor a storm sewer trench on the north side of Walnut Street, MacDonald elected to go himself.

Within a couple of hours the backhoe had opened up a trench about 1.5 metres wide and 20 metres long from Walnut Street north towards the planned location of a new catchbasin/manhole. In the bottom of the trench, which was slightly over a metre deep, were exposed portions of several prehistoric pit features. It was a pattern that would repeat itself time and time again throughout the field season. Everywhere that the contractor needed to dig a hole, we found paleosol and features filled with artifacts, requiring careful excavation. By the end of the day, MacDonald and two crew members had managed to salvage the deposits.

It had been a very busy week, and, as we sat on the tailgates of our vehicles scraping the mud from our boots, we gazed over at the many more absorbing weeks of work that stared mutely up at us like so many huge black eyes from the exposed subsoil. Although we complained and kidded each other about the unusual field conditions and weather, the physical and mental challenge of it all had a certain appeal. Indeed, it was partly the rigours of the out of doors which had attracted us to the field of archaeology in the first place, although none of us would have likely imagined that our career paths would have led us on an archaeological expedition to Fort Erie in late winter.

The following week saw a large crew from both offices arrive at the site. MacDonald walked over to where Williamson stood at the edge of the excavation surveying the scene. Together they stepped down into the site, and as they walked across to the east side, MacDonald reviewed the progress since Williamson's departure the previous Wednesday. Williamson in turn explained how he had been lobbying for a design for the truck yard, which would not require excavating the features. He outlined his plan to have the crew continue mapping the features, since this would need to be done anyway now that they had been exposed, but to hold off excavating them until the Peace Bridge Authority had made a decision, having consulted with their engineers and contractors.

Walking back to the west side of the site, they explained the revised game plan to the crew who by now were about to get work underway. They then proceeded over towards the construction site where the above-ground foundation for the new commercial customs building was taking shape. Stopping to inspect the storm sewer trench that had been salvaged on Friday, they saw that the Stephens and Rankin crew was already busy installing the new sewer pipe. As they watched the work, Doug Campbell approached and asked if someone could meet the backhoe over on the north side of the building where they were about to dig another sewer trench. Thus the new week started in much the same manner as the previous one had ended — with our crew monitoring construction operations hundreds of metres apart but in equally rich settings.

Williamson was faced with a new problem. As soon as the media had caught wind of the fact that we were back in town, they had started coming around the site to see if any interesting discoveries had been made. The orange tarpaulin that was protecting the Early Woodland burial in the centre of the truck yard was obvious to any visitor, but to the media it was like a flashing red light. While from our perspective it was the preservation of such a vast array of archaeological features under a heavily developed urban landscape that was the most significant story at the site, we were resigned to the fact that it was the discovery of human bones that sold newspapers.

We had been very circumspect about the burial, as we and the aboriginal community wanted it treated with the utmost respect, and we didn't want anyone snooping around it after hours, particularly on the weekends. Williamson realized that, as the story would come out one way or another, he had better ensure that it was done right. Fortunately, during the Snake Hill dig, Williamson had cultivated contacts with key local media personnel that he could count on for thorough and sensitive reporting. Having consulted with the local aboriginal community, he brought these people together and briefed them on the results of the project to date. He was not disappointed when the news items came out later that week.

Our nine-person crew was divided between mapping the truck yard and salvaging features in storm sewer trenches north of Walnut Street. The trench that was begun earlier was extended northward another 15 metres to the catchbasin location, and then, turning 90 degrees to the right, was extended eastward by another 30 metres to another catchbasin location. As we proceeded eastward along the trench, we encountered another animal burial, consisting of a mature dog, the bones of

Ron Williamson poses with dog skull for media.

(Leonard LePage, *St. Catharine's Standard*)

which were gracile enough to mean it was probably prehistoric. Later analysis would confirm the diagnosis.

Soon after, word came down that the new truck-yard surface had been redesigned in order to avoid the necessity of excavating all of the features. The only portion that would require mitigation was the subdrain trench on the east side, since it would still be excavated below the current grade. While Williamson greeted this news with enthusiasm, he knew that it raised a new question: How to go about capping the features in a way that would satisfy the Ministry of Citizenship, Culture and Recreation? Immediately he contacted Neal Ferris, the Plans Review Officer, in order to set up an on-site meeting.

The following morning, Williamson and MacDonald drove across the bridge to the Peace Bridge Authority's administration building for a meeting with Stephen Mayer and Cliff Elwood. Surrounded by Peace Bridge photos and memorabilia in Mayer's spacious office, Williamson and MacDonald reviewed the work to date and briefed their clients on issues surrounding the proposed capping of the truck yard. Later that afternoon, Elwood joined Williamson and MacDonald in the Merit construction trailer. There, together with several other key people, including Bob Smith, John Brucato, Sto Tritchew, and Doug Campbell, they hammered out various capping protocols and procedures with Neal Ferris.

When the meeting broke up, Williamson offered to give Ferris a tour of the site. He handed Ferris a spare hard hat and the two headed out across the wind-swept construction site. MacDonald went to check on the progress in the sewer trench and then rejoined them at the truck yard. With business out of the way, the three colleagues entered into an animated discussion on a shared passion; the discoveries and interpretations of an extraordinary archaeological site.

The weather the following week remained dismal, with three centimetres of snow falling throughout the day on Monday. Later in the week the snow turned to driving rain. Williamson, MacDonald, and Pihl were working at the end of the sewer trench, where it widened out into a large three-by-three-metre square to accommodate the catchbasin.

We were having some difficulty interpreting the complex stratigraphy which seemed to involve more than just discrete or overlapping pits. Despite the downpour we carried on with our work, having found three Genesee tools, including a complete point, a complete drill, and a drill base from one of the features. Interestingly, several other drill fragments were recovered from features that were part of the complex. Over a hundred specimens of large mammal bone, most of which were burned or calcined, were also recovered from the area, although none were human.

The eastern end of the trench was especially difficult to interpret as virtually all of it comprised intersecting cultural deposits. In order to interpret the deposit, multiple cross-trench profiles were excavated while the nine-square-metre area at the end of the trench for the catchbasin was excavated in one-metre squares. This provided multiple profiles of the pits which intruded into the matrices as well as multiple profiles of the matrices themselves. While this methodology helped to confirm the plan view of the various deposits, it was next to impossible to render any meaningful interpretation of their interrelationships, because of the limited exposure that was available.

On the other hand, we were rewarded for our diligence when MacDonald encountered a large sandstone metate or grinding stone that had probably been left where it had last been used. Our thoughts naturally turned to a group of people at this very spot, 4000 years before, grinding nut meats in the stone bowl.

Meanwhile, having finished mapping the roughly 1100 square metres that had

Debbie Steiss and Deb Pihl sorting through their screens in the catchbasin trench.

(Leonard LePage, *St. Catharine's Standard*)

been exposed in the truck yard, Williamson supervised a crew from Stephens and Rankin, who began the capping procedure that was established during the meeting with Neal Ferris. They began by spreading 10 centimetres (four inches) of clean sand over the truck-yard features. This was followed by the placement of a woven plastic fabric, which would help to prevent physical impact to the underlying features, but would allow water to permeate through as it would naturally. Should there ever come a time when a portion of the site has to be re-excavated, the long-lasting geotextile would also serve to mark the top of the sand cap and caution a Peace Bridge crew or contractor that something sensitive was present. The geotextile material was then covered by a metre or so of granular and the asphalt surface.

The capping operation soon reached the burial that had yielded the limestone pipe and flint drill. In keeping with the spirit of the protocol, it was time to return the artifacts to the grave and ensure that it was similarly protected from future disturbance. As Williamson knelt respectfully at the side of the truck-yard grave, he removed the plastic tarpaulin for the last time and placed a small quantity of burning tobacco beside the remains. Standing solemnly behind him were Debbie Steiss, and Robert von Bitter. Unwrapping the tubular pipe and the flint drill, which had been in safe-keeping until this moment, he returned the grave offerings to their rightful owner. Then, taking a sheet of geotextile, he carefully shrouded the remains. Williamson, Steiss, and von Bitter then gently shovelled sand onto the textile until

Genesee period drill (2000–1500 BC).

they were satisfied that no harm would come to the artifacts or their keeper. They then watched as the backhoe completed the capping of this section of the yard. Slowly, they turned away to join their colleagues who were working on the final features in the truck-yard subdrain trench.

With the capping operation in the truck yard nearing completion, we were eager to finish salvaging the remaining subdrain trench features as soon as possible. This wish, however, was thwarted by the many large features that were exposed in this area, their frequency perhaps a reflection of the proximity of the shoreline. Many of the features yielded large quantities of fish scales and articulated fish vertebrae as well as deer bone and some charred hickory, walnut, and seed remains. The recovery of so many fish scales and articulated vertebrae suggested to the team that initial processing of fish was occurring in this locale, close to the shoreline.

The definition of features in this area was complicated by the presence of several large historic disturbances and the dense, overlapping nature of features from all time periods. There was one pattern in the soil, however, that especially caught our attention. We detected two parallel rows of post moulds about 5.9 metres apart on either side of, and overlapping a feature cluster, and immediately recognized these stains as the remains of a wood-framed, bark-covered house structure.

Inside these walls, at a distance of about 1.5 metres were a number of much larger posts, also aligned and parallel with the outside walls. These we interpreted as both support posts for the main rectangular frame of the building and as main posts for the bench rows on the inside of the structure. Unfortunately, no other posts could be seen in the difficult field conditions. The walls seemed to terminate only five metres from exposed bedrock, indicating that the structure had no formed end. On the opposite northern end, the walls extended into the unexcavated area.

Large sandstone metate or grinding stone.

The capping operation in the south truck yard. Note the placement of sand followed by the geotextile material to protect the features from future accidental disturbance.

One of the posts yielded a bone tool handle found standing on its end. As bone tools on the site were relatively rare, everyone gathered around to examine the piece. Fortunately, it was Stephen Cox Thomas, the animal bone specialist, who had found the artifact. He immediately identified the bone as deer antler. The antler handle was 10 centimetres long and three centimetres wide, well-worn and slightly polished with finely etched single and paired lines extending along its body, although no pattern was discernable. One end had a small excavated socket eight millimetres in diameter, presumably for hafting of a tool.

While open-ended houses have been documented at special purpose Late Woodland sites elsewhere, we were not sure of the age or cultural affiliation of the structure. The recovery of a serrated Neutral projectile point less than 10 metres north of the house and the radiocarbon-dated seventeenth-century maize kernel from a feature less than 100 metres to the southwest suggested the possibility that the house was historic Iroquoian. On the other hand, the morphology of the structure, in particular its width of 5.9 metres, was more in keeping with earlier structures dating to the period between AD 800 and 1200. Moreover, a number of the features within and around the structure yielded ceramics, many of which had cord-marked surfaces suggesting a Transitional Woodland affiliation for the house (AD 600–900).

Indeed, the main Woodland occupation evident on the east side of the excavation area was Transitional Woodland. Feature 158, located just 10 metres north of the house structure, for example, yielded the remains of a collapsed ceramic vessel, radiocarbon-dated to AD 675, the date having been run on carbonized food debris encrusted on the interior surface of the vessel. It had been placed within a ring of large fire-cracked rocks and flint nodules and had collapsed with rim portions falling inward and laterally encompassing the contents of the pot within the vessel fragments. Articulated fish vertebrae and a portion of a deer shoulder were found in the contents of the pot and were later analyzed by Stephen Cox Thomas.

Thomas concluded that the pot contained the remnants of a stew or soup consisting primarily of pickerel, bass, venison, nut meats, and purslane (a wild pot herb). The feature also contained four other Transitional Woodland rim sherds, three of which had cord-wrapped stick stamping. Within days of the find, the story of the discovery of the pot was in the regional newspapers, the media having kept an eye on the team's progress throughout the month.

Other features in the east trench area containing Transitional Woodland ceramics yielded significant quantities of animal remains, including pickerel, white bass, sturgeon, channel catfish, deer, dog, woodchuck, squirrel, chipmunk, passenger pigeon, duck, grouse, and turtle. A number of the deer lumbar vertebrae from one of the features even had a series of semi-parallel cuts in the bone, likely representing butchering of the animal. A predominance of pickerel, passenger pigeon, and migratory waterfowl clearly indicated that this portion of the site had been occupied mainly in the spring. While no pattern was discernable in the large number of other posts in the area, it was thought that they represented the remains of activities conducted outside of the houses in warm weather, such as fish and meat processing. The recovery of numerous netsinkers from the area also suggests that net preparation for fishing was a major activity.

We were certain that similar hunting and fishing activities were carried out by the previous Late Archaic occupants of the site. Many of the Genesee features, for example, yielded in addition to Genesee lithic tools, similar kinds of animal remains. The recovery of large quantities of spring-spawning fish and juvenile bird bones reinforced the notion of spring occupation of the site, regardless of the period of cultural affiliation of the occupation. One of the features contained a large number of calcined mammal bone fragments along with other burned and calcined animal remains, a pattern which was consistent with the Late Archaic Broad Point burial practice documented in one of the caissons the previous year. While many of the recovered remains could only be identified as medium to large mammals, an extremely worn human molar was among them.

Flint tool production had obviously also been a major activity in the area for all periods of occupation, as attested to by the recovery of large numbers of bifaces from features as well as significant quantities of flake debris and hammerstones.

Once we had completed our work in the truck yard, we monitored and salvage excavated several installation trenches: a catchbasin/manhole here, an electrical vault trench there, or an oil interceptor somewhere else. By now, Williamson and MacDonald had arranged to split the supervisory duties through the week, in order to allow themselves time at their respective offices to take care of other responsibilities. While on site we would monitor the backhoe as it stripped the overburden, then assign staff to undertake the necessary salvage work. When not supervising the backhoe, we would assist in the excavations.

The most difficult challenge during this period was simply keeping track of all the places on the site where we had been working. The customary grid of wooden stakes was impossible to install on the bustling asphalt construction site. Fortunately,

John Brucato and Doug Campbell were able to provide us with detailed site plans on which we could identify the various underground installations. When digital plans were provided at the end of the project, our CAD technicians were able to plot the excavation trenches onto the computerized base map.

By the middle of the last week of April, the ground floor for the new commercial customs building was virtually complete, and we were surprised at the rapidity with which the steel superstructure rose, day by day. It had come time for the next major excavation in preparation for the concrete truck pad which would abut the south side of the building. This pad would support the vans and semi-trailers that would be pulling up at the many truck bays that faced onto Walnut Street. The removal of the asphalt and granular proceeded as it had for the truck yard, with the large, toothless backhoe bucket being used to achieve the final grade.

Work began on the east half of the pad, as the west half was still occupied by a complex of office portables. A wide swath of overburden would be removed, to the extent of the reach of the backhoe, and stockpiled for reuse. Once any necessary feature salvaging was done, the swath would be backfilled through the established capping procedure. Since there were initially piles of building materials preventing access to the site of the truck pad immediately adjacent to the new customs building, the stripping and salvaging began at the southern edge of the pad and moved northward over the ensuing weeks.

As in the truck yard, the original topsoil had been either removed or heavily disturbed by previous parking lot construction activities. There were also extensive late nineteenth- and early twentieth-century features related to the row of houses that once made up the Walnut streetscape. These included large backfilled cellars and outbuilding foundations as well as numerous privy and refuse pits. The result was a dense hodgepodge of features, with many twentieth-century refuse pits intruding into prehistoric ones.

Together with the construction contractors, we were relieved to discover that the final grade to which they needed to cut was mostly at or slightly above the level at which the features became exposed. In the southeast quadrant of the truck pad this meant that they could implement the capping procedure without even fully exposing the underlying features. For the remainder, we would need to map all the features and salvage those that were threatened by a network of subdrain trenches which crisscrossed the pad, connecting to the previously installed catchbasins. As soon as the recording grid was in place, we began shovel-shining the five-metre squares and recording and salvaging the threatened features.

Although the historic features were mapped, they were not considered archaeologically significant for several reasons. The artifacts they contained were essentially modern, including domestic debris, such as china, condiment bottles, pop, beer and liquor bottles, plastic combs, light bulbs, tinware, old shoes, and other familiar items. There were also large quantities of pharmaceutical glassware from a nearby dental laboratory (the Antidolar Manufacturing Co.), including dozens of beakers and jars and hundreds of pipettes and ampules. While archaeological investigation of these remains might have yielded some information, there was no compelling reason to do so. Had there been a reason to research the early twentieth-century residents of Walnut Street, much more useful information would have been available through documentary sources or by searching out and interviewing surviving occupants and other long-time local residents.

As the truck-pad excavations got underway, other smaller excavations were still happening around the construction site, and Doug Campbell or Rob Bivollotto would periodically stop by the dig to make a request for monitoring. Frequently, the

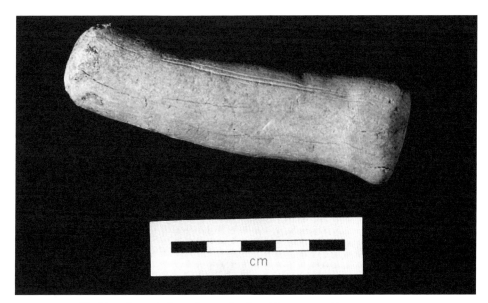

Tool handle made from deer antler, found in post mould.

request would be answered by Bruce Welsh, our monitoring specialist. Welsh had developed a reputation as something of a lone gun because of his competence doing solo work, which often involved rising at the crack of dawn to get to a distant site, or working alone under adverse conditions.

Contrary to the common stereotype of a lone gun, however, it was Welsh's affable personality and easy-going nature which endeared him to both our staff and the construction workers, who were often his only company. He had been our advance scout at the Peace Bridge site, and it was now a common sight to see his yellow hard hat bobbing across the construction site, a shovel slung casually over his right shoulder and the tip of a trowel projecting from his back pocket. He would monitor a gas-line trench, several electrical conduit trenches, lamp standard excavations, and several more catchbasins, allowing the rest of us to stay focused on the truck pad.

The discovery of human remains continued to occur, almost invariably right in the path of a proposed drainage installation. Fortunately, there was always enough latitude in the construction design to permit avoidance of the graves. One burial in the truck pad was bypassed by re-routing the flexible corrugated subdrain pipe around the pit. Similarly, part of a human hand that had been previously disturbed was avoided by re-locating a catchbasin a few metres to the south. While the sight of human remains was quite familiar to us, the reaction of the construction workers tended towards apprehensive curiosity. To everyone's credit, though, no matter how inconvenient the encounters with human graves became, the remains were always treated with the utmost care and respect.

As the backhoe revealed the final swath of subsoil in the truck pad, immediately adjacent to the new commercial customs building, Campbell and Bivollotto traced out on the ground the path of the subdrain trenches with orange spray paint. Unfortunately, the subdrain trench was heading straight through a very complex set of features, which seemed to extend throughout and beyond a single five-metre square. The key to this feature complex seemed to be a large, amorphous blob in the centre, which did not have the discrete circular or ovate plan shape of most pits. It did not help that the sun was drying the sandy soil within minutes of its trowelling, thereby fading the differences in shade brought out by the soil moisture.

Cross-sectioning the blob we could see that the profile had much better definition, so we used this to guide our interpretation of the plan. To improve the view even more, MacDonald suggested excavating a perpendicular cross-section as well. By excavating the feature in quadrants, we would be able to see the profile in three dimensions, rather than two. In this way the pit gradually resolved itself into a large oval more than a metre across.

It took nearly three days for us to excavate the 120 centimetres to the bottom of the pit, draw and photograph the profiles with their multiple layers and pockets of different-coloured soil, and then screen the remainder of the fill, taking soil samples as we went. When we reached the bottom, MacDonald noticed that the prehistoric site inhabitants had stopped digging the pit when the soil had turned from sand into a stiff, reddish clay. Noticing that the clay contained minute snail and clam shells, MacDonald collected a sample just in case his colleagues in the Earth Sciences Department at the University of Waterloo might be able to shed any light on the origins of the clay. He then turned his attention to the remainder of the feature complex.

Collapsed vessel found in Feature 158. Note the large sections of the vessel that had fallen inward encapsulating the contents of the pot.

It is common to find two or more pits which, having been dug sequentially over time, have intersected each other like dirty olympic rings. Usually, provided there is some difference in shade or texture between intersecting pits, it is possible to sort out which came first, as it will be visibly truncated by the intrusive pit. In contrast, this feature complex had very few well-defined edges, the staining changing subtly from place to place.

Excavating a series of long sections across the square to help us define discrete features, we were able to confirm several pits this way, as well as a hearth, a common feature of prehistoric dwellings. Yet these discrete features were surrounded by general staining which seemed to extend into the soil by 20 or 30 centimetres without any good definition. Since it contained the odd artifact, we concluded that this might be a type of feature called a living floor. Such features are formed by the accumulation of organic material within a structure. Over time, foot traffic and other activities within the structure mix this organic material into the soil horizon. We speculated that in this loose sand it would not be difficult to produce such a deposit in a relatively short period.

What interested us most, however, was the possible date of the structure. The majority of the artifacts recovered from the feature complex were Genesee tools dating to 3800 years ago. This was one of the best-documented structures to have been excavated for that period, and the team had already identified several more likely candidates.

Animal remains found from archaeological features.

Indeed, over the next several days we salvaged over 30 cultural features, including one more of the Late Archaic living-floor complexes. As we carefully sectioned this second living-floor feature, we encountered a drilled and polished fragment of translucent rose quartz-like stone, no larger than a fingertip, which we recognized as the central portion of a winged bannerstone. Bannerstones are generally interpreted as sliding weights that were attached to the shaft of an atlatl, or spear thrower, in order to increase the momentum of the spear. Although very rare, they are occasionally found on Archaic period sites.

Later that day, we encountered a similar fragment in an adjacent feature. Washing the pieces off under the tap of our water jug, we were astonished as the two fragments, which had been rent asunder almost 4000 years ago, meshed perfectly together like the halves of a mystical talisman. It was indeed magical, for in the instant that the bannerstone fragments were reunited, so too were the two features that had contained them, linked together again in time.

Nineteen of the east truck-pad pits yielded Late Archaic stone tools, mostly of the Genesee type. Although fragments of pottery were recovered from several features, no Woodland period stone tools were recovered. Collectively, these features also yielded dozens of complete and partial bifaces as well as tens of thousands of flint chips that underscored the importance of stone-tool manufacturing on this site.

The recovery of dozens of netsinkers — sometimes in clusters suggesting that they had been buried while still attached to the net — highlighted the importance of fishing. So, too, did the numerous fish bones that were recovered from the dozens of green garbage bags full of soil samples that had been collected. But the processing of the soil samples and the analysis of the artifacts would not occur until many months from now. Until then, we would have to be satisfied with an impressionistic understanding of the site, gained through hours of staring into bipod screens and trowelling through the refuse of the past.

Once archaeological salvage operations in the east half of the truck pad were completed and the area capped, the next few months would be again spent responding to calls for monitoring of excavations for asphalt and granular removals, storm sewers, electrical conduits, sluice-gates, bollards, fire hydrants, and oil interceptors.

Two of us would spend one or two days per week on site, sweltering in the summer heat with the Stephens and Rankin crew. The conditions in the truck yard were far from ideal. Surrounded by shimmering asphalt and circling semi-trailers, the sun beating relentlessly down on us through a noxious haze concocted from truck exhaust and clouds of dust, it was not always pleasant. While the breeze from the lake provided some respite from this daily assault, it just as often blew the choking dust into the faces and eyes of the enervated crew.

It wasn't until mid-August that there was a need for a sizeable crew back in the truck yard. MacDonald had been monitoring asphalt and granular removal for a truck lane, south of Walnut Street, when he encountered a number of the large black cultural features. Having called for help, he supervised a crew over the next week in the recording of the pits. It was difficult work with the constant throbbing of the tractor engines and the squealing of their air brakes. We could feel the gaze of an endless stream of truck drivers as they looked down from the cabs of their tractors trying to determine what these odd-looking construction workers were up to.

Within a few days we had managed to define the features within an eight-by-seven-metre trench. So far, the exposed features in the western two-thirds of the trench lay below the finished grade, so they would only need to be capped once they were recorded. When Campbell and Bivollotto checked the east end, however, they discovered that several features rose above the required grade and would have to be salvaged.

As we trowelled off one large pit that was nearly two metres long and one and one-half metres wide, we could see that a 30-centimetre-wide utility trench had been cut through the centre of the feature at some time in the past. This discovery was rendered more tragic when we discovered disturbed human remains within the pit. Fortunately, the remains were low enough in the pit that by excavating the upper pit fill down to the required grade, we were able to leave the burial where it was. Another large pit with a human burial, located about seven metres to the east, was dealt with in a similar manner. Considering the difficulty of discretely exhuming a skeleton in this location, Williamson and MacDonald were glad that they had been able to identify the pits as human interments without the onlookers having seen a single bone.

Gazing back along the trench at all the other large pits which were about to be capped, we wondered how many of these were also graves and how far the burial area extended. An answer to that question would come a few months later when Williamson was back supervising a crew to the south of that very area. Having exposed two long trenches, we encountered the usual density of black features but found that most contained human remains. One of the first features we investigated contained the remains of an adult and an infant in a red ochre layer, red ochre being iron hematite that was sometimes ground into powder and spread on burials in Late Archaic and Early Woodland times (1000–300 BC).

Other nearby features were found to contain the burials of infants, older children, and adults of both sexes. Once the extent of these burials was documented, the construction design was modified to permit capping, thereby protecting the burials from any further disturbance. The profusion of the burials in these trenches and the adjacent truck lane suggested that this was another discrete burial area on the Peace Bridge site, not unlike the Surma and Orchid components excavated in the 1960s.

When we were almost finished with our work in the truck lane, Doug Campbell came by to see if someone could monitor a subdrain trench excavation over by the

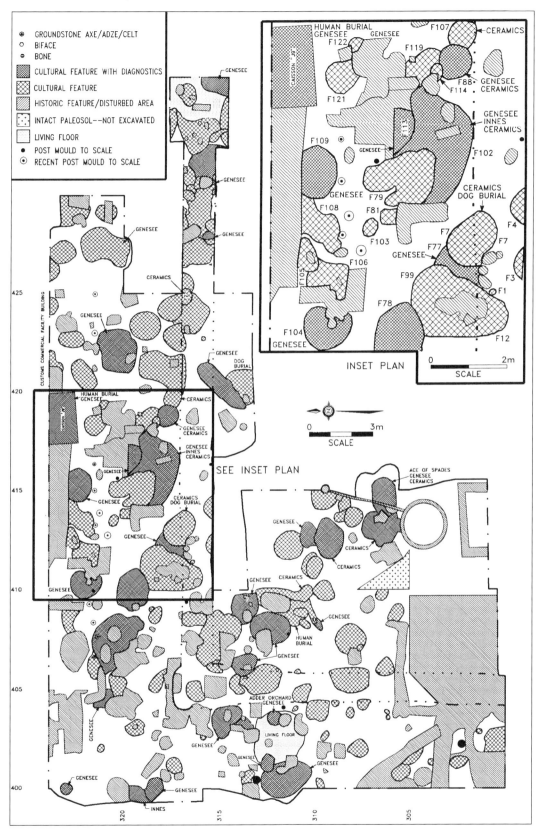

Features in the east truck pad. Note the pattern of the features in the inset area, which is also shown on Plate 10 of the colour photograph section.

north side of the bridge. Seeing that the trench would run parallel to the bridge, no more than 10 metres from the southwest corner of where we had salvaged dozens of features in the truck yard that spring, we knew that there was a good chance of hitting something. With the first few scrapes of the bucket, the outline of a black pit came into view. By the time we reached the other end of the one-metre wide, 25-metre-long trench, we had exposed parts of four more features. Immediately, our four-man crew swung into action, with MacDonald and Williamson mapping the trench, and Welsh and Robert von Bitter drawing and photographing the features. Soon the salvage excavations were underway, each pair selecting one of the larger pits to work on. Although it was already well after five pm, we decided to finish the work rather than stay the night in Fort Erie.

Less than an hour later, we were richly rewarded for our diligence. Williamson was shovelling black earth into the screen for MacDonald as they investigated a remnant of artifact-laden paleosol at the east end of the trench. Behind MacDonald, near the centre of the trench, Welsh was sorting through a screen load of soil while von Bitter was further exposing the feature profile. Suddenly, von Bitter yelled out, "Holy shit, holy shit, holy shit," each expletive a little louder and more impassioned than the last. MacDonald snapped his head around to see what was the matter, while Williamson dropped his shovel and started running towards von Bitter.

Thinking that something was wrong, MacDonald and Welsh dropped their screens and converged on the feature in time to see von Bitter triumphantly hand Williamson a dark gray, palm-sized stone. Williamson stared at it in disbelief. Clearly engraved into the face of the stone was a figure of a thunderbird, and the bottom half of a second, similar figure extended from the bottom edge which had been broken off. MacDonald grabbed a paintbrush from the tool box and handed it to Williamson, who gently cleared away the adhering soil.

Taking turns to examine and admire this find we knew that, as unassuming as it might appear to the casual observer, this was truly an extraordinary artifact, since representational art in any form is rarely found on archaeological sites in the lower Great Lakes region.

After carefully wrapping the slate gorget for safe keeping, we returned to our work, spurred on by our desire to find the other half of the thunderbird. Von Bitter began gingerly trowelling through the remaining pit fill, using his fingers to cautiously probe through the loosened soil in fear that the metal trowel might damage his quarry. When it did not emerge, he shovelled the rest of the dirt into Welsh's screen and sat down to finish filling out the feature record form. Still buoyed by the thrill of his discovery, and with his customary unbridled jocularity, he brashly penned the following words for posterity: "It must be noted that I, Rob von Bitter, was the skilled individual who recovered this artifact from its dark layer where it had been waiting for me for all of these thousands of years. So today, I am the best archaeologist in Ontario." Months later, when reviewing von Bitter's field notes, we would break into hysterical laughter as we fondly remembered the occasion.

We were all disappointed that the other half of the gorget had not appeared in the remainder of the pit fill, but we carried on with our tasks, finally wrapping things up in the dwindling light. With the exception of a couple of monitoring excursions by Bruce Welsh, this would be the last we would see of the Peace Bridge site for another eight weeks. In the meantime, however, the image of the thunderbird made its way onto the front pages of the regional and national newspapers. Shortly after returning to Toronto, Williamson even received a call from his friend and colleague Bill Fox in Inuvik, congratulating him on a nice find!

When MacDonald returned to Fort Erie in October, he was impressed by the changes that had taken place. All the structural work for the new commercial customs building was done, and workers were busy finishing the exterior, erecting interior partitions, and installing plumbing, wiring, and the rest of the internal hardware. Outside, the east half of the concrete truck pad was already in use, as contractors backed their vans up to the docks to unload equipment and materials. Meanwhile, in the west truck pad, a crew was finishing preparations to load the office portables onto flatbed trailers and truck them off to a new location.

Peter Flake was waiting patiently in the cab of his backhoe when MacDonald arrived. With a few words of greeting, MacDonald hurried into the Merit trailer to get his instructions from John Brucato. Moments later he was out the door again with a large plan tucked under his arm. We would start the day by excavating a series of metre-deep holes around the north and east perimeter of the new customs building as well as around the perimeter of the new parking lot on the north side of Queen Street, where large trees would be planted in the coming weeks. Flake had been retained by the contractors since their machines were already busy.

The work went relatively quickly as most of the 15 excavations were in previously disturbed soil. In three holes, we encountered features at the very bottom of the excavation, and while initially protected, they were later excavated to allow for a deeper planting of the trees. Stopping by the Merit trailer to report that we had completed the tree excavations, Brucato suggested that we redeploy Flake and his machine in the west truck-pad area. There, the portables were being hoisted up on slings by a large crane and deposited on flatbed trucks. Soon the only evidence of the structures was the grid of cylindrical concrete footings projecting from the ground, and the miscellaneous flotsam and jetsam which had accumulated under the buildings over the years. As a crew began cleaning this up, a large excavator with a crab-like claw began hauling the footings up out of the ground and stacking them for removal.

Back in early June, work had been started on a catchbasin trench, but it could not be completed because the portables were in the way. Now they needed to complete the sewer and catchbasin installation in advance of stripping the west half of the truck pad. Flake had the remainder of the trench stripped within hours. As we began shovel-shining the 1.5-metre wide by 20-metre long trench, we could see the evidence of our excavations the previous June.

Pushing westward, we encountered several large historic pits which had truncated some smaller prehistoric ones. Then, a little west of the halfway point, we noticed an indistinct transition to a slightly darker soil. As this deposit contained the odd artifact, we made note of it as a possible cultural feature and continued shining. A few metres to the west we came upon three large features that seemed to be surrounded by the mysterious deposit. Realizing that we had discovered another living floor, we carried on to see if we could define its other edge. Unfortunately, a utility trench and several other recent disturbances had obliterated portions of the feature, although we expected to be able to see more of the feature once the adjacent area was excavated.

The following week, Williamson and MacDonald were back on the site with Debbie Steiss and Bruce Welsh to begin monitoring the backhoe as it stripped the overburden from the west half of the truck pad. The area of the living floor turned out to be extremely complex and perhaps layered. In an attempt to better define the stain, the area was shovel-shined again, removing approximately five centimetres of the deposit in the process. At this slightly lower level, a number of features were resolved. Interestingly, immediately adjacent to one of the features were two large post moulds which may have been structural supports with which the floors were associated.

The recovery of a complete Genesee drill from one of the features suggested a Late Archaic age for the living floor complex. This same feature was filled with waste related to the processing of game birds, which along with fish remains from an adjacent feature, indicated springtime subsistence activities. Also recovered from these features were 22 bifaces and eight netsinkers. All of the evidence pointed to ancient Genesee house structure(s), occupied during the spring to fish, hunt game birds, and procure flint.

One of the features in the complex was especially interesting as it was later found to contain 262 calcined bone fragments, most of which were considered by Stephen Cox Thomas to be human. While Thomas suggested that the remains might represent another cremation event, similar to the one the crew had found the year before in the excavation for one of the caissons, the significant difference was that no concentration of calcined bone was noted in the field, nor was there any evidence of *in situ* firing as in the other case. Regardless of where the cremation had occurred, it is likely that we had also come across the remains of one of the people that had inhabited the structure 4000 years ago.

Once the topsoil of the entire west truck pad was stripped, Williamson and MacDonald conferred with Rob Bivollotto about the grade of the exposed subsoil. As in the east half, the features exposed in the west half of the truck pad were sitting at or below the required grade, such that only those threatened by subdrain trenches would need to be salvaged. As Bivollotto pointed to where the trenches would extend, MacDonald marked their paths on the ground with orange spray paint, so they could see exactly which features would be intersected.

Once the grid was in place and the features trowelled, we started mapping those five-metre squares which were least complex. These included several containing nothing but historic disturbance, as well as others along the western side which contained neither historic nor prehistoric features. Noting that feature density dropped away to

The Meadowood cache of bifaces in the profile of the feature.

zero as one moved from east to west away from the river, we speculated that this probably represented the western limit of the occupation, at least in that area of the site. It soon became apparent that, not only was the feature density much lower in this area, but the degree of historic disturbance was high, particularly along the south lip of the truck pad where we encountered large, in-filled cellars with concrete foundations. A complete nineteenth-century white clay pipe was found, nevertheless, in one of the historic features.

By the end of the following week, we had recorded and excavated those features that were threatened by the subdrain trenches. The pleasant fall weather had made for an enjoyable week, although the glare and low angle of the late October sun had made it difficult to see subtle changes in soil colour. At one point, Campbell had come over to ask for someone to monitor an excavation for another catchbasin/oil interceptor. MacDonald obliged, walking the short distance to the north edge of Walnut Street where the big excavator was pulling into position. Once the asphalt and granular had been removed, MacDonald noticed a dark stain in the subsoil and motioned for the operator to stop the machine. Clearing it off with his shovel, he discovered a single, relatively large pit, roughly a metre and a half in length and three-quarters of a metre in width.

Realizing that the feature would need to be salvaged before they could proceed, the construction crew left to pursue other tasks. Returning to the truck-pad area, MacDonald conscripted Austin and Cottrill to look after the salvage excavation. Half an hour later, just as we were preparing to pack up our equipment for the day, we heard a shout from Austin to come over and see what they had found. In the centre of this otherwise unassuming pit was a cache of 29 Early Woodland period Meadowood bifaces, including 15 complete, exquisitely made specimens. Williamson was elated. Caches similar to this one had rarely been found in the field in the last 30 years, most having been disturbed by ploughs and subsequently collected by avocational archaeologists during the late nineteenth and early to mid-twentieth centuries. They were now in museum collections. One of the interesting aspects of these caches is that the bifaces are invariably made from Onondaga flint.

For years, Williamson and Bill Fox, his colleague in Inuvik, had been studying these caches and had been trying to teasingly convince the acknowledged leading expert on Meadowood bifaces, Joseph Granger (the same man who had excavated at the Orchid component), that these biface caches were made on the Canadian side of the river. Granger, naturally, argued that they were made on the American side. It certainly wasn't long before a media report of the find had made its way via fax lines to the University of Louisville in Kentucky. It was our collective opinion, however, that Austin's luck at unearthing prized artifacts had come through again.

Although we would respond to additional requests to monitor a variety of construction activities that might have threatened archaeological deposits through that winter and early spring, the major excavations of the site were essentially completed by the end of the fall of 1995. That did not mean, however, that our work had been completed. Several hundred thousand artifacts remained to be examined in light of all of the other data collected at the site. It would be another two years before we found rest.

The Meadowood cache of bifaces, close up.

7 Life on the Site

Ron Williamson was in his office making some notes when Bev Garner strode in and lowered herself into the chair across the desk from him. While she waited for him to finish, her eyes were immediately drawn to the low counter behind his desk, where the magnificent 1300-year-old pottery vessel rested on a small stand. It was the one that had been recovered from the truck yard of the Peace Bridge site and painstakingly reconstructed by Monicke Thibeault in the laboratory downstairs. Standing 37 centimetres high and 32 centimetres in diameter, it sat as a mute reminder of why Williamson had called this meeting — to review the progress in the processing of artifacts from the site.

As laboratory coordinator, Garner and lab technician Thibeault had been working hard to keep pace with the surges of artifact bags from Fort Erie that had flooded into their hands over the last couple of years. They had even farmed out dozens of boxes for processing at our ASI branch office in Stratford in order to stay ahead of the game. Just as they were finishing one batch, the crew would roll in with another vanload of material. Hour after hour they would be parked on stools at the counter with a basin of water before them, gently scrubbing every artifact with a toothbrush. Each glistening item was then placed with its bag mates and the bag label onto a two-by-two-foot frame with one-by-two-inch wooden sides and window screen lining the bottom. The frame was designed to slide into a rack that held many other such frames as well as a small fan in the bottom which circulated air throughout the rack to dry the artifacts.

Thibeault, with meticulous care and penmanship, then wrote the provenience information directly onto the artifact with indelible ink, that was later covered with lacquer. A catalogue number would also be added, consisting of the official archaeological site registration code plus a serial number. The remaining artifacts were sorted into lots by category, such as ceramic sherds, flint flakes, bone fragments, and then catalogued, labelled, and bagged. Each artifact category was sorted by provenience into corrugated cardboard bankers' boxes, ready for analysis.

Williamson laid down his pen and looked up at Garner. "Bev," he said with a bemused smile, "how many artifacts would you guess we brought back from Fort Erie?" Garner rolled her eyes at the very thought. "Too many," she replied, recognizing this as a rhetorical question. "That's right," he said, "so we'd better get organized or we'll never get this report out in our lifetime," and he started going over his game plan notes with Garner, scheduling the analysis that was yet to be completed and reviewing the amount of work it would take to write their report. In fact, he outlined plans for two reports. One was a technical volume, probably 500 pages long, that would eventually be submitted to both the Buffalo and Fort Erie Public Bridge Authority, and the Ontario Ministry of Citizenship, Culture and Recreation, the licensing agency, and the other a volume that would summarize the discovery and importance of the site for the general public. The Peace Bridge Authority had even indicated that they would support the publication of the latter volume, a commitment well beyond their legislative obligation.

Popular portrayals of archaeology often characterize its practitioners as nothing more than highly educated tomb robbers or artifact miners, the most celebrated example being Indiana Jones of the highly acclaimed *Raiders of the Lost Ark* movie series. This is perhaps not surprising, since the fieldwork component of the work has the greatest public profile. First, there is the sense of adventure which comes from travelling to exotic — or at the very least unfamiliar — locales. Second, there is the constant aura of discovery and the possibility of making a really significant find. Third, it has great visual appeal, as demonstrated by print media depictions of archaeologists with their latest finds and by popular television programs that re-create the moment of discovery.

To be fair, fieldwork holds a great deal of appeal to many archaeologists as well, and the discipline's unique blend of rigorous outdoor work, meticulous laboratory investigation, and scholarly discussion has tended to attract a unique — some might say eccentric — breed of practitioner. Fieldwork is also a critical aspect of archaeology since there are no second chances to observe and record crucial details, such as the spatial relationships between artifacts and features. But the goal is not to fill museums with antiquarian curiosities: it is to use archaeological data to derive meaningful inferences about past human behaviour, to use these inferences as the basis for making important contributions to the social sciences, and to enhance the cultural heritage of living peoples, many of whom have no other tangible record of their own collective past. This explains the archaeological maxim that every day in the field results in a day in the lab, for retrieval of artifacts and field data is only the beginning of the process, not the end.

Over the duration of the various 1993 to 1995 investigations at the Peace Bridge site, we had been constantly monitoring the initial processing of artifacts in the lab, and ensuring that, as soon as a given provenience lot had been washed and catalogued, the various classes of material were immediately turned over to the designated specialists for analysis. By early 1996, we already had a growing stack of preliminary reports as well as an assortment of computer databases containing detailed inventories and descriptions of what had been recovered. The organizational conundrum that Williamson had alluded to in his conversation with Bev Garner was that the dozens of physically discrete excavations which had been undertaken over the last two years were, in fact, just small windows through which we were seeing mere glimpses of a much larger site. To treat them — as well as the earlier investigations including the Orchid and Surma excavations of the 1960s — as separate entities would not do justice to the site. The challenge would be to integrate and synthesize the plethora of diverse data that even now was growing, as various analysts continued to carve away at the mountain of material which lay neatly stacked in our basement repository.

To help organize and coordinate this effort, we knew that it would be enormously helpful to have detailed site plans showing every excavation unit and what had been encountered there. Accordingly, Williamson had set Jane Cottrill to the task of turning the hundreds of pages of field forms and maps into a computerized map of the site. Given the nature of archaeological consulting, we could not afford the luxury of dedicated task specialists, relying instead on versatile employees with complementary skill sets. Cottrill was a good example, adept not only as a field archaeologist, but also as a CAD technician, among other things. Her experience on the site also made her an ideal person to tackle the extremely challenging task of stitching together so much dirt-smeared paper into a digital whole.

With base maps provided by the engineering companies involved in the various projects and help from our other CAD technicians, Andrew Allan and Andrew Clish, and after producing dozens of drafts that would be edited and corrected by us, the goal would finally be achieved through a set of small-scale key plans and larger-scale details. This set of plans would not only detail exactly where excavations had taken place, but what archaeological features, post moulds, and historic disturbances had been encountered there. Labels and hatching would help to distinguish historic from prehistoric pits, excavated from unexcavated features, human burials from other feature types, pits with temporally diagnostic artifacts from those without, and wherever possible, the cultural affiliation of the diagnostic artifacts contained within a given pit.

Determination of the latter attribute of course required analysis of the artifacts, and this was already well underway. Rob Pihl, one of our senior archaeologists and a ceramic specialist, had taken the ceramics away to his office for study, while Debbie Steiss and Bruce Welsh had spent months compiling databases of the chipped stone tools, including bifaces as well as more formal items such as projectile points, drill bits, and hide scrapers.

To speed up the process they worked as a team, one using a caliper to read off various key measurements and noting other attributes, while the other entered the data directly into the computer. The metric attributes included standard measurements, such as length, width, and thickness, but for tools such as spear points, might also include such characteristics as stem length and width. Non-metric attributes included standard observations such as tool type, temporal/cultural affiliation, completeness, portion of tool, and flint type, as well as comments which might include descriptions of reworking of broken tools or resharpening of dull ones.

Once these data were entered, the database could be queried to explore various trends in the data or to average key variables for comparison with figures from other sites. The data could also be sorted and printed out to facilitate other analyses, for example, sorting all the Genesee period artifacts by provenience to see if they were concentrated anywhere on the site. Indeed, such a printout would be used by Cottrill to label the features on the various site plans.

Databases were also compiled of the flint debris, although the strategy for this was somewhat more complicated. As time went on during the various excavation projects, it had become apparent that recovering every single flint chip was counter-productive. Logistically, this would have involved processing and inventorying thousands of kilograms of flint flakes. The sampling procedures worked out with Neal Ferris were, therefore, implemented in an attempt to keep the recovered assemblage to a manageable size. As it was, over 300 kilograms of flint chipping debris were recovered, representing on the order of 275 000 individual flakes. This was still not a workable assemblage, so a process of triage was implemented once the samples had been processed in the lab.

First, certain key samples were isolated from features that had been dated with some degree of confidence on the basis of temporally diagnostic artifacts and in some cases radiocarbon dates. These were subjected to very detailed analysis. Second, samples from features in selected areas were subjected to a preliminary analysis. Third, all remaining samples, including debitage from all paleosol and some features, were inventoried and weighed. In the end, over 40 000 flakes were analyzed in detail.

Since the analysis of the chipped stone tools and flake debris had taken many months, involving different analysts working on separate aspects of the assemblage, the final challenge would be to synthesize the results into a coherent whole. This job

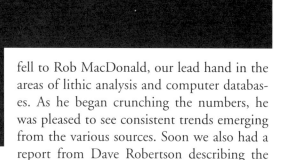

(opposite) Fish bone, freshwater Drum dentary (part of the jaw of a freshwater Drum – twice actual size).

(below) A Lamoka ground stone gouge – actual size (2000 BC).

fell to Rob MacDonald, our lead hand in the areas of lithic analysis and computer databases. As he began crunching the numbers, he was pleased to see consistent trends emerging from the various sources. Soon we also had a report from Dave Robertson describing the refined and decorated ground stone artifacts. This report also compared artifacts such as the thunderbird gorget to artifacts with similar iconography that had been documented in other aboriginal contexts. Descriptions of the ground stone tools, including axes, chisels, mortars and pestles, and netsinkers, had been started by Bruce Welsh and Martin Cooper, and MacDonald finished the analysis and integrated the results with Robertson's report.

At the same time that the artifact analyses were happening, two long-time associates of ours, now proprietors of their own firm, Bioarchaeological Research, had been working on a subcontract basis to analyze the animal bone and plant remains that had been recovered from the site. Stephen Cox Thomas had studied the dog remains, prepared inventories of the faunal remains, including the bone tools, and had done a more detailed analysis of bones that had been found within the collapsed pottery vessel in the truck-yard pit. Using reference collections at the University of Toronto and the Royal Ontario Museum, he had identified a wide variety of mammals, birds, amphibians, and fish, including several species which are either extinct or no longer found in the Niagara Frontier. He also identified the human cremation that we had originally thought was burned food waste. Thomas's associate, Stephen Monckton, had processed all the soil samples to extract the carbonized plant remains by water flotation. He had then sieved the dried samples through a nested set of graduated screens and spent days staring at the trays of floral remains through his binocular microscope, tabulating the remains of nuts, seeds, and fleshy fruits, and identifying wood charcoal to the individual tree species.

Rob Pihl's report on the ceramic analysis arrived as we were putting the finishing touches on the ground stone tool descriptions. Now, together with detailed maps and a complete database of every recorded feature, we had everything we needed to begin compiling the final report. It was time to start re-assembling the four dimensional puzzle to see what pictures lay concealed and to see what insights they might yield.

THE LATE ARCHAIC: A Genesee Camp

The opening scene of this 4000-year tableau would have been a treeless expanse of the Niagara River floodplain, mostly flat, with a few subtle stream runoff scars where spring floods had left their marks in the sandy soil. For centuries this 400-metre-wide landscape had lain submerged under the waters of the swollen river, a product of ongoing changes in the Great Lakes drainage system since the retreat of the Laurentide Ice Sheet thousands of years before. Now, as the drainage system matured, the Lake Erie waters were dropping and with them the level of the Niagara River.

As the landscape continued to dry out, plants began to colonize the former river bed, grasses and sedges at first, but gradually dogwoods and trees such as red maple and black ash. Even as the plants were beginning the succession that would lead to a mature hardwood forest, Late Archaic families were coming to the river-front, as they always had, although now they would reside down on the flats rather than on the crest of the upland scarp, which by this time lay far to the west of the river.

In the early years of this new camp, there were still a few old timers who had known a slightly different landscape and different ways of doing things. Some of them still had a few of the old narrow stone spear tips. Most people, however, now used the broad stone spear point, shaped like the pine tree. Not only had this become the most popular style among their people, but all of their neighbours were also using this style, making them from whatever suitable material they had at hand. These people knew they were lucky, however, for when the lake had receded, it had exposed limitless beds of high quality flint, and they wasted no time taking advantage of it. They harvested the flint for their own use and shared it with their neighbours through trade in stone tools.

Such a description is based almost entirely on the evidence from the site itself. The oldest stone tools that we had found, for example, were four Lamoka points, including two from the same pit in the west half of the truck pad. Named after the Lamoka Lake site of central New York, where they were first professionally documented, Lamoka points are one of several types belonging to a Late Archaic technological complex called Narrow Points, which were popular between about 4500 and 3800 years ago (*circa* 2550–1850 BC). Interestingly, the same pit also yielded several Genesee tools which belong to the later Broad Point complex and date to around 3800 years ago (*circa* 1850 BC). Assuming that the contents of this pit were all deposited at the same time, the association of Lamoka points with Genesee tools suggests a certain degree of continuity between these technological traditions.

This is not too surprising since overlap often occurs as older technology is replaced by newer forms, and such continuity between Lamoka and Genesee has been documented elsewhere in the Northeast. The recovery of several 4000 to 3900-year-old (*circa* 2050–1950 BC) Adder Orchard broad points, which some consider to represent a transitional form between narrow and broad points,

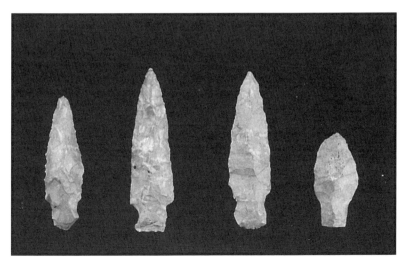

Various Late Archaic Lamoka-like narrow points (2000 BC).

A Genesee preform (2000–1500 BC).

provides additional evidence that the site was occupied from the earliest stages of the Genesee stone tool tradition.

Genesee tools were by far the most common temporally diagnostic chipped stone artifacts recovered from the site, representing almost two-thirds of the total. An assemblage of this magnitude, which included 127 projectile points, 56 preforms, nine drills, and four hide scrapers, was completely unprecedented, and it provided a rare opportunity to study Genesee tool-manufacturing from flint acquisition through to finished product. Given that the Genesee artifacts had come from virtually every corner of the site, including features that contained much later artifacts, it was apparent that the Genesee people had lived here for centuries and during that time had produced thousands of chipped stone tools: if the recovered tools represented the "dust" which had fallen through the cracks of this "shop floor," then the output must have been staggering.

Indeed, it seemed likely that these people had laid down a blanket of manufacturing waste over the entire area that had become incorporated into the topsoil over time. Later, whenever their descendants would dig a pit, they would dig through this blanket, inadvertently mixing their own and their ancestors' refuse as they filled in the hole again. Later groups would also contribute to the artifact load of the topsoil, and it would be this topsoil that would be preserved as a paleosol under the streets of Fort Erie. It was the accumulated cultural debris in that topsoil that led to the early twentieth-century descriptions of the site as "one continuous refuse heap."

The debitage analysis revealed much about how the flint had been quarried and worked. Since flintknapping is a process of reduction, the earliest flakes removed from a block tend to be large and chunky while the latest flakes removed tend to be small and flat. Between these extremes there is more or less a continuum, and by breaking up this continuum into arbitrary types, we could classify the flake assemblage to see how the various stages of lithic reduction were represented.

The results of the preliminary debitage analysis were rather surprising. It was expected that, since the Peace Bridge site was considered to be a flint quarry, the earliest or primary stage of lithic reduction would be very evident. This is the stage at which "blanks" are produced, either by striking off very large flakes or by working a block into a rough biface. This work is often done right at the quarry, since it significantly reduces the weight of material that needs to be carried away, and if there are flaws in the material, they will likely show up during the initial stages of reduction.

While there were trace levels of primary reduction flakes in the site assemblage, most of the flakes represented the secondary stages of reduction. Thus, in spite of the proximity of the flint outcrop, the site occupants seem to have preferred to bring prepared blanks back to camp for further refinement, rather than large blocks of flint. We could almost see the people at work.

A typical reduction sequence from block to Genesee preform.

As the Genesee flintknapper moved over the flint outcrop, he took care not to slip on the slick, algae-encrusted flint that rose in massive slabs from the grey lake beyond. Glancing around, he selected a good-sized block of flint, held it to his ear, and gave it a few solid taps with his large hammerstone, listening for the bell-like tone that would tell him the block had no hidden cracks or flaws. Once he had collected a dozen or more such blocks, he sat down on a ledge of flint. Then, with the hammerstone he drove huge flakes off the blocks, quickly trimming them into rough bifacial blanks. With the blanks safely stowed in his leather bag, he returned to camp.

A few days later he took out one of the blanks and, with his smaller hammerstone, repeatedly raked the feather edges of the blank to dull them and provide a strong platform for further flake removal. When he was satisfied that the blank was ready, he switched tools, selecting his antler billet, a nearly cylindrical tool about a foot long with a short, tapered tip.

Sizing up the blank, he searched for a previous flake scar ridge that would become the spine of the flake he planned to remove, as well as just the right striking platform upon which to land the blow that would detach the flake. By abrading the platform a few more times with the hammerstone, he ensured that the tip of the billet would not skate across the hard flint surface. Then, with an experienced touch he swung the antler hammer down within a millimetre of his target, driving off a nickel-sized flake with a sharp crack.

He repeated this process dozens of times, each successive flake removing ridges left by its predecessors, gradually thinning the piece while slightly reducing its size. He worked along one edge and then flipped the piece to work the other side of the same edge in order to maintain bifacial symmetry. Since he was very skilled and experienced, he usually succeeded in removing the flakes, most of the failures being caused by invisible flaws in the flint itself. Although he took great pains to properly support the blank with the flesh of his hands and with leather pads when necessary, occasionally a blow sent a shock wave through the flint causing it to shatter. Unfortunately, it happened more frequently the thinner and more refined the piece became.

The finished preform was pentagonal-shaped, about two-thirds the size of his outstretched hand and with one point longer than the others. While he might have worked all of the blanks to this stage, then refine some or all of them *further into tools, or stash them for refinement later, he decided instead to further refine the piece into a projectile point. The others he placed in his bag with the thought of trading them, since preforms were a valuable commodity in their own right, being an easily transported, generic item that could easily be refined into one of several possible tool forms. To finish his projectile point, he needed to create a notch between the base and the shoulder that would define the sides of the stem and the bottom of the blade.*

To do this he began by using a small billet to initiate the notch. Soon, however, he did not have enough room to manoeuvre without the risk of damaging the piece, so he resorted to the final item in his tool-kit — an antler pressure flaker. Made from a robust antler tine, the tip of this tool could be used to deliver enough force to detach small flakes with great precision. First, he ground the edge of the preform with the hammerstone to roughen the flint. Then, with the preform held tightly against a leather pad in the palm of his hand, he placed the tip of the flaker against the edge where the flake was to be removed. Finally, with the vice-like action of his knees pressing against the backs of his straining forearms, he exerted enough pressure to lever a small flake off the lower surface of the preform into the leather pad. He repeated the process until he held up the finished product — a beautifully thinned spear point that had the shape of a pine tree.

About one-fifth of the flakes that we recovered from the site were retouch flakes, the by-product of such pressure-flaking activities. Approximately two-thirds of the flakes were produced in the course of thinning bifacial blanks into preforms, and preforms into finished tools. The predominance of this activity was also indicated by the more than 1500 bifaces and biface fragments that were recovered, representing the full spectrum of biface refinement. Although many could not be dated with certainty, it was noted that most were large enough to have been Genesee bifacial blanks. Genesee preforms were much easier to identify, since they had the unique, pentagonal shape, a clear precursor of the finished Christmas tree shape of the Genesee point.

The Genesee camp may have existed on the river-bank for over 500 years. The features which were tentatively identified as living floors suggested that they may have lived in large huts up to four or five metres in diameter, although no post mould patterns were identified that would confirm this hypothesis. While the possible living floors were five to 10 metres apart, there was no way to determine which, if any, were contemporary with any other. In other words, they may all have been there at once, or only a few at once, or only one at any time over the 500-year occupation. Nor was there enough information to know how big the Genesee camp was, or whether they camped on different parts of the site at different times. While there seems to have been a concentration of Genesee deposits in the truck-pad area, Genesee artifacts were recovered from nearly every part of the site.

It seems most likely that the Genesee people only occupied the site seasonally, although it was probably one of their principal base camps. The site may have been part of the territory of one of many bands which occupied the Niagara Frontier at

All of the recovered flint artifacts from Feature 73, one of the cultural features in the east truck pad. Note the projectile point fragments, bifaces, and flake debris.

this time. It may also have been a spot where two or more bands briefly came together to engage in social activities and rituals, including burying their dead. Now, however, we even had evidence upon which to base a reconstruction of Genesee burial practice.

The man carried his brother's body out of the structure and laid him on the ground. Stricken with sorrow, he cried in anguish at his life having been taken so prematurely. His brother had only seen 20 winters and he should have lived as much again. Now, however, he had to ensure that the soul of his brother made the journey to the sky world without the burden of his body and with enough food and tools to sustain the effort.

He turned and walked a few steps back to the hide that was draped over the entranceway to the small, round structure in which he and his family lived while they were hunting and fishing by the lakeshore. It was not a large house but it was sufficient to store their belongings, including the tools with which he worked the stone from the lakeshore. He and his brother had always come to this place together because of its magic and beauty, magic because of the flint that littered the shoreline as far as you could see, and beauty, because of the view across the river and lake.

He found his antler tools, and returning to his brother's side, lifted and moved him to beside the others gathered around the fire. First, he accepted offerings of food from other band members, acknowledging their words and respect for his family's grief. After everyone had spoken, he tenderly placed his brother's body in the raging fire, which was surrounded by large stones to capture the heat and to ensure that there was nothing left of the flesh — just the purified whiteness of the bones. He then added deer meat and his antler tools to nurture his brother on the long journey.

Nearing the end of the ceremony the shaman stepped forward and, holding his talisman, called on the thunderbirds to help the man and protect his soul from the serpents of the underworld. Once the ritual had been completed, the community feasted and celebrated, not only the life that was but the life that would be.

Portrait of Joseph Brant with his dog, by William von Moll Berczy, *circa* 1807.

FROM WOLF TO FRIEND

That a dog is a man's best friend is not a recent reality but an ancient one. In fact, 4000 years ago, the aboriginal residents of the Niagara Frontier were burying their dogs in much the same manner as people do today — with reverence for a dear departed friend.

There is only a limited amount of evidence upon which to reconstruct the appearance of these animals, namely, a few archaeological examples and a small number of eyewitness descriptions from early European visitors to the region. The French missionary Gabriel Sagard, for example, described the dogs of Huronia in 1634 in the following way:

> The dogs in this country howl rather than bark, and all have upright ears like foxes, but in other respects all are like the moderate-sized mongrels of our villages ... They also very frequently put their pointed noses into the savages' pot.

In another published account of native American dogs, in the *Philadelphia Medical and Physical Journal* in 1805, J.S. Barton provides a more detailed description:

> The Indian dog [I mean that which is most allied to the wolf] is frequently called, by the traders and others, "the half-wolf-breed." His general aspect is much more that of the wolf than of the common domesticated dogs. His body, in general is more slender than that of our dogs. He is remarkably small behind. His ears do not hang like those of our dogs, but stand erect, and are large and sharp-pointed. He has a long, small snout, and very sharp nose. His barking is more like the howling of the wolf.
>
> His teeth are very sharp, and his bite sure. When he snarls, which he is wont to do upon the slightest occasion, he draws the skin from his mouth back, presenting all his teeth to view ... For the purposes of hunting, the Indian dogs are very useful; but in other respects, they are by no means so docile as common dogs ... If my information has been correct, this

species or breed is still preserved in the greatest purity among the Six-Nations, from whom the Delawares acknowledge that they received it.

While early twentieth-century descriptions of aboriginal dogs are consistent with earlier accounts, some include notations of colouration as well — usually black or black with white patches. The only reliable images that exist of prehistoric examples, however, are found on the artistic renderings on recovered artifacts.

Bone comb depicting dog and swan recovered from the Boughton Hill site, New York State. (Reprinted from Museum Service Bulletin of the Rochester Museum of Arts and Sciences, January–February, 1965)

The bands of people may have moved to the site in early April to collaborate in the netting of spawning walleye in the Niagara River and to exploit the huge flocks of migrating birds. Walleye bones were the most common fish remains recovered from the site. The fishery may have sustained them throughout the spring, although it would have been difficult to support even a single band of 30 to 50 people in one location for more than a few months, particularly after the spawning runs had stopped. In summer, part or all of the band may have moved off to other base camps in localities such as Point Abino, where ecologically diverse habitats containing a wide range of plant and animal resources could support them for a few more weeks. This might explain why summer-bearing fruits, such as strawberries, were poorly represented in the Peace Bridge site floral assemblage.

In the fall they seem to have returned to the site, using it as a base from which hunting parties would go out in search of game, such as deer and wapiti as well as fur-bearers such as raccoon, muskrat, and beaver, all of which are well-represented in the Peace Bridge site animal bone assemblage. Many of these parties would have been accompanied by their canine companions — small gracile dogs with a curled tail.

This would also have been the time of year that various nuts and ripening fruits were harvested. Plant remains floated from the soil samples included fruits such as black nightshade, grape, bramble berry, elderberry, plum, and hawthorn, as well as seeds from other plants, including cleavers, chenopod, knotweed, small grass, purslane, and sumac. While these may all have been part of the foraging diet, ethnohistoric records show that many were also used by aboriginal peoples for their medicinal properties. The most abundant plant food remains recovered from the site, however, were those of nuts, including walnut, hickory nut, beech nut, and acorn, and the Genesee people may have used the large stone mortar and pestles to process these.

Nut shell from two pits containing Genesee stone tools were submitted for radiocarbon dating. Unlike wood charcoal that may come from a much older tree, nuts are the product of annual mast crops and are unlikely to have been stored for more than a few months. They are, therefore, a more reliable source of radiocarbon dates. The nut shell from one pit yielded a calibrated date range of 4070 to 3700 years ago (2120–1750 BC), while the other sample returned a range of 3880 to 3570 years ago (1930–1620 BC), both of which are consistent with dates from other Genesee sites in the Northeast.

Genesee broad points made of Onondaga flint are most densely concentrated in central and western New York and in southern Ontario. At the same time, virtually identical points are also common from Vermont through Pennsylvania, northern Ohio, eastern Indiana, and eastern Michigan, although away from the Onondaga flint deposits they are more commonly made from locally available materials. It is not clear to what extent Genesee points and preforms manufactured at the Peace Bridge site were exported beyond the territories of local populations, although Genesee tools made from Onondaga flint have been found several hundred kilometres away from the Fort Erie outcrop. On the other hand, Onondaga flint occurs for some distance along the Lake Erie shoreline and while there are geophysical and palaeontological tests to differentiate among various flint sources, such techniques have rarely been used to distinguish artifacts made from flint sources from within the same formation.

Nor is it clear to what extent various regional populations had access to the Fort Erie Onondaga flint outcrops, although studies elsewhere in the world suggest that

The two sherds on the right are Vinette I ceramics – the earliest pottery in northeastern North America (500 BC).

hunter-gatherer groups seldom exert exclusive ownership rights over such resources. Until more sites from this period are studied to shed light on this issue, a reasonable working hypothesis would be that the site lay within the traditional territory of one or a few local bands who enjoyed frequent access to the flint and had a rewarding sideline in producing points and preforms for trade.

At the same time, other bands, with which they had reciprocal relations, may have occasionally sent envoys to the site to acquire flint, either through their own quarrying efforts or through trade with the resident band. Eventually, through trade networks, Genesee tools from Fort Erie may have found their way into the hands of far distant people who had never visited the site. In light of this model, the Peace Bridge site can be interpreted as a major node in the Genesee cultural network.

The importance of the Peace Bridge site in this regard seems to have waned around 3600 to 3500 years ago (*circa* 1650–1550 BC). Genesee points are thought to have been replaced by other styles towards the end of the Broad Point tradition, and two of these types — represented by a single Perkiomen point and a single Susquehanna point base — were recovered from the site. From that time until around 2700 years ago (*circa* 750 BC), Broad Point styles were replaced by Small Point styles, the last of the Late Archaic projectile-point traditions in the Northeast.

Although 27 Small Point tools were recovered from various parts of the Peace Bridge site, few were found in feature contexts that would indicate discrete occupations. It was, therefore, difficult to learn much about what was happening at the site during this period other than to say that Late Archaic hunter-gatherers were using the site, but apparently not as intensively as during Genesee times.

Making Pots and Caching Tools: Mysteries of the Early Woodland Period

The next most noteworthy occupation of the Peace Bridge site seems to have occurred somewhere between 2850 and 2350 years ago (*circa* 900–400 BC) at the beginning of what is called the Early Woodland period. Known as Meadowood, named after an estate in central New York where the first site of this period was excavated, these people were among the first pottery makers of the lower Great Lakes region. It would seem that ceramic vessels had been made during the Late Archaic period in the southeastern United States, the technology having arrived even earlier from Central America.

In the Northeast, bowls made from stone appear to have foreshadowed the arrival of ceramics from the Southeast, although ceramic vessels offered better capacity for storing large quantities of foodstuffs. Eventually, they were used for collecting and retaining water and cooking soups. As people became less mobile and their require-

Early Woodland Meadowood projectile point (500 BC).

ments for food storage and cooking technology changed, ceramic vessels evolved in form and function to meet the needs.

Remains of 10 Early Woodland ceramic vessels were recovered from the site, nine of which were classic undecorated Vinette 1 ware pottery. With the exception of one fragmentary rim sherd from a truck-yard feature and another from a caisson for the new customs building, all of the vessels came from the trench which crossed Niagara Boulevard at Forsythe Street. The pottery is characterized by fine- to medium-textured grit temper, and both the interior and exterior surfaces of the pots have marks on them indicating that their makers had used paddles wrapped with cord to shape them. Some vessel surfaces were subsequently smoothed as were most of the lips.

Of the 56 diagnostic Meadowood chipped stone tools recovered, 22 came from the sewer and water main excavations along Niagara Boulevard, mostly from the same trench as the ceramic vessels. It is tempting to speculate that this would have placed their main camp closer to the edge of the river than the earlier Late Archaic camps. Unfortunately, though, it is difficult to say precisely where the river was at that time, since the evidence suggests that the water level likely fluctuated over time. There does, however, seem to be a strong association between temporally diagnostic Meadowood artifacts and netsinkers, indicating that fishing may have been the most important activity other than flint quarrying to these people. Otherwise, the hunting and gathering lifestyle of the Meadowood people was likely very similar to that of their Late Archaic ancestors.

The Meadowood people were also renowned for their production and distribution of caches of large, thin, exquisitely made bifacial preforms. Twenty-nine bifaces were recovered by Shaun Austin from a cache encountered while salvaging the pit threatened by an oil interceptor near the west side of the truck pad. All of the preforms were skilfully and completely flaked from Onondaga flint and only one specimen showed any sign of having been used. There were no flakes found in the feature relating to the manufacture of the bifaces. Of considerable interest, however, was the observation of two directions of regular oblique pressure-flaking, suggesting the presence of at least two knappers contributing to the cache, a first for features of this nature in the Northeast.

It was also interesting to note that while the complete preforms and projectile points recovered from the Niagara Boulevard excavations and elsewhere ranged in length from 40 to 50 millimetres, those from the cache ranged from 60 to 90 millimetres in length. This suggests that there was a tool production system for making projectile points, drills, and various other tools from one kind of biface, distinct from the system responsible for the production and distribution of cache bifaces.

Not only do the lengths set the cache preforms apart from the others on the site, but they are also significantly larger than those from most other caches in southern Ontario and New York State. While their size probably relates to the unlimited availability of large blanks at the flint source, it does not explain why they were placed together in a pit never to be reclaimed.

Thus, the cache represents a mystery. Indeed, the frequent discovery of caches from the bottom of bogs or swamps or from locales along lake shores or river-banks far from settlements suggests that many of these were never intended to be retrieved. This, in turn, indicates that the bifaces in these caches probably don't represent stored or surplus items from which a variety of tools were to be produced. In thinking about why people may have placed groups of flint artifacts in the ground with no apparent thought of returning to them, we wondered if there might be a clue to such a behaviour in ancient aboriginal belief systems.

We found that in both Algonquian and Iroquoian cosmology, the appearance of flint on the earth is linked to the Gods. In the Iroquoian-Huron creation story, for example, a woman falls from the sky world and subsequently lands on the back of the turtle upon which the earth is formed. The exploits of her two grandsons eventually result in a conflict where the elder brother, named Iouskeha, uses the horns of a stag as a weapon, while Tawiscaron, the younger brother, uses a branch of a wild rosebush. Iouskeha strikes his brother so hard that his blood flows abundantly and becomes the stone known as Tawiscara, the stone we call flint.

That tools made of the blood of Gods find their way into the ceremonies of their children is not too surprising. While the placement of stone tools, either individually or in caches, with human burials is easily understood in the context of providing for the afterlife, perhaps other biface caches in more isolated contexts should also be thought of in a religious light and not necessarily in terms of a public ceremony. There is no evidence, for example, that caching was a public act, or that it always marked important social occasions and events.

Indeed, there is no evidence to suggest that isolated caches involved anything other than a single feature containing the cache. It very well could have been an entirely private act on the part of an individual carried out at some distance, both spatially and socially, from the rest of the community. In this way, the offering of stone tools in burial contexts, sometimes in large numbers, may have been part of the sacred realm accessible to everyone or perhaps only to the kin group of the deceased,

Early Woodland Meadowood bifaces (500 BC).

HOW TO GET A DATE
Radiocarbon Dating

Prior to the early 1950s, the only way archaeologists could determine the age of an artifact or cultural deposit was by trying to link it with something of known age. For example, if decorated Iroquoian pottery was excavated from a pit that also contained glass trade beads known to have been imported by the French in the early seventeenth century, it would be concluded that the pottery was of roughly the same age.

Once this age relationship was established, pottery of that type could itself be used as a temporal marker. While there was some imprecision in the method, due to factors such as much older "antique" pottery being curated well beyond its time of popularity, the method proved quite useful, particularly in parts of the world with long historic records to authenticate the relationships.

This process is called relative dating, since it indicates whether something is older, younger, or about the same age as something else, but not by how much, and it remains a cornerstone of archaeological method. The problem with relative dating, though, was that it left archaeologists without any way of gauging the time depth of prehistoric cultures, and these represented the vast majority of human history. What was needed was an absolute dating technique, a way to quantify the age of an object.

In the late 1940s, scientists at the University of Chicago discovered certain properties of carbon isotopes that would permit the absolute dating of organic materials. Carbon occurs naturally in three forms, the vast majority being the stable C12 (98.89%) and C13 (1.11%) isotopes. However, for every trillion (1×10^{12}) atoms of stable carbon, there is one unstable, or radioactive, C14 atom. Carbon 14 is constantly being produced in the upper atmosphere by the bombardment of nitrogen 14 atoms with cosmic ray neutrons.

At the same time, however, carbon 14 is constantly reverting to its stable isotope forms through radioactive decay. What the scientists had discovered was that this radioactive decay occurs at a constant rate. This rate is known as the half life, since it is based on the length of time it will take half of a given quantity of radioactive material to decay. The half life of carbon 14 is now known to be about 5730 years.

Since carbon is one of the building blocks of life on earth, plants and animals take up carbon from their environment in the course of their lives, and the carbon they take up is in the ratio of one trillion C12 atoms to every C14 atom. When an organism dies, it stops taking up carbon, and this has a result similar to starting a stopwatch. Without a continuing supply of carbon 14, the ratio of C12 to C14 in the organic tissues begins to change, as the C14 continues to undergo radioactive decay. In 5730 years, a piece of wood or a bone will contain half as much C14 as it did on the day the tree was cut down or the animal died. In 11 460 years it will have one-quarter as much C14, and so on. Therefore, by measuring the ratio of C12 to C14 isotopes in a sample of charred wood or a bone, the time since the death of the organism can be calculated.

Subsequent research discovered that there had been fluctuations in the concentrations of atmospheric C14 over time, so to correct for this, dates were run on tree ring sequences from long-lived species such as bristlecone pine. Since the precise age of any given tree ring sample could be calculated by checking its position in the ring sequence, correction factors could be determined to realign the radiocarbon dates with the calendrical dates. Radiocarbon age determinations that have been corrected in this manner are referred to as calibrated dates.

Radiocarbon dates can be acquired from a wide variety of organic materials, including wood charcoal and other carbonized plant remains, bone, and shell, as well as artifacts made from these materials. Unfortunately, conventional radiocarbon dating requires the destruction of around 10 grams or more of the item being dated in order to release enough carbon in a gaseous or liquid form for isotope counting.

Traditionally, wood charcoal has been used to date archaeological sites since it is often plentiful, but there is always the possibility that wood from a very old tree will render a date which is centuries earlier than the deposit from which it is obtained. Since 1977, the use of the Accelerator Mass Spectrometry (AMS) method of direct C14 isotope counting has revolutionized radiocarbon dating, since this method requires only milligram-sized samples. At the Peace Bridge site, AMS dates were obtained from several samples of carbonized nut shell, a 10-milligram sample of corn, and carbonized food residue from the inside of a pottery vessel.

```
          ISOTRACE RADIOCARBON CALIBRATION REPORT
             Output by calibration program C14CAL
                    Copyright (c) R.P.Beukens


                          9-Nov-95


    TO-5243  encrustation on ceramic vessel 540-230 Feature 158

    Radiocarbon date :  1330 ±  60 BP

    All solutions, with a probability greater than 50%  for the calibrated age
    of this radiocarbon date  have been calculated from the dendro calibration
    data. The 68% and 95% confidence intervals, which are the 1σ and 2σ limits
    for a normal distribution, are also given. A probability of 100% means the
    radiocarbon date intersects the dendro calibration curve at this age.
    All results are rounded to the nearest multiple of 5 years.

       Probability       cal Age         68.3 % c.i.          95.5 % c.i.
    ─────────────────────────────────────────────────────────────────────
           100 %        675 cal AD     655 AD -  725 AD     625 AD -  820 AD
            56 %        750 cal AD     655 AD -  775 AD     620 AD -  870 AD


    Calibrated with the bidecal data set INTCAL93 from:
       M.Stuiver and P.J.Reimer; Radiocarbon 35 (1993) 215-230

    This data set uses the dendro calibration results from:
       M.Stuiver and G.W.Pearson; Radiocarbon 35 (1993) 1-23
       G.W.Pearson and M.Stuiver; Radiocarbon 35 (1993) 25-33
       T.W.Linick, A.Long, P.Damon, C.W.Ferguson; Radiocarbon 28 (1986) 943-953
       B.Kromer and B.Becker; Radiocarbon 35 (1993) 125-135
```

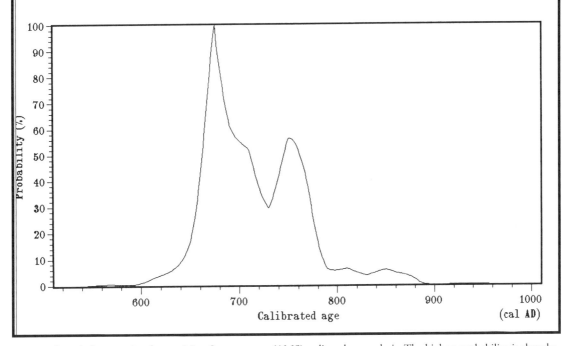

An actual result from an Accelerator Mass Spectrometry (AMS) radiocarbon analysis. The highest probability is that the pot involved dates to over 1300 years ago.

whereas isolated caches, often in smaller numbers, may have also been a ritual event, but accessible only to the individual participant.

Isolated caches may also have been special offerings in the sense that they were meant in gratitude for the stone itself. It is conceivable that there was a long-standing tradition of ceremonial behaviours, on the part of knappers, or individual hunters who relied on stone for their weapons and hunting tools, that at times required returning to the earth the stone that was so essential in their lives.

It was a giving back of God's blood or body, or a refocusing of the object's value in the sacred realm, itself a reinforcement of the basic philosophical tenet of aboriginal worldview that everything, including material culture, had a spiritual context. While this might explain the caching of well-used or expended items, it may also be true of the Peace Bridge and Snake Hill quarry caches, where flint was the focus of life.

The only other Early Woodland event of interest on the site was the burial documented in the truck yard. While the bones of the individual were in very poor condition, due to their placement directly on bedrock in a shallow pit along the shoreline, the truly remarkable finds were the artifacts that had accompanied the person on his or her journey to the afterlife. The stone pipe, while significant because of its rarity, was made of a limestone from Ohio. That this individual was buried with an obviously prized object, made from an exotic stone, points to the importance of the trade in goods and burial ceremonialism that occurred throughout the Early Woodland period.

After the Early Woodland period, there is a glaring gap in the archaeological record of the site, in that no artifacts dating from the Middle Woodland period were recovered. Given that such a small percentage of the Peace Bridge site was excavated, it is possible that the occupation from this time occurred elsewhere on the site. Yet if this were so, one would still expect to see some occupational evidence, however faint. Indeed, the evidence for the other time periods, although perhaps somewhat more concentrated in some areas than in others, was generally found to be scattered across the entire site.

We were therefore forced to conclude that the site had not been occupied at that time. The most compelling hypothesis to explain such an absence was that the site was uninhabitable during the Middle Woodland period, perhaps as a result of fluctuations in water levels which inundated the site. Unfortunately, the geological models to support the flood theory are not yet refined enough, although Jim Pengelly's research on lake levels has already suggested rises at 2170 and 1350 years ago. It will be interesting to see what future evidence will tell us about the history of the Peace Bridge site environment between about 2150 and 1350 years ago (*circa* 200 BC—AD 600).

FROM CAMPS TO VILLAGES: People in Transition

From the end of the Middle Woodland through the Late Woodland periods, aboriginal culture in the Northeast experienced a profound sequence of transformations that began with the adoption of corn agriculture. There is considerable evidence that the Peace Bridge site was occupied from the very beginning of this sequence, sometimes referred to as the Transitional Woodland period, although no direct evidence for experimentation with horticulture was found at the site.

Much of the evidence for Transitional Woodland occupation was in the form of small, undecorated pottery sherds that were found in pits containing either no other temporally diagnostic material, or stone tools from earlier times. This was thought to

PEACE BRIDGE SITE
Projectile Point Types

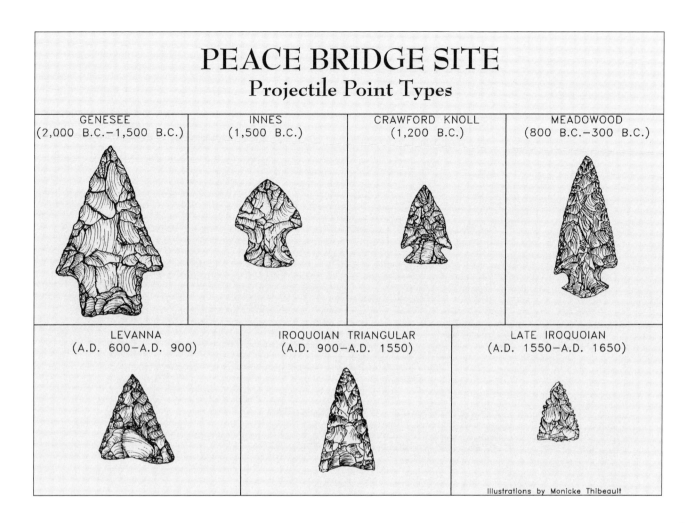

GENESEE
(2,000 B.C.–1,500 B.C.)

INNES
(1,500 B.C.)

CRAWFORD KNOLL
(1,200 B.C.)

MEADOWOOD
(800 B.C.–300 B.C.)

LEVANNA
(A.D. 600–A.D. 900)

IROQUOIAN TRIANGULAR
(A.D. 900–A.D. 1550)

LATE IROQUOIAN
(A.D. 1550–A.D. 1650)

Illustrations by Monicke Thibeault

be the result of earlier artifacts becoming incorporated in pit fill when Transitional Woodland peoples excavated through the artifact-laden paleosol.

Many of the Peace Bridge site burials were also thought to be the remains of Transitional Woodland peoples, since artifacts from this period were often noted in the fill of the pit. One such burial produced three Levanna points, small isosceles to equilateral triangular points roughly four centimetres long by three and one-half centimetres wide. A number of the burials from the Surma area of the site, excavated in the 1960s, also contained several Levanna points. Much smaller than most of the earlier projectile tips, many archaeologists believe that Levanna points are the first true arrowheads, marking the advent of bow and arrow technology in the Northeast.

Projectile points were not the only aspect of Transitional Woodland flint technology that seemed different from earlier periods. An interesting contrast to the kinds of flakes that characterized the majority of the site was provided by a detailed analysis of the flakes from a feature containing Transitional Woodland ceramics. Analysis of this assemblage, as well as those from several other key features, was undertaken by Dr. Andrew Stewart, a specialist in chipped flint technology. Stewart noted that there was a much higher proportion of flakes that had been removed directly from the original block of flint, and conversely a much lower proportion of later biface thinning flakes in this feature than had been noted elsewhere. He also noted that one of the bifaces from this feature had been produced on a large flake removed from a block rather than a bifacial blank, and that one side exhibited very little flaking at all.

Together, this evidence suggested that Transitional Woodland flintknapping stressed the production of large flake blanks which could be used as all-purpose or "expedient" tools, or refined into unifacial tools such as scrapers or bifacial tools such as projectile points. As he pointed out, the apparent deterioration in flintknapping technology, indicated by the shift in emphasis from producing bifacial tools to producing flake tools, has been noted elsewhere in eastern North America at about this time. This shift is usually attributed to a more sedentary lifestyle resulting from the adoption of agriculture.

The theory is that when people are highly mobile, they require bifacial blanks or cores from which they can produce flakes to use for immediate tasks or they might use the bifaces themselves as tools. Less mobile peoples either established their settlements close enough to flint sources, or transported sufficient material to those settlements, to satisfy all of their immediate needs without resorting to biface technology. In the case of the Peace Bridge site, the pattern suggested that the Transitional Woodland peoples were residing at the site for a longer period of time than their Late Archaic or Early Woodland predecessors and were using whatever was easily accessible for flint tool production.

Two house structures that possibly date to the Transitional Woodland period support the contention that people from that period were staying at the site for longer durations. The first of these was the collection of post moulds and Transitional Woodland pits situated in the Niagara Boulevard, close to where contemporaneous material had been recovered from the Orchid component in the 1960s. Unfortunately, not enough of the structure was exposed to be able to say much about it.

Andrew Stewart working at his desk at the Royal Ontario Museum.
(Richard Douglas)

The second structure, which was identified while excavating in the truck yard, consisted of two parallel walls of post moulds, approximately 5.9 metres apart, together with several pits containing Transitional Woodland pottery. Also within the structure were several larger post moulds that were interpreted as supports for the roof and bench structures. Architecturally, this structure appeared to be similar to, but smaller than, the well-known Late Woodland longhouse. Given the effort to construct such a house, it is likely to have been occupied for a substantial period of time.

The most vivid glimpse of life at the Peace Bridge site in Transitional Woodland times was provided by the collapsed vessel and its contents excavated from a pit a few metres away from the truck-yard house. All of the pieces of the pot had been returned to the laboratory in Toronto where it had been carefully reconstructed. We were very interested in the shape of the pot since it has a conical base, an attribute that is usually associated with much earlier vessels of the Middle

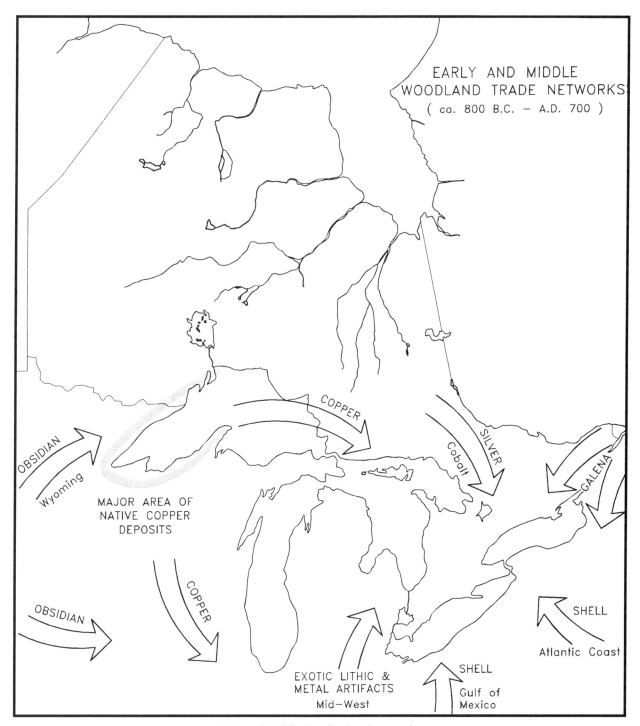

Early and Middle Woodland trade networks.

Woodland period.

The radiocarbon date of AD 675 taken on encrusted food debris from the vessel's interior surface, however, clearly indicated that the vessel had been made and used during the Transitional Woodland period. The contents of the pot were also analyzed and identified as the remains of a fish stew or soup, some of which was fresh and some of which had obviously been in the pot for a longer period of time. The bones of the fish that had been in the pot for some time were almost completely leached. While we rarely have an opportunity to reconstruct a ceramic vessel, we almost never get the chance to identify a 1300-year-old meal! Indeed, we usually have to satisfy ourselves with lists of the animals and plants that were used by the site inhabitants.

Once the story of the pot and its contents hit the media, it wasn't long until we received one of the strangest calls of the project. It came from Mike Vogel, a first-class journalist with the *Buffalo News*. Vogel has an abiding interest in the past and in archaeological projects in particular and has covered our projects in the Niagara

A variety of Levanna points (AD 600–900).

area since the time of Snake Hill. In this case, however, he was also calling on behalf of the food editor of his newspaper. They wondered if we could come up with a recipe for the soup which they would then pass on to the Aboriginal Culinary Course at Niagara College.

The plan was to recreate the soup and then hold a media event to explain how the archaeological project had led to an experiment in an ancient culinary art. The event proved to be memorable for all those involved. In fact, while discussing the event, one student was overcome with the emotional connection she had just made with her ancestors, and her tears, in turn, had a profound emotional effect on us. It is a rare and treasured moment when the humanity of an archaeological enterprise shines through the sterile trappings of science.

Not only was the experiment a success, but the program coordinator, Beverly Hill, agreed to serve it to the public at an event sponsored jointly by the Greater Fort Erie Chamber of Commerce and the Fort Erie Native Friendship Centre. The evening was also a resounding success and by the end of the night, more than 100 people had tried the meal that had been cooked and lost the day the vessel collapsed in a hot ember fire, 1300 years previously.

The old woman was crouched on the beach beside a small pile of rocks only 100 feet from the shoreline. It was a warm spring morning and the women of their house had decided to build a fire outside of their structure to cook the day's meals. As she was digging a shallow hole in the sand she called to her younger daughter to bring some hot embers from the house, and to her older daughter to bring the soup pot. The old woman placed the large rocks in a circle, being careful to pad sand around them. Some of the rocks were actually large blocks of flint that had been scattered about the beach. When she was finished, she took the hot embers from her daughter and laid them on a bed of dried twigs and leaves in the middle of the circle of rocks.

The two women then watched as the older daughter emerged from the wooden, bark-covered structure with the main soup pot, cradling it in her arms and struggling with the weight since it still contained soup from the previous few days. With great care, she lowered the pot into the shallow hole over the hot embers until it rested against the rocks, still leaving room to add logs should the fire need fuel. The old woman sighed in relief that the transfer had been made without damage to the pot. It was a cherished one having been made in a style that her grandmother had taught her.

The younger women called to their children, who were playing in the water, to be careful and to not venture too far into the river's currents. They were not overly concerned, however, as there were other women nearby, who were also watching the children from where they were washing some hides. A moment later, one of the boys yelled that he could see the canoe with the men coming along the lakeshore.

Within minutes, it arrived and the boy's father stepped from the canoe holding several large fish. It was a good time of year to catch these type since they came close to the lakeshore among the rocks to lay their eggs. The men had set their nets the night before and had gone out at sunrise to check on them. They had returned with enough fish to feed their household for two days and they all looked forward to the morning meal.

The old woman took three of the fish, gutted them, cut them into small pieces, then dumped them into the pot. Adding some more water, she noted that the soup still contained a shoulder of venison from a few days ago as well as a few old pieces of fish. The new fish, however, would freshen the stock considerably along with some walnut and purslane, a pot herb which she and her

HOW TO MAKE ANCIENT TEN-FISH SOUP

Have ready:

Three fresh pickerel
Three white bass
One piece river sturgeon
One venison shoulder (bone in)
Lake Erie water (may substitute)
One bowl shelled walnuts
One generous handful purslane

Method:

Place venison in large clay stew pot and cover with water. Bring to boil, reduce heat and simmer until the venison is tender and falls off the bone. Meanwhile, clean fish and cut into small two-inch chunks. Include head and tail. When venison is tender, add fish chunks and shelled walnuts. Cook an additional 30 minutes. Just before serving add purslane and heat through.

Serves the extended family

grandchildren had collected the day before. Leaving the soup to simmer, she returned to the house to get the wooden bowls for the meal, cautioning the boys, who were now running around wildly, to stay away from the pot while they were playing.

She had just entered the house when she heard an awful clamour coming from the cooking area. She backed out in time to see her daughter help one of the boys to his feet, after which he sunk to his knees over the fire, aware of what he had done. With great trepidation, he stood up to face his grandmother. The old woman walked slowly over to the fire staring at it in disbelief; not only had the meal spilled into the dirt, but the pot had cracked into hundreds of pieces, collapsing inward over the fire. A few pieces of fish could be salvaged but most was lost and the pot could never be fixed. As she turned to walk back to the house, she glanced at her grandson and, seeing his anxious face, smiled at him, reassuring him it was not the end of the world.

PEOPLE OF THE LONGHOUSE: Iroquoian Occupation of the Site

Although we knew from the 1964 and 1988 excavations at the Orchid site that Late Woodland peoples had frequented the site, we found very little new evidence of Late Woodland occupation. A total of 16 Late Woodland triangular projectile points and four pottery sherds were recovered from features and paleosol in various parts of the site. The style of the projectile points and the decoration on the potsherds all indicated that the people were Iroquoian-speakers, probably belonging to the Neutral or their ancestors.

There was also a glimpse of a possible Late Woodland house structure, near the intersection of Walnut Street and Niagara Boulevard. A small exposure revealed part of a row of post moulds that was reminiscent of an Iroquoian longhouse wall. Had we been excavating on a research site and not reacting to the demands of present-day development, we almost certainly would have continued to delineate the walls of the house.

Other Late Woodland (or Iroquoian) evidence was gathered almost by accident. In the truck yard, nut shell from a pit which contained a Genesee point, a Meadowood biface, and a fragmentary Vinette 1 pottery rim returned a calibrated radiocarbon date ranging from 750 to 664 years ago (*circa* AD 1225–1286). While we had been trying to date the Early Woodland component, it would appear that the pit had been used by Early Iroquoians to process nuts. Clearly, earlier artifacts from the paleosol had been incorporated into the feature when it was filled.

Without doubt the most interesting Late Woodland feature at the Peace Bridge site, however, was the one which produced the piece of slate with the thunderbird effigies. A kernel of corn from the same level in the pit from which the fragment came returned a calibrated radiocarbon date that pointed to a mid- to late seventeenth-century origin for the find. While we thought that the piece may have dated to an earlier period, on the basis of the artifacts from adjacent features, we were glad to have evidence of occupation of the site at that time.

Fitting in the palm of your hand, the piece likely represents part of a polished stone gorget, which had hung around a person's neck. It had been broken both longitudinally and laterally prior to being deposited in the pit. One of the thunderbird figures had survived on the recovered piece. It is of an abstract linear form, with the body and wings represented by single lines, the head by a pair of short gashes, and the tail by a somewhat fan-shaped element consisting of at least seven incised lines.

The incomplete figure, which is more representational, is suggested by a Y-shaped tail, lower torso, and right wing. Greater effort has been made to model this figure three-dimensionally through use of incisions of variable direction and depth, and overall, the image has a rather more curvilinear outline. Three lightly incised lines extending down from the right wing may represent wing feathers or power lines.

With the knowledge that representational art on portable stone artifacts was relatively rare in eastern North America, we assigned David Robertson to conduct a thorough review of the archaeological literature in search of comparable artifacts and images. Robertson, who found research of this nature interesting and stimulating, attacked the task with vigour and thoroughness.

He found that thunderbird figures occur on a variety of artifacts throughout the Northeast on sites that have been ascribed various ethnic affiliations. Inscribed ground stone items, bearing images similar to the Fort Erie linear figure, and assumed to be of Algonquian origin, have been recovered from sites in Lambton and Oxford counties in southwestern Ontario. Other comparable motifs have been found on artifacts collected from sites that are likely to be of Late Iroquoian affiliation in Elgin and Wellington counties.

A similar image even appears in the central Illinois River valley as a decorative element on a late tenth-century ceramic vessel and on a rock painting from Rainy Lake, near Fort Francis, Ontario. He also found that the incomplete motif has a widespread distribution within the Great Lakes region. Close counterparts appear as petroglyphs or rock paintings in northern Ontario, Pennsylvania, Minnesota, and Vermont.

What was even more widespread, however, was the use of a celestial thunderbeing, engaged in a constant struggle against malevolent underworld powers. Robertson found that similar notions were held by virtually all of North America's aboriginal populations and throughout much of northern Eurasia as well. In North America, the Thunderer is typically understood to be a great raptorial bird, whose flapping wings cause thunder while lightening emanates from its eyes or mouth.

Thunderbird is the most common manifestation of the upperworld thunderbeing in the Northeast, appearing among many of the Algonquian-speaking groups of the western Great Lakes. Robertson found considerable variation, however, in the manner in which it was conceptualized. Among some Algonquian-speakers, the Thunderers could be either bird-like or human, or could take a hybrid form, as seems to have been the case among some Iroquoian-speaking groups.

Two smoking pipes, recovered in the early twentieth century from Iroquoian sites in Oxford and Norfolk counties in southern Ontario, for example, bear composite figures (bird torso and human head). Among the New York Iroquois and several eastern Algonquian-speaking groups, on the other hand, the Thunderers appear to have been conceived as fully anthropomorphic beings.

In addition to controlling the rain, wind, and thunder, Thunderbird, as the protector of humans, waged a constant battle against the evil Great Lynx or Panther and Horned Serpent of the

Illustration of the thunderbird gorget, drawn by Monicke Thibeault.

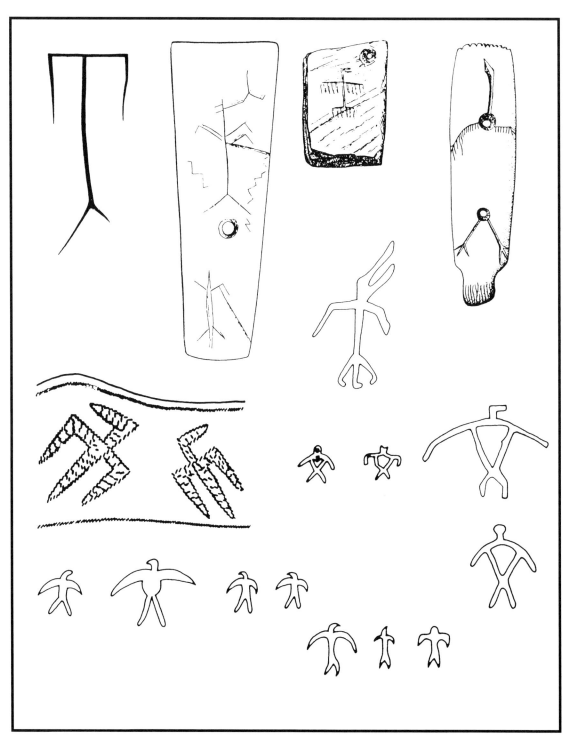

Similar thunderbird figures on artifacts recovered from archaeological sites.

underworld. The ferocity of Thunderbird in these battles also resulted in its becoming linked with human hunting and military prowess. This connection must be considered, however, within the context of a more widespread and generalized association between raptors and warriors. In the southeastern United States, for example, there was a large and powerful ceremonial system characterized by complex iconography that was shared by many regional populations. Artifacts bearing such Mississippian motifs have been found on a number of mid-seventeenth century Neutral sites in southern Ontario.

It has also been suggested that Thunderbird played an important role in bestowing powers upon and serving as protectors of shamans, particularly the Ojibway Jiissakid or tentshakers. In this way, the frequent occurrence of Thunderbird combining both human and bird elements may have hinted at the ability of shamans to transcend human form and to assume the shape and features of another being. Some of these images then are perhaps a manifestation of the widespread importance of bird symbolism in ecstatic rituals involving soul-flight.

Thus, the widespread distribution of motifs that are similar to the Fort Erie figures, together with the widespread nature of bird symbolism in general, and the concept of the thunderbird in particular, led Robertson to conclude that it would be unwise to attempt to assign a cultural affiliation to the individual who had made the gorget. Moreover, given the degree to which both objects and people travelled in prehistory, the individual who made the object might not have been the same person who had last worn or carried it prior to it's having been discarded in the pit.

We received another surprise, however, when a second polished and inscribed gorget fragment was discovered among the ground stone artifacts that had been brought back from the site. The importance of the piece wasn't discovered until it was washed some time later. It was a fragment of very dark greyish-brown shale that was extremely friable and had been recovered from a feature that contained both Late Archaic (Genesee) and Transitional Woodland material. It, too, had been broken, laterally and possibly longitudinally, prior to its placement in the feature. The remaining piece was 85.3 millimetre or about four inches in length.

Another slate gorget found at the Peace Bridge site, drawn by Monicke Thibeault.

Robertson examined the piece carefully and conducted a similar search of the literature looking for comparisons. A total of 20 lines had been lightly scratched onto the surface of the artifact, at least 12 of which clearly represent deliberate incisions made with a pointed tool. The cumulative effect of this decoration, which forms a series of overlapping tri-anguloid motifs, is that of a highly abstract image. The clearest motif consists of a triangular human or anthropomorphic spirit figure of a type that belongs to the general class of humanoid figures found on petroglyphs, pictographs, and birch-bark scrolls.

Joan and Ron Vastokas, experts with images of this kind, suggest that in the case of such motifs, there is a correlation between the degree of abstraction and the degree of spirituality and sacredness, in that a distinction is intended between human shamans, which are depicted in a representative mode, and shamanistic spirits, which are highly abstracted. In terms of basic form, however, the closest parallels with this figure may be found on two Iroquoian pipes found in southern Ontario, which depict Thunderbird as a composite figure with a bird torso and human head.

A second discernable motif on the fragment, above the triangular spirit figure, is one that is reminiscent of zoomorphic figures found on two ceramic vessels from a site in central Illinois, which have been interpreted as sitting birds that are symbolic representations of upperworld themes. This figure may also incorporate a third motif; that of the "bisected angle," which has also been found on Late Woodland ceramic vessels in Illinois.

This motif has been associated with serpentine beings that have underworld associations. Although the identification of the bisected angle motif overlapping or merged within the avian figure is perhaps the most unconvincing of those suggested for the artifact, such intimate associations between upper- and underworld beings are a predominant aspect of Northeastern cosmology and its symbolic representation.

Finally, the two gorgets found by us were not the first to be discovered at the site. Indeed, two inscribed gorgets were recovered during the 1965 University of Toronto excavations of the Transitional Woodland burials at the Surma site. While one specimen is fragmentary and the other is complete, the designs on the two items are very similar.

The fragmentary artifact was associated with the interment of a flexed adult male, along with an unspecified number of beaver incisors and a whetstone. The piece is rectangular in shape and manufactured from well-polished fine-grained black slate. While it is broken laterally, a single two-millimetre diameter hole that had been drilled from both surfaces is still visible. Polish on the edges of the hole indicates that the artifact was suspended from a thong. One surface of the artifact is decorated with a finely inscribed motif consisting of a pair of lines running along the longitudinal axis of the gorget, from which extend 24 opposed pairs of oblique lines.

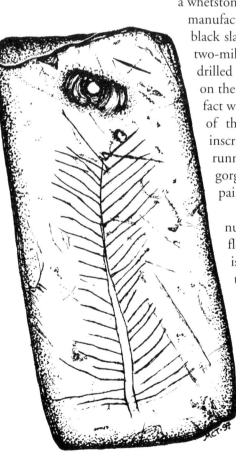

The complete specimen is one of numerous grave goods recovered from the flexed burial of a 27–30-year-old male. It is a "boat-shaped" pendant manufactured from highly polished dark greenish-grey banded slate. Reconstructed from three fragments, the piece measures 191 millimetres (eight inches) in length and 40 millimetres (one and one-half inches) in maximum width, and also has a small, neatly drilled hole. The artifact is heavily encrusted with a mineral coating on one side, partially obscuring the finely incised decoration, which consists of a single line that serves as the axis for

Broken black slate gorget from the Surma site, drawn by Monicke Thibeault. Note the "X-ray" image.
(University of Toronto Collection)

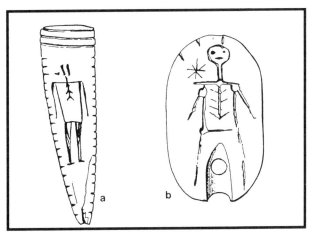

Human figures rendered in "X-ray" style.

31 pairs of alternating and paired obliques.

Robertson, having researched these designs thoroughly and having found other examples from southern Ontario of human figures rendered in a similar manner, decided that the images on these two gorgets had several possible interpretations. Perhaps the most prosaic explanation is that they are simply depictions of feathers. It is more likely, however, that they relate to one of two other notions. One is that of a tree, possibly even that of the original "world tree" growing at the "cosmic axis," which links the earth and sky, or humanity and the spirits.

This concept is central in Northeastern shamanistic belief systems as is the other notion of skeletonization — the abstraction or reduction of human or animal forms to their essential elements. In this interpretation, the "X-ray" representational style depicts the spinal column and rib cage, and would be especially effective if the gorget was worn on the chest. One of the other images that Robertson found was that of a pipe with a very similar image illustrated in the chest area of the figure. Mircea Eliade, a world authority on shamanism, once noted that the ability of shamans to reduce themselves to the skeletal condition was equivalent to

Complete "boat-shaped" gorget from the Surma site, drawn by Monicke Thibeault. Note the "X-ray" image.

(University of Toronto Collection)

re-entering the womb of primordial life, that is, to a complete renewal or mystical rebirth. Perhaps these pieces had been intended to enable the deceased at Surma to achieve such a rebirth.

Whatever their original intent, these artifacts underscored the profound differences in worldview between the peoples who had occupied this landscape for some 4000 years, and our own. Hints of these differences were also seen in the caching of the Early Woodland stone tools and the cremations of the Late Archaic Genesee people. To a large extent, these ideological differences were rooted in the close relationship these aboriginal peoples had with the land, and in their much more intimate connection to the ever-present cycle of life and death. At the same time, however, we were keenly aware of the basic human desires and needs which we had in common, and our shared experience of the Peace Bridge site landscape.

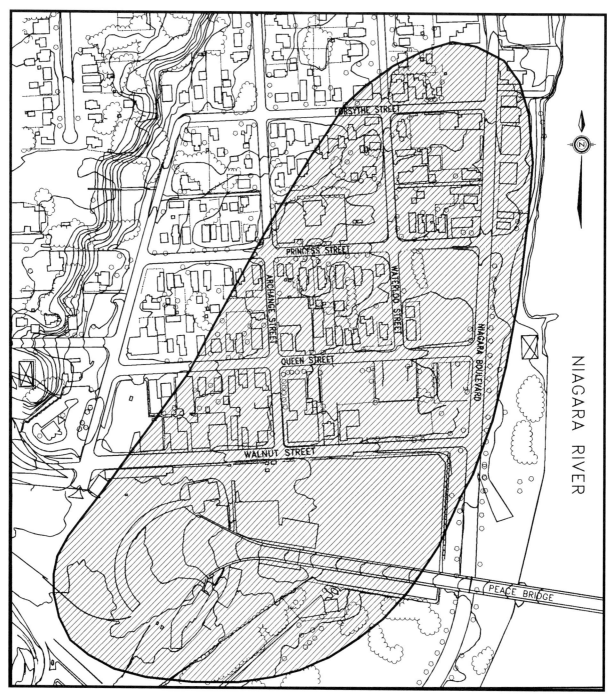

Areal extent of the Peace Bridge site.

8 The Town That Came Before

TOUCHSTONE — *that which serves to test or try the genuineness or value of anything.*
(Oxford English Dictionary)

It is a nearly universal human practice that those people, things, institutions, and events which we hold in greatest reverence — whether as individuals, families, or a society — are often commemorated in stone. These range from the small and personal, such as a grave marker or historical plaque, to imposing and public, such as a seat of government or religious edifice, to grandiose such as an Egyptian pyramid or the Great Wall of China.

Stone is the medium of choice because it symbolizes permanence. Yet the essential ingredient in the longevity of a monument is the human values it symbolizes, regardless of the tenacity of the stone. Witness the many defunct monuments, such as statues of dictators or the Berlin Wall, which have fallen throughout human history. By symbolizing human values, therefore, stone monuments not only remind us of the past, but also serve as touchstones for comparing our own values to those of our ancestors.

The prehistoric inhabitants of the Peace Bridge site left no lasting monument in any form which would still be easily recognizable. Yet the flint which was a cornerstone of their existence must be considered as permanent a monument as any that could be constructed today. At the same time it is a touchstone which tests the genuineness or value of our concern for our human heritage and especially the heritage of those aboriginal members of our society. Let us then consider the legacy of the Peace Bridge site people.

It can be argued that the preoccupation of populist archaeology with temples, pyramids, towns buried by volcanic ash, ancient cities lost in the jungle, and massive architecture in general, overlooks much of interest in the past, since the average person had little or nothing to do with these creations of the cultural élites. In the lower Great Lakes region, where such stratified societies never developed in prehistoric times, to overlook the lives of the common people is to overlook everyone!

It is, therefore, important to recognize that the real monument left by the people of the Peace Bridge site is the physical remains of their day-to-day lives. Many of these remains they themselves may have considered to represent the most mundane aspects of their lives, since the majority of the archaeological deposits are essentially prehistoric trash. But because so little is known about life at that time, even the trash is interesting to us, since it can shed light on many other aspects of life, not just refuse disposal patterns.

Perhaps the most impressive attribute of the Peace Bridge site, to both the general public and archaeologists, is the immense areal extent of the deposit. Estimated to cover 24 hectares, it is actually hundreds if not thousands of small camps superimposed on each other like raindrops on a windshield. This makes the archaeologist's task of teasing apart and interpreting these occupations extremely difficult.

The investigations which have taken place on the site since the 1960s have exposed approximately 6000 square metres, or roughly 2.5 percent of the entire site. Trying to understand the site on the basis of such a small sample could be compared to trying to grasp the subtleties of plot and character development in a two-hour movie based on three minutes' worth of footage divided into 18 clips of 10 seconds each. As impossible as such a task may seem, we have actually been able to start fleshing out the culture history of the Peace Bridge site, largely because archaeological interpretation is not done in a vacuum. Rather, it builds upon knowledge from other sites and from other sources of information, including early historic records of aboriginal life in the Northeast as well as ethnographic studies of hunter-gatherers in other parts of the world.

The picture will also continue to fill in as the site is studied by professional archaeologists. Since its earliest discovery, there has been a slow but steady trickle of information published about the site, in newspaper accounts as well as academic journals. With the recent work at the site, this trickle has grown to a stream, including publication of a 540-page technical volume on our 1993 to 1995 ASI investigations, numerous newspaper articles, television news features, and a short piece in the popular magazine *Archaeology*, which also appeared on their web site.

The artifacts and data which have been recovered from the site to date will continue to be studied, and use of the information by graduate and other students has already started. Since the major excavations of 1994 and 1995, additional windows have been opened on the site in advance of the continued development of the commercial customs facilities and, more recently, the twinning of the Peace Bridge.

Archaeological investigations will undoubtedly continue far into the future, as the urban landscape is perpetually remodelled. While it may be frustrating to some to see our understanding of the site evolve so slowly, it must be treated as a non-renewable heritage resource of utmost significance, worthy of the long-term stewardship and care of the Town of Fort Erie. Certainly the existence of an archaeological resource as large and as significant as the Peace Bridge site within the town's jurisdiction must be viewed as both a weighty responsibility and an incredible endowment to the people of Fort Erie.

Moreover, we can look forward to filling in the gaps in our understanding of the site. So far, we have learned that while the Peace Bridge site may have been occupied before about 4000 years ago, any evidence of such occupations was apparently scoured away by the river during the Great Lakes high-water stage known as the Nipissing Transgression. Late Archaic hunter-gatherers then colonized the site sometime after the retreat of the water. These people were known for making a distinctive Christmas-tree shaped projectile point which archaeologists have termed "Genesee," and this point was a regional variant of a class of similar points, common throughout eastern North America at this time, known as the Broad Point complex.

For the next 400 to 500 years, these Genesee people frequented the site as they moved on an annual round of their territory to exploit seasonally available game and plant foods. As such, we were not surprised to find animal remains in their refuse pits, which indicated that these people had come to the site in the spring to harvest spawning walleye and other fish, and that they had returned in the fall to use the site as a base camp for hunting deer, wapiti, raccoon, beaver, and muskrat. Nor were we surprised to find charred evidence that work parties had gone into the local forest to harvest walnuts, hickory nuts, beech nuts, and acorns.

It was evident to us that the unprecedented scale of the Peace Bridge site occupations was the result of a combination of factors coming together at this one location. First, it was a major source of Onondaga flint, one of the highest quality tool-stones in the lower Great Lakes region. Second, the rich fishery and other local resources could sustain foraging bands in this locality for months at a time. Third, it was strategically located with respect to transportation across the Niagara Frontier at a spot where canoeists could avoid the hazards of a river crossing by paddling out across the lake.

The Genesee people certainly seem to have capitalized on this lucky chain of circumstances. Judging from the enormous quantities of stone tool manufacturing debris they left behind, they could have been supplying a huge hinterland of neighbouring bands with preforms and finished tools. Indeed, the distribution of Genesee points manufactured from Onondaga chert throughout the lower Great Lakes indicates that the Peace Bridge site was likely one of a small number of major manufacturing and distribution nodes in an extensive Late Archaic trade network.

We were struck by a certain irony in this fact almost daily as we excavated at the site. Indeed, as we watched the semi-trailers wheel through the truck yard and the new commercial customs facility rise from the ground, we realized what a crucial role geography had played in creating this trade and transportation hub, both then and now.

At the same time we were still unclear as to how this Genesee production and distribution system had actually operated, although we had several theories. One possibility was that one band had occupied the site nearly continuously, controlling all access to the flint and concentrating significant effort on tool manufacturing and export. We considered this scenario to be unlikely, knowing that craft specialization and exertion of ownership over natural resources is very rare in band-level foraging societies. Nor was there strong archaeological evidence to suggest a year-round occupation of the site.

Another possibility was that many different

WHAT SHOULD HAPPEN TO THE ARTIFACTS?

This editorial was taken from the August 2, 1994 edition of the Fort Erie Review Weekly.

It's time Fort Erie reclaims and celebrates its past. Last week, archaeologist Ron Williamson revealed several artifacts he has found while inspecting Peace Bridge property.

They include projectile points (arrowheads), scrapers, net weights and grinding tools. A stone hearth was also unearthed.

These items date back more than 4000 years and were found in what was camp site and quarry used for more than a 1000 years. Mass burial sites, discovered in the early 1960s, were also part of this camp.

Skeletons of hundreds of native bodies were taken to Ottawa for study, where they remain.

So much of this history has been taken from town, few people realize the significance that the land that makes up Fort Erie had before the birth of Christ. What the town needs now is a way to display these artifacts and detail the progression of the ancient people who lived there.

As well, the return of the bodies taken from town would no doubt be a welcome gesture to our native community.

A burial site has been approved for use on the grounds of Old Fort Erie in order to allow these people a final resting spot. Such a move could be the first step in recovering this lost history.

The next step would be to find a way, in co-operation with local natives, to display the thousands of artifacts Williamson has uncovered in his numerous excavations here.

There is a great deal of talk about building the town's tourism industry. If we embraced our past and created, in some way, an accessible portrait of early life in Canada, perhaps others would be drawn to the rich tableau of history that was the foundation of Fort Erie.

bands had come to the site at different times, camping there for a few days while they availed themselves of the flint and the local food resources. Although not impossible, we considered this scenario to be somewhat improbable, as it would require some bands to travel vast distances across other band territories, an inefficient and potentially hazardous method of acquiring flint. We think that the most likely scenario falls between these two extremes.

One or a few local bands may have seasonally occupied the site, perhaps joining up as a so-called "macroband" to cooperate in communal fishing and hunting activities in the spring and fall, respectively. Over the weeks that they resided at the site, they would have replenished their own tool inventory and made a surplus which they could trade with other bands with whom they had regular contact. While such contact may have occurred when the bands encountered each other during seasonal travels, it more likely occurred through trade envoys, either travelling out from the Peace Bridge site or coming to the site from distant bands.

We felt that this scenario was most consistent with the archaeological observations of seasonal occupation, inhabiting houses large enough to accommodate extended family groups. The presence of numerous burials also suggested to us that the site had been occupied by fairly large groups over extended periods of time.

Like our predecessors, we were also astonished by the unprecedented quantity of Genesee artifacts that we recovered from virtually all parts of the site. We noted that the Genesee activity seemed to be concentrated near the new commercial customs building at the corner of Queen Street and Niagara Boulevard. Many of these artifacts came from pits that were thought to date to Late Archaic times, and radiocarbon dated nutshell from several pits tended to confirm this. In some cases, however, we had found Genesee artifacts incorporated into the fill of later pits, and we attributed these to later occupants digging through the artifact-laden topsoil and accidentally encountering earlier artifacts.

It was clear to us that no other time period was as well represented at the Peace Bridge site as Genesee. We also noted that, in the final stages of the Late Archaic period, during which broad points such as Genesee were replaced by small points, there was much less evidence of intensive use of the site. Indeed many of the small points we had recovered were from pits with later artifacts, suggesting that they had been inadvertently incorporated into the pit fill from the topsoil. We acknowledge, however, that it is possible that the main Small Point occupation was located on a part of the site that has not yet been investigated.

Just as the Genesee period occupation seemed to have been concentrated near the corner of Queen Street and Niagara Boulevard, the Early Woodland period occupation seemed to have been concentrated along Niagara Boulevard, between Princess and Forsythe streets. It was apparent that the main Early Woodland occupation was by hunter-gatherer bands who were part of a cultural tradition known as Meadowood. Renowned as the first potters in the Northeast, they counted amongst their ranks highly skilled craftsmen who produced large, thin, exquisitely made biface preforms and projectile points of Onondaga flint.

Like their Genesee ancestors, the Meadowood people seem to have used the site extensively, spreading occupation debris far and wide and manufacturing large quantities of stone tools for domestic consumption and export. We encountered at least one Early Woodland burial at the site, and together with the occupational evidence, including many netsinkers and fish remains, we concluded that the site had been seasonally occupied by at least one entire band.

Perhaps the most intriguing puzzle of the Peace Bridge site was the apparent abandonment of the site during Middle Woodland times, from about 2150 to 1350 years ago (*circa* 200 BC–AD 600). As we pondered this mystery, we came up with two theories. One possibility was that these people had inhabited a part of the site that had not been investigated yet, although we think that some evidence of occupation would have turned up, however scanty.

Another possibility was that the site had been uninhabitable through this period, perhaps as a result of periodic or permanent flooding. Turning to our colleagues in various earth science disciplines for help, we established that parts of the site would have most certainly experienced occasional seasonal flooding. Furthermore, given the current elevation of Lake Erie, it would only have taken a rise of a few metres to partly or completely flood the site; hence a sustained period of high lake levels could have cut off the site to Middle Woodland peoples. Indeed, there was evidence from dune paleosols along the northeastern Lake Erie shore, as well as geological evidence, to suggest that several lake level rises had occurred around this time.

In 1997 we were elated when salvage excavations for one of the new Peace Bridge companion span piers revealed direct evidence for prehistoric flooding at the site. Whereas a prehistoric topsoil, or paleosol, capped with modern fill had been widely documented on the site, two paleosols were encountered at this locality, one immediately above the other.

Analysis undertaken by University of Guelph scientists revealed that the lower layer was a well-developed soil that had been exposed as a stable ground surface for hundreds, if not thousands of years. Above it was a deposit of alluvial sand which had been laid down on top of the original soil by the river. This new ground surface had remained exposed as a stable surface long enough that soil development was well underway, although it could not be considered a mature soil. Finally, these soils had been covered with the modern fill which capped most of the site.

We initially hypothesized that the alluvial deposit might date to the Middle Woodland period, when it was thought that the site might have been flooded. The subsequent recovery of Transitional Woodland artifacts from the lower paleosol refuted this hypothesis, however, indicating that the alluvium had likely been laid down during the Late Woodland period. Nevertheless, it clearly demonstrated that prehistoric flooding of the site had taken place, prompting a renewed effort to find similar evidence elsewhere on the site in future excavations.

When occupation of the Peace Bridge site resumed sometime after about 1350 years ago (*circa* AD 600), aboriginal life in the Northeast was entering into what archaeologists, worldwide, consider to be one of the most profound periods of change in the history of any culture: the adoption of agriculture. While there is evidence to suggest that people had been tending plants for food and medicinal use since Late Archaic times and earlier, there could only be minimal commitment to this enterprise, since the people were mobile and the plants were not.

If, for example, people at the Peace Bridge site planted or otherwise encouraged the growth of certain plants during their time there in the spring, they would do so in the hope of reaping a harvest on their return in the fall. While such yields might be an important supplement to their diet, neither the quantity nor the reliability of the crop would be much to bank on.

Only plants which required little or no ongoing care would be suitable for such low-maintenance horticulture. Sunflower is one such plant, and it appears to have been domesticated from wild ancestors in the American Midwest by Late Archaic times. Squash, which was likely domesticated in Mexico in Early Archaic times, also appears in the Midwest during the Late Archaic period. Exactly when these cultigens appeared in the lower Great Lakes region is unclear, but the full suite of historic aboriginal cultigens was likely in place by the beginning of the Late Woodland period,

The discovery of two separate paleosols at the site in the fall of 1997 in one of the piers for the proposed companion span of the Peace Bridge.

namely, corn, beans, squash, sunflower, and tobacco.

Corn was the engine which drove this economic revolution, since it was capable of yields which would eventually provide for up to half of the Late Woodland diet. Like squash, it had been domesticated in Mesoamerica during Early Archaic times, although it had taken somewhat longer for the plant to adapt to a more northerly environment. Not only could corn produce vast quantities of food, but when eaten with nutritionally complementary beans, it constituted a high-quality source of protein.

Relatively quickly the commitment to producing food through agriculture was established, involving abandonment of the group mobility which had characterized aboriginal life for thousands of years. Instead, a semi-permanent village was established and land cleared around it for the crops, while hunting, fishing, and gathering parties were sent out to satellite camps to harvest the traditional natural resources.

In the end, we could not tell if a semi-permanent village had ever been established at the Peace Bridge site. While we found the remains of two probable Transitional Woodland period houses, too little had been exposed to learn much about them. At least one of these houses had possessed the classic structure of a Late Woodland longhouse, although it was somewhat smaller.

They could have been part of a cluster of houses in a small settlement, or single, warm, season shelters used to house work parties on the site. Based on the frequency of Transitional Woodland pits and burials, however, we suspect that more than one or two houses once stood somewhere on the site.

The economic shift from hunting and gathering to agriculture resulted in other changes besides a different residential pattern. Over time it would have contributed to various developments in other spheres of life, including a kinship system or "family tree" which traced descent through the mother's side rather than the father's.

While the significance of such a change in kinship system may not be immediately apparent, except perhaps to those who dabble in genealogy, it was actually a fairly profound change, considering that in band- and tribal-level societies such as these, the entire social and political system is based on kinship, in this case maternal lineages and clans. Indeed, the development of the Iroquoian longhouse as a communal residence was related to these changes in social structure.

We could see evidence of cultural change right down to the level of technology, with an increasing emphasis on multi-purpose stone tools rather than single-purpose ones. Often such multi-purpose tools were simply large flakes that could be used or adapted to a particular task and then thrown away. The reduced investment in time and skill to make such tools seems to have been reflected in the flint debris from the Transitional Woodland period.

The site continued to be used through the Late Woodland period, although it is unclear to us what the precise nature of this usage was. During the 1997 salvage work for the new companion span piers, we were thrilled to find the first concentration of artifacts dating to the beginning of the Late Woodland period, a sub-period known as the Early Iroquoian period. Although the exposure was too limited to identify remains of structures, this discovery lent support to our contention that occupations from different time periods were situated on different parts of the site.

In this same pier location, we also encountered the foundation of an early pioneer homestead dating to the 1850s. Made from mortared blocks of flint and limestone, this discovery was a further reminder of how the past was intricately layered on the site with the flint running through as a common theme. This same point had been made even more powerfully when we had arranged to review the Surma artifacts from the University of Toronto collections. In with the gorgets and flint tools from the site was an American infantry button from the War of 1812.

The most significant Late Woodland feature that had been documented on the site was the ossuary that was excavated during the 1960s at the Orchid component, near the intersection of Forsythe Street and Niagara Boulevard. While we subsequently recovered Late Woodland projectile points from scattered pits throughout the site, we found very little pottery from this period. Outside of the scattered probable Late Woodland pits that we documented, the only structural evidence was a wall segment that may have been part of a Late Woodland longhouse.

Given this relative dearth of occupational evidence, we wonder whether there was ever a substantial Late Woodland presence at the site. Unfortunately, the presence of the ossuary sheds little light on this question, as such communal burials were typically situated away from the main village and might contain the accumulated dead of several different communities from over a decade or more.

An 1850s flint block foundation found in one of the piers for the proposed companion span of the Peace Bridge.

Perhaps the Peace Bridge site had only been used as a satellite camp for hunting, fishing, and quarrying flint during this period. Considering the harsh winter winds off Lake Erie, we consider it unlikely that any group would have wintered at the site, let alone established a large, year-round settlement.

Whether or not there had ever been a substantial Late Woodland occupation on the site, the radiocarbon-dated corn from the pit that produced the thunderbird effigy gorget made it clear that aboriginal people had continued to use the site right up to the point when European brass and iron rendered the flint obsolete as a vital material for tool manufacturing.

There is something fittingly ironic that such a potent symbol as a thunderbird should be one of the last vestiges of 4000 years of a lifestyle with such an intimate connection to the flint, for in certain European folk mythologies, flint tools were called thunderstones, in the belief that they were created by lightning striking the ground.

Although we have merely glimpsed the prehistory of the Peace Bridge site, it is clear that this is truly a town beneath a town. Throughout the world, having such archaeological remains under the streets of a modern town is not such an uncommon phenomenon. But here in northeastern North America it is extremely rare, and virtually unique that such remains should be prehistoric and not the remains of more recent historic settlement. Certainly, there are prehistoric sites buried elsewhere be-neath urban landscapes, but few, if any, approach this size or complexity.

How can anyone who is aware of this site walk these streets now without trying to imagine what life may have been like here so long ago, or thinking about the ancient ones now resting below their very feet? The Peace Bridge site is indeed an extraordinary heritage legacy for aboriginal and non-aboriginal people alike.

Epilogue
LEGACY OF STONE

SUNSET ON A SPRING DAY IN 1883 BC

The man had come to the sandy, lakeside hill that afternoon, alone, to reflect on his good fortune and to thank the earth for her bounty with an act of both humility and submission. He was a tall and heavily muscled man with brown weathered skin and a mass of black, wild hair. Although he had seen 40 winters and summers, he was as agile as a lynx and was good with his hands, making many of the tools that his family needed.

His band, including his brothers' families, had come to this lakeshore for as long as he could remember to fish and hunt, but mainly to find the stone from which they made their spear points, knives, and scrapers. It was stone made from the flesh of Gods and left to them by the mother of his people in the far distant past.

His grandfather had told him that this ancient mother had first given birth to the four winds and then to flint, who had jumped out of her womb tearing her body to pieces. As a consequence, the Great Hare had fought with Flint and pieces were chipped off his body, pieces that the Hare told him may be of use to humans some day.

As the shaper of stone for his family, he felt a closeness with the spirit of Flint and believed that he must return stone to the earth to thank him for the gift of his body. It was not so much that the idea originated in his head or from the elders' teachings but it had come from within his whole being, as if some hidden force was instructing him on the appropriate balance for his life.

The sun was setting and the sky had turned to crimson, a good omen for the drama that was about to unfold. As he knelt in the sand, next to the hill, he dug a hole with his hands until he could reach no further with his extended arm. He opened his bag and removed the items he intended to offer to the earth. In all, he had brought 29 of them, one for each day of the new moon, symbolic of his affirmation of the unalterable but cyclical nature of life and of his commitment to return to the earth that which had been provided.

He placed all but eight of the pieces at the bottom of the hole, along with his favourite shaping stone. As he filled in the hole with the sand he had excavated, he called upon the spirit of Flint and offered thanks and assurance that he had replenished the earth with objects that he could easily transform into finished tools.

He then took the remaining pieces and kneeling, placed them on the outcrop along the partially submerged shoreline. Here he asked the spirit of the lake to honour his people's need to visit this place and collect the stone. His grandfather had told him of times when the lake had grown with anger until the stone was beyond reach. While that had never happened in his lifetime, he was careful to thank the lake for its kindness.

With these simple acts, the man felt at one with the land, and he rose and returned to his people, who were camped at their favourite spot — where the river of the great falls leaves the lake and Flint had left his legacy.

Glossary

artifact	any item that has been created by humans through design and conscious effort
artifact assemblage	all artifacts of one culture or time period found within the context of an archaeological site
BP	before present (1950)
biface	a stone tool that has been worked on two faces to produce a cutting or scraping edge (see retouch)
chert	a fine-grained stone similar to flint, used by prehistoric peoples for the manufacture of tools; differences in chert properties (colour, texture, mineral composition) are often indicative of the specific bedrock source
cortex	the coarse outer surface of a chert nodule (or bone)
debitage	debris produced during the manufacture of chipped stone tools
decortification	the removal of cortex from a chert nodule
diagnostics	artifacts which can be assigned to a specific culture or time period
feature	a generic term for any recognizable soil stain or discolouration found on an archaeological site, including cultural features such as pits, hearths, post moulds, as well as natural features such as rodent burrows or tree root disturbances. A pit, for example, is produced by the excavation of a hole in the soil that penetrates both the topsoil and the subsoil, followed by infilling of the hole with mixed soils that are noticeably different in colour or texture from the surrounding soils.
flint	see chert
flotation	a process whereby the soils from archaeological features are collected and subjected to a water separation process that allows for the retrieval of carbonized plant remains and other organic material.
glacio-	pertaining to glaciers
lithics	stone tools manufactured by the selective removal of flakes, or by grinding, to achieve a desired form
morphology	the structure and form of objects
osteoarchaeologist	an archaeologist who specializes in the study of animal bones in order to examine past dietary practices
osteobiography	the measurement of bones in an effort to identify the age and sex of the animal or human that they represent
paleosol	a topsoil layer that has been covered by additional soil, either deliberately (for example, filling in areas during landscaping) or as a result of natural processes such as flooding
physiography	the study and description of the landscape
post mould	a soil stain left by a post or stake that was driven into the ground, but which has subsequently decayed
projectile point	an arrow- or spearhead
retouch	the removal of fine flakes to change the shape or sharpen a stone tool; may occur on one face of the object (unifacial) or on both faces (bifacial)
stratigraphy	the study of the sequence of soil accumulation and deposition. The basic premise underlying this interpretive approach to archaeological sites is that if one deposit overlies another, it must have accumulated later in time than the lower, which could not have been inserted beneath a layer already there. Study of the stratification, or ordering of soil layers, and of the different artifacts recovered from the various layers is a method of estimating the dates (relative to one another) of various events that occurred on an archaeological site
stratum	a soil layer or deposit (pl. strata)
uniface	a stone tool that has been worked on one face to produce a cutting or scraping edge (see retouch)

Index